On Consolation

ALSO BY MICHAEL IGNATIEFF

The Ordinary Virtues: Moral Order in a Divided World

Isaiah Berlin: A Life

The Warrior's Honor: Ethnic War and the Modern Conscience

Blood and Belonging: Journeys into the New Nationalism

Fire and Ashes: Success and Failure in Politics

The Lesser Evil: Political Ethics in an Age of Terror

Scar Tissue

The Russian Album

The Needs of Strangers

On Consolation

Finding Solace in Dark Times

MICHAEL IGNATIEFF

PICADOR

First published 2021 by Metropolitan Books, New York

First published in the UK in paperback 2021 by Picador

This edition first published 2022 by Picador
an imprint of Pan Macmillan
The Smithson, 6 Briset Street, London EC1M 5NR
EU representative: Macmillan Publishers Ireland Ltd, 1st Floor,
The Liffey Trust Centre, 117–126 Sheriff Street Upper, Dublin 1, D01 YC43
Associated companies throughout the world
www.panmacmillan.com

ISBN 978-1-5290-5377-7

1 3 5 7 9 8 6 4 2

A CIP catalogue record for this book is available from the British Library.

Printed and bound by CPI Group (UK) Ltd, Croydon, CR0 4YY

Visit www.picador.com to read more about all our books
and to buy them. You will also find features, author interviews and
news of any author events, and you can sign up for e-newsletters
so that you're always first to hear about our new releases.

For Zsuzsanna

CONTENTS

PREFACE

This book had its origins in an unusual invitation. In 2017, I was invited to give a talk about justice and politics in the book of Psalms as part of a choral festival in Utrecht at which four choirs would sing settings of all 150 of the Psalms. My lecture was to take place in an interval between performances. Apart from what nearly everyone knows—"the Lord is my shepherd" and "though I walk through the valley of the shadow"—I knew little about the Psalms, but I accepted anyway, telling myself I had time to learn. I studied them over a summer in the King James Version of the Bible, read Robert Alter's translations from the Hebrew, and gave the lecture. Afterward my wife, Zsuzsanna, and I sat with the rest of the audience, over a Saturday and Sunday, to listen to the choirs, with the words of the Psalms projected in Dutch and English above the stage. The music was beautiful, the words were resonant, and the experience had a cathartic effect I have been trying to understand ever since. I came to give a lecture about justice and politics, but I discovered consolation—in the words, the music, and the tears of recognition in the audience.

So that is how the project began: trying to understand the impact of the Psalms on me and others in that concert hall in Utrecht. How had ancient religious language exerted such a spell upon us, especially upon a nonbeliever like me? And what did it mean, exactly, to be consoled?

As I pursued this project over the next four years, it became more enthralling but also more difficult. I felt that I was wading against the current, working on a subject that bewildered friends and colleagues, who often asked me, Why consolation? Why now?

Then in March 2020, COVID-19 sent us all into recurrent lockdowns for a year or more. In the online world that became our global commons, there was a veritable explosion of attempts to provide consolation, to give meaning to our shared feelings of disorientation, fear, loneliness, and raw grief, as the death tolls rose from the scarcely believable to the mutely accepted. Artists, writers, singers, musicians, and thinkers sought to bear witness to the moment and bring comfort to those around them. Zsuzsanna and I, for example, joined thousands online to listen to a Rotterdam orchestra, who, unable to be together, played Beethoven's "Ode to Joy" on Zoom, the musicians in their homes, coordinating their timing through earphones. A pianist, Igor Levit, played Beethoven sonatas every night from his room in Berlin; Simon Rattle accompanied Magdalena Kožená as she sang songs by Brahms; poets read poems of solace from their bedrooms; people read aloud from their copies of Camus's *The Plague* or Defoe's *A Journal of the Plague Year*; rappers rapped; singers sang; intellectuals declaimed.

This outpouring validated the impulse that led me to take counsel from great men and women who lived through times darker than our own and who found consolation in works of art, philosophy, and religion. These works are still there to help us in our hour of need, to perform their ancient task once again.

This book is not a working through of private griefs, but it remains a deeply personal project. The form it has taken—portraits of particular men and women in history struggling to find consolation—puts special stress on how ideas and meanings are forged in the crucible of experiences at once singular and universal in their significance.

On Consolation is a return to work I did as a historian of ideas in *The Needs of Strangers*, back in 1984. My understanding of Hume, Condorcet, and Marx, who figure in this book, was formed by my time at King's College, Cambridge, between 1978 and 1984, as codirector of a project on the history of classical political economy. The philosopher Bernard Williams was the provost of the college during this period; Gareth Stedman Jones and John Dunn were guiding inspirations for the project; and my codirector was that incomparable scholar István Hont, whose death in 2013 at sixty-five is a loss to all who knew him.

During the twelve years that I knew Isaiah Berlin and worked on his biography, I never discussed consolation with him, since he was one of those irrepressibly buoyant people who seemed not to need any at all. But my understanding of Anna Akhmatova, who consoled herself with the hope that her poetry would constitute an imperishable record of Stalin's Terror, was shaped by Berlin's recollection of his encounter with her in Leningrad in 1945.

As I wrote this book, I became ever more indebted to traditions of scholarship that have made my work possible. The fact that we have some of these texts at all—the book of Job, the book of Psalms, Paul's Epistles, Marcus Aurelius's *Meditations*, Cicero's letters, for example—is a testament to the fidelity, over many centuries, of anonymous scholars, copyists, scribes, and translators who saved them from the mice, from fire and plague and human indifference. My modern contemporaries are faithful heirs of these traditions. Here I would like to express thanks to particular individuals who helped me as the project took shape. Yoeri Albrecht issued the original invitation to give the lecture at the festival in Utrecht. I am grateful to Robert Alter for his wonderful translation of the Hebrew Bible and for his reading of Job and the Psalms as works of literature; to Nicholas Wright for his interpretation of Paul and his trenchant criticism of my own; to Christian Brouwer for his work on Boethius; to Arthur Applbaum for sharing his knowledge of Hebrew and for his writing on Montaigne; to Moshe Halbertal for sharing his understanding of Job with me and for his essay, "Job, the Mourner"; to Leon Wieseltier for acute editorial suggestions throughout; to Sarah Schroth for her study of El Greco, published more than forty years ago; to Emma Rothschild for her scholarship on Condorcet; to Gareth Stedman Jones for his biography of Marx; to Adam Gopnik for his writing on Lincoln; to the musicologist and conductor Leon Botstein for his knowledge of Mahler; to Karol Berger for sharing his understanding of Wagner and Nietzsche; to Lisa Appignanesi for years of dialogue on Freud and other matters both weighty and frivolous; to Tim Crane for thinking with me about whether we have a right to religious consolations if we do not share religious belief; to János Kis for his thoughts on the relation between consolation and being at peace with fate; to Maria Kronfeldner for her critique of my treatment of "hope" in Primo Levi; to Carlo Ginzburg for his close and critical reading of my treatment of Primo Levi; to Mark Lilla for his reading of Camus; to Michael Zantovsky, Jacques Rupnik, and Havel's exemplary translator Paul Wilson for sharing their friendship and their understanding of Václav Havel; to Győző Ferencz for reading and correcting the section of a chapter devoted to the Hungarian poet Miklós Radnóti; to the curators of the Anna Akhmatova Museum in Saint Petersburg who shared their love of the poet and their intimate knowledge of her lodgings in the Sheremetiev Palace; to David Clark who enriched my view of Cicely Saunders; and to Tom Laqueur for the luminous scholarship of his *The Work of the Dead*. All these scholars and friends shared their knowledge with me but bear no responsibility for what I have done with it.

I also want to thank my brother, Andrew, who cares for the family roots from which this book also took its sustenance.

I owe a special debt of thanks to the chief librarian of Central European University, Diane Geraci, and her team, for their constant assistance. Thanks also to my resourceful assistant, Noemi Kakucs.

I am grateful to the editorial team that devoted such care to the manuscript: Jane Haxby for her copyedit, Brian Lax for moving the process along, and Sara Bershtel and Anne Collins for editorial suggestions that clarified arguments and reduced repetitions. Sara and Anne, joined by Ravi Mirchandani and my agent and lifelong friend Michael Levine, each committed to the book before they knew how it would turn out, and this act of faith helped me to sustain my own.

Speaking of acts of faith, I cannot conclude without mentioning Zsuzsanna Zsohar, who was there in Utrecht when it all began and who, as always, has listened to every word and improved it all. The book is dedicated to her.

On Consolation

Introduction

After Paradise

I am visiting a friend who lost his wife six months ago. He is frail but unsparingly alert. The chair where she used to sit is still in its place across from his. The room remains as she arranged it. I have brought him a cake from a café that they used to visit together when they were courting. He eats a slice greedily. When I ask him how things are going, he looks out the window and says quietly, "If only I could believe that I would see her again."

There is nothing I can say, so we sit in silence. I came to console or at least comfort, but I can't do either. To understand consolation, it is necessary to begin with the moments when it is impossible.

Console. It's from the Latin *consolor*, to find solace together. Consolation is what we do, or try to do, when we share each other's suffering or seek to bear our own. What we are searching for is how to go on, how to keep going, how to recover the belief that life is worth living.

But here, in this moment with my old friend, I am reminded

how difficult this is. He is truly inconsolable. He refuses to believe that he can live without her. Trying to console him takes us both to the limits of language, and so words trail off into silence. His grief is a deep solitude that cannot be shared. In its depths, there is no place for hope.

This moment also lays bare what it is like to live in this time after paradise. For millennia, people believed that they would see their loved ones again in the afterlife. They imagined it vividly, and the great artists depicted it: clouds, angels, celestial harps, unending plenty, freedom from toil and illness, but above all the reunion, this time forever, with the beloved.

Paradise was the form that hope has taken for thousands of years, but what Shakespeare said of death is also true of paradise: it is the country from which no traveler returns. By the sixteenth century, Europeans began to suspect that no such country ever existed. In the twenty-first century, unbelief now commands the hearts and minds of many, though not all, of the people I know. What unleashed unbelief, among many other forces, was an ideal of truth. If my old friend succumbed to his own longing to believe, he would feel he had betrayed himself.

This is where we are today, heirs both to traditions of consolation and to the centuries of revolt against them. What consolations can we still believe in?

Today the word has lost the meanings once rooted in religious traditions. In these times, the consolation prize is the one you don't want to win. A culture that chases success does not devote much attention to failure, loss, or death. Consolation is for losers.

Consolation used to be a subject for philosophy, because philosophy was understood to be the discipline that taught us how to live and die. *Consolatio* was a genre unto itself in the Stoic traditions of the ancient world. Cicero was a master of the art. Seneca wrote three famous letters to console grieving widows. Marcus Aurelius, the Roman emperor, wrote his *Med-itations* essentially to console himself. A Roman senator, Boethius, wrote *The Consolation of Philosophy* while awaiting a death sentence at the hands of a barbarian king in AD 524. These texts still linger on in humanities courses for undergraduates, but professional philosophy has left them behind.

Consolation has also lost its institutional setting. The churches, synagogues, and mosques, where we once consoled each other in collective rituals of grief and mourning, have been emptying out. If we seek help in times of misery, we seek it alone, from each other, and from therapeutic professionals. They treat our suffering as an illness from which we need to recover.

Yet when suffering becomes understood as an illness with a cure, something is lost. The religious traditions of consolation were able to situate individual suffering within a wider frame and to offer a grieving person an account of where an individual life fit into a divine or cosmic plan.

This is the wider frame in which the great languages of consolation offered hope. Such frames remain available to us even now: the Jewish God who demands obedience but whose covenant with his people promises that he will protect us; the Christian God who so loved the world that he sacrificed his own son and offered us the hope of eternal life; classical Roman Stoics who promised that life would hurt less if we could learn how to renounce the vanity of human wishes. More influential today is the tradition that takes shape in the work of Montaigne and Hume, who questioned whether we could ever discern any grand meaning for our suffering.

These thinkers also gave voice to a passionate belief that religious faith had missed the most crucial source of consolation of all. The meaning of life was not to be found in the promise of paradise, nor in the mastery of the appetites, but in

living to the full every day. To be consoled, simply, was to hold
on to one's love of life as it is, here and now.

Both ancients and moderns did share a sense of the tragic.
Both accepted that there are some losses that are irremediable;
some experiences from which we cannot fully recover; some
scars that heal but do not fade. The challenge of consolation
in our times is to endure tragedy, even when we cannot find a
meaning for it, and to continue living in hope.

To live in hope, these days, may require a saving skepticism
toward the drumbeat of doom-laden narratives that reach us
from every media portal. In 1783, when Britain had just lost
its American colonies and public affairs were in turmoil, James
Boswell asked Samuel Johnson whether the "turbulences" of
public life had not "vexed yourself a little, sir." Johnson reacted
in his grandest and most dismissive mode. "That's cant, Sir.
Publick affairs vex no man, Sir. I have never slept an hour less
nor eat an ounce less meat."

We can take this today as an injunction to retain some skeptical self-command in the face of the narratives that invade our
consciousness and frame the times in which we live. If it was
cant in 1783 to lose sleep over the loss of America, it would
be cant, in our times, to let our own resilience buckle before
the tide of public commentary that predicts environmental
Armageddon, democratic collapse, or a future blighted by
new plagues. None of these challenges, as daunting as they
are, are made easier to overcome by believing they are unprec-
edented. In this book we will encounter men and women who
lived through plague, the collapse of republican freedom, campaigns of mass extermination, enemy occupation, and catastrophic military defeat. Their stories set our times in context
and enable us to draw inspiration from their lucidity. To see
ourselves in the light of history is to restore our connection to

the consolations of our ancestors and to discover our kinship
with their experience.

We will be astonished when we do. We might suppose
that religious texts—Job, the Psalms, Paul's Epistles, Dante's
Paradiso—are closed to us if we don't happen to share the faith
that inspired them. But why should we be required to pass a
test of belief before we can derive consolation from religious
texts? The religious promise of salvation and redemption might
be closed to us, but not the consolation that comes from the
understanding that religious texts can offer for our moments of
despair. The Psalms are among the most eloquent documents
in any language of what it is to feel bereft, alone and lost. They
contain unforgettable descriptions of despair as well as exalted
visions of hope. We can still respond to their promise of hope
because the Psalms recognize what we need hope for. This is
why, even at this hour, someone, somewhere, is picking up the
Gideon Bible in a hotel room and reading the Psalms, and why,
as I discovered in the choral festival in Utrecht where this project began, when music and words come together, they hold out
a promise of hope that makes our unbelief somehow irrelevant.

Consolation is an act of solidarity in space—keeping company with the bereaved, helping a friend through a difficult
moment; but it is also an act of solidarity in time—reaching
back to the dead and drawing meaning from the words they
left behind.

To feel kinship with the psalmists, with Job, with Saint
Paul, with Boethius, Dante, and Montaigne, with modern figures like Camus, to feel our emotions expressed in the music
of Mahler, is to feel that we are not marooned in the present.
These works help us find words for what is wordless, for experiences of isolation that imprison us in silence.

We are still able to hear these voices from the past thanks to chains of meaning maintained over thousands of years. Eight hundred years after Boethius consoled himself by imagining a wise Lady Philosophia who visited him in prison, Dante, in exile from his native Florence, read Boethius's *Consolation*, and it inspired him to imagine a journey, also in company with a wise lady, from the inferno through purgatory to paradise. A further six hundred years later, in the summer of 1944, a young Italian chemist trudged through Auschwitz with a fellow prisoner. As they walked, the Italian suddenly remembered lines of Dante:

> We are not born to be brutes. We are men, created for knowledge and virtue.

This is how the language of consolation endures—from Boethius to Dante, from Dante to Primo Levi—human beings in extremity drawing inspiration from each other across a millennium. This solidarity in time is the essence of the consolation that this book hopes to make accessible, once again.

There are many other words we use, beside consolation, when we confront loss and pain.

We can be comforted without being consoled, just as we can be consoled without being comforted. Comfort is transitory; consolation is enduring. Comfort is physical; consolation is propositional. Consolation is an argument about why life is the way it is and why we must keep going.

Consolation is the opposite of resignation. We can be resigned to death without being consoled, and we can accept the tragic in life without being resigned to it. We can derive consolation, in fact, from our struggle with fate and how that struggle inspires others.

To be resigned to life is to give up, to forgo any hope that it could be different. To be reconciled to life, on the other hand, allows us to hold out hope for what the future might bring. To be reconciled we must first make peace with our losses, defeats, and failures. To be consoled is to accept these losses, to accept what they have done to us and to believe, despite everything, that they need not haunt our future or blight our remaining possibilities.

The essential element of consolation is hope: the belief that we can recover from loss, defeat, and disappointment, and that the time that remains to us, however short, offers us possibilities to start again, failing perhaps, but as Beckett said, failing better. It is this hope that allows us, even in the face of tragedy, to remain unbowed.

When we seek consolation, we are seeking more than just a way to feel better. Serious losses cause us to question the larger design of our existence: the fact that time flows inexorably in one direction, and that while we can still hope for the future, we cannot unlive the past. Serious reversals cause us to reckon with the fact that the world is not fair and that, in the larger domain of politics and the smaller world of our private lives, justice can remain cruelly out of reach. To be consoled is to make peace with the order of the world without renouncing our hopes for justice.

Finally, and most difficult of all, loss and defeat force us to confront our own limitations. This is where consolation can be hardest to achieve. In the face of our failures, we are tempted to take refuge in illusion. There is no true consolation in illusion, so we must try, as Václav Havel said, "to live in truth."

This book is a collection of portraits, arranged in historical order, each devoted to a single person in extremity who used the traditions they inherited to seek consolation. As we shall see, they did not always succeed, but we can learn from their struggles and find hope in their examples. It begins with the book of Job and concludes with Anna Akhmatova, Primo

Levi, Albert Camus, Václav Havel, and Cicely Saunders. I hope
my choices will not appear arbitrary. Another book could have
been written about what Europeans learned from Asian, African, or Muslim sources of consolation. I have tried to show how
traditions of consolation forged over thousands of years in the
European tradition remain capable of inspiring us today. What
do we learn that we can use in these times of darkness? Something very simple. We are not alone, and we never have been.

One

The Voice in the Whirlwind

The Book of Job and the Book of Psalms

Consolation is possible only if hope is possible, and hope is possible only if life makes sense to us. If we genuinely believed that life were absurd, one random event after another, without letup or respite, ending in death, then resignation, heedless pleasure, flight, suicide—anything at all—would make sense, but not consolation. The hope we need for consolation depends on faith that our existence is meaningful or can be given meaning by our efforts. This is the faith that allows us to live in expectation of recovery and renewal. Consolation depends on that faith and is thus an unavoidably religious idea, even if, as we shall see, the meaning that gives us hope can take nonreligious and even anti-religious forms. Yet it is with the religious search for the meaning of suffering that we must begin. Religions fulfill many functions, but one is to console, to explain why human beings suffer and die and why, despite these facts, we should live in hope.

From the beginning of the human record—when ideas were first put down on clay tablets in cuneiform or on papyrus strips with ink made from ashes—thinkers have asked the essential question: how to sustain faith in the human experience in the face of suffering, loss, and death. Jewish and Christian religions begin with a refusal to accept that we are born only to suffer and die.

The Hebrew prophets begin this search for hope, and hence are the originators of the Western idea of consolation. They imagined a monotheistic God, all-powerful and all-knowing, a divine lawgiver, but they then had to explain why such a God could allow the righteous to suffer and the iniquitous to prosper. In supposing that the world was the creation of a just God, the Hebrew prophets bequeathed to us the problem that human beings have been trying to solve ever since: how to preserve hope and faith in the face of the injustice and harshness of life. Without a solution to this problem, there is no consolation.

Many texts in the Hebrew Bible, the Old Testament, are a sustained, anguished search for an answer. One of these is the book of Job. Another is the book of Psalms. Of these texts, we will ask two questions: how they solved the problem, and why, even today, when the solution—faith in God's justice and mercy—no longer commands belief, these books still retain their power to console.

We know next to nothing about the book of Job's author or authors. Robert Alter, who translated the book of Job into English, surmises that the author was a brilliantly sophisticated poet with a mastery of Aramaic verse, working somewhere in the Middle East in the fifth or sixth century before the Christian era. It is also possible that the book of Job does not have a single author but is instead a compilation of writings by a number of authors over a long time, working from primeval myths, folktales, or oral traditions going back still further. If so, the book of Job can be seen as the collective imagining of whole peoples, borrowing from Aramaic and Canaanite sources and from tribes who warred with the Jews only to make peace and share traditions. The fact that the text survived and was incorporated into the Hebrew Bible may be an example of beauty saving itself, words striking so close to the heart that anyone who read them felt bound to save them from destruction.

The book of Job imagines a man who once enjoyed a plenitude of good fortune—robust health and a contented family, barns full of animals and grain, expanses of tilled fields—losing everything because God decides to try his faith. This is an all-powerful God, but also one who is human in his susceptibility to temptation and bad counsel. A figure in the tale known as the "satan," which Alter translates as the "adversary," insinuates that Job's faith depends only on his prosperity. A fortunate man, he suggests, would turn against God if fortune turned against him.

God tests Job's faith by sending marauding tribes to slaughter Job's cattle, set fire to his buildings, and slay his children. When the messenger brings Job this news—"And I only am escaped alone to tell thee"—Job mourns, tears his garments, shaves his head, bows down before God, but his faith does not buckle. Instead of giving in to rage or sorrow, he declares, in the words of the King James Version, "the Lord gave and the Lord hath taken away; blessed be the name of the Lord."

The adversary then whispers in God's ear that "A man will give all he has for his own life." Strike his bone and his flesh and see whether he keeps his faith. And so God turns Job over to the adversary, cautioning only that his life be preserved. The adversary gives Job the plague, but Job survives, ill and destitute, by the ashes of a cold hearth, scratching at his sores. His wife berates him. "Curse God and die," she cries. Still, though his despair is as black as night, Job refuses to abandon his God.

At this point in the story, three friends, Job's comforters, sit down beside him and at first share his dejection in silence.

"None spake a word unto him: for they saw that his grief was very great." Each in turn then tries to talk him into accepting his fate. Your faith is being tried, they tell him, and you must endure the trial. Job listens with clenched teeth, bitterly unconvinced. He is inconsolable. The God in whom he placed his trust, the God he loved, is punishing him for no reason at all. Why does God keep him alive, he cries, when he longs for death "but it cometh not"?

The comforters then become more critical. Job's despair will disperse, they tell him, only when he recognizes his faults. "Shall mortal man be more just than God?" Instead of repining, Job should be positively grateful for his afflictions. They are just punishment for his wrongdoing.

Job will have none of it. It is not only God's errant malignity that torments him, but also a new sense of mankind's cosmic insignificance. "Man that is born of a woman is of few days and full of trouble." The most trifling plant or tree dies away with the autumn and then renews itself each spring; man dies only once and his bones waste away to nothingness. Hope, Job is saying, depends on faith that human life has significance in God's eyes. What if we don't matter at all?

The comforters seize on Job's admission of his own insignificance to humble him further, but Job fights back. His very despair is a way of insisting, despite everything, on his own importance in the ultimate scheme of things. In his despair, Job edges toward blasphemy, asking, what is this God he worships? Why do we obey someone who torments us?

The comforters try to convince him that the road to consolation lies in accepting blame for his misfortunes. Job refuses. He has kept faith with God. He has accepted what God has given, and what God has taken away. What more can be asked of him? That he should confess guilt, when he believes he is innocent? "My righteousness I hold fast and will not let it go."

Humbling himself, Job retorts, is the path not to consolation, but to humiliation. He will not take further counsel from these "physicians of no value." I am not being heard, he tells them, not by you, not by God. There is no consolation if you are not heard. He no longer cares what humans have to tell him. His quarrel is with God. "I would speak to the Almighty, and I desire to reason with God."

This figure covered with sores, destitute and abandoned, in rags, is a stupendous invention: the true ancestor of all the great wronged and self-wronging giants of literature up to King Lear and beyond. Job shakes his fist at the sky. "I would speak," he thunders, "and I will not fear him for that is not the way I am."

Job takes upon himself the right to talk back, to demand answers. Here is worship as dialogue and argument. In Job, and in the prophetic Hebrew tradition, the human search for consolation becomes a demand for divine validation, a cry insisting on its right to be heard.

Job's God does not keep silent. He speaks out of the whirlwind in a majestic tirade. Who, he demands to know, dares to challenge him? Does Job have any idea of his power? "Where wast thou when I laid the foundation of the earth?" How can a mere human being dare to question the power of the one who put the morning stars in the sky, who created the sea, who girdled the earth with clouds? Who are you to tell me what to do? How dare you, God cries, accuse me of your suffering? "Wilt thou condemn me, that thou mayest be righteous?"

In God's eyes, Job is impermissibly arrogant, for he dares to blame God for his torments. Job must make peace with what he cannot understand.

The voice from the whirlwind insists on obedience but it also confers recognition. Once the voice ceases speaking, Job knows that God has heard him and he accepts that he must reconcile with a divine power he cannot hope to understand.

His reconciliation with God begins with an admission of ignorance, but not of guilt. "I have uttered that I understood not . . . things too wonderful for me, which I knew not." Having spoken and having been heard, there is now a dignity in his surrender: "Therefore, do I recant, and I repent in dust and ashes."

A learned friend tells me that the Hebrew for "And I repent" here is *v'nikhamti*, from the root N-Kh-M. It is the same as the word for consolation. When the King James Version renders the lines in Isaiah as "Comfort ye my people," the Hebrew is *nakhamu*, from the same root, N-Kh-M, which is more literally translated as "You be consoled." The Hebrew connects the idea of consolation with a change of heart toward grief itself. Grief can be a single-minded obsession, and Job's grief is of this kind. He is inconsolable so long as he can think only of himself and his fate. When he accepts that God is inscrutable and unknowable, when he ceases to fixate on his innocence and accepts God's unknowable order, he is restored to his former life. Consolation may not require admission of guilt, but it requires repentance and acceptance.

Is this how we are to understand what God demands and Job accepts? That God will not console Job unless Job repents? If this were so, consolation is possible, in God's world, only if mourners throttle their grief and submit to God with unwavering obedience.

Yet this is not all there is to this dark tale. The book of Job also wants us to notice that instead of thanking Job's three comforters, God reproves them. "Ye have not spoken of me the thing that is right, as my servant Job hath."

Job's comforters had sought to relieve his despair by explaining his suffering. They had offered a rationale for God's infliction of torments on an innocent man. This may be why God reproaches them—for presuming to explain. False consolation of the kind offered by Job's comforters fails to console precisely because it presumes to explain, because, in the case of Job, it implies that he got what he deserved.

In the Job story, God demands absolute obedience as the condition of consolation, but he also demands something else: fidelity to one's truth. Job refused to admit his guilt. He demanded that his innocence be recognized, both by God and by the false comforters. He kept faith, paradoxically, by demanding justice. To demand justice is to have faith that the world is sufficiently meaningful for justice to be possible and that God has the power to grant it. If this interpretation is correct, the teller of the Job story wants us to understand that if there is consolation in obedience, there is none in helpless resignation. If we apply this idea to our own lives, consolation can lift us from the depths of despair only if we have the courage to demand recognition, from ourselves and from others, for the reality of our suffering and refuse the false consolations of those who deny what we have endured or who claim that it is justified. The story also counsels us to stop asking the question that so often torments us in grief: Why me? God tells Job, and thus tells us, this is a question for which there is no good answer.

In the final lines of the parable, as if rewarded for this new understanding, Job is restored to his riches, his family, his home, and his health. The book of Job concludes by telling us that Job died eventually, "old and full of days," at peace with his God.

The book of Job is an account of the order of the world in which consolation is possible, because the heavens are not silent. Human beings are part of this world, not estranged from it, and while its order may be inscrutable, it is possible for Job to accept that his suffering, however unendurable, has meaning in God's eyes as a trial of his faith. The injustice of God's world may be hard to bear, but it is the work of an intelligence that surpasses our understanding, not random and meaningless chance.

Today, those who still talk to God, like Job, live in hope that their prayers will be answered, yet they also know that God may not answer. The comfort of prayer is in the saying of them and in the communion with the self that results. Prayerful people no longer expect the voice to speak out of the whirlwind. In modern times, we have become used to waiting for God in silence. The great religious thinker and mystic Simone Weil, who died in 1943, reflected deeply on the story of Job. She always thought of her relationship to God as a form of waiting, in patience and in hope. She was not waiting to be consoled, she said, merely to feel that he was there. In Beckett's *Waiting for Godot*, this vision of the human relation to the divine grew darker and more comic. Vladimir and Estragon wait and talk and wait, and no one speaks to them out of the ambient air. We have got used to the silence.

How then is an identification with the Job story possible for those who will never bring themselves to accept Job's God or wait for him to speak? Whatever we think of Job and his God, we must begin any history of the idea of consolation here, for the story describes the human situation so clearly. Job's story tells us we are fated to endure sorrow and suffering that have no apparent meaning, moments when existence is a torment, when we know what it is to be truly inconsolable. But like Job, we must learn to endure, we must hold on to the truth of what we have lived and refuse false consolations, like believing that we deserve to suffer. We should refuse the burden of guilt and struggle as best we can to understand the meaning of our lives. We are not condemned to eternal silence, to meaninglessness. There is an answer to be found in the whirlwind, in human beings' unendingly troubled encounter with our fate, but to find the answer that is true for us we will have to be as courageous as the man in rags who dared raise his fist to the sky.

> The Lord is my shepherd; I shall not want.
> He maketh me to lie down in green pastures; he leadeth me beside the still waters.
> He restoreth my soul; he leadeth me in the paths of righteousness for his name's sake.
> Yea, though I walk through the valley of the shadow of death, I will fear no evil: for thou art with me; thy rod and thy staff they comfort me.
> Thou preparest a table before me in the presence of my enemies: thou anointest my head with oil; my cup runneth over.
> Surely goodness and mercy shall follow me all the days of my life: and I will dwell in the house of the Lord forever.

These are some of the most consoling words ever written. If you are grieving, Psalm 23 can help you through the night. If you are in prison, they are the words a chaplain may read out to you. Once, when men and women mounted the scaffold, these may have been the last words they heard.

In the book of Job, Job is consoled by God's appearance in the whirlwind, by his recognition of Job's dignity even in his suffering. But what about us? If we do not have Job's faith, if we do not believe in God, why does the psalm move us? Why were the eyes of the people in the Utrecht hall filled with tears of recognition?

It's easy to see why these words bring comfort—they are beautiful, rhythmically phrased, incantatory. But consolation is something more. How do they contain a message of hope? And why do we believe it?

Job is consoled because he ends his life secure in his submission to God's cosmic order, even if he does not comprehend it. Today we can admire the beauty of this conception and even wish it were true, but elegiac nostalgia for discarded certainties is a passing comfort. Consolation should have some element of enduring plausibility, or else the hope it gives us will not survive the tests in store.

We cannot read the Psalms, as the faithful do, as testaments of faith in a divine order, but we can still draw consolation from being connected to a chain of meaning stretching back to the very dawn of recorded human expression and, if the chain remains unbroken, stretching far into the future, offering consolation to generations as yet unborn.

While the texts themselves have survived, their authors have vanished. We call them the psalmists, but we know nothing about them. Were they votaries of a cult, or rabbis of the early Jewish faith? Could there have been women among their number? In an age when we know our authors' lives as well, if not better, than their books, it is salutary to be moved by authors about whom we know nothing.

The Psalms are a palimpsest, a layering of meanings built up over generations from Baal worship, Canaanite metaphysics, and the emergent monotheism that became Judaism. They are texts that borrow, steal, and mediate among faiths whose doctrines are lost but whose fears and exaltations survive in the fragments that have come down to us.

The Psalms haven't survived unscathed. Scholars can show where lines break off, where a copyist made a mistake. We can't figure out what certain lines mean or why one line follows another, what metaphysics is implied, for example, in the original Hebrew word that the King James Bible translates as *soul*, but which, according to Robert Alter, might actually mean something closer to *vitality* or *life force*. The text of the Psalms is not settled. Christian readings have contended with Jewish ones for thousands of years. Modern translations vary so significantly that you wonder whether they are of the same psalm. So their survival—and the continuity that consoles—cannot be due to the reverent handing on of a holy text from one set of scribes to the next, but to something more like a fierce argument, in which the text has been manhandled, snatched from one faith and tossed to another, saved from flames, hidden underground, smuggled to safety, treasured but also manipulated, in good faith and in bad.

The Psalms are songs, both of praise and of lamentation, and the texts that have survived contain markings for musicians along with indications that certain instruments should be used, possibly as part of a cultic worship whose traces have vanished. We no longer know what these musical instruments were or what they might have sounded like. But that has not prevented musicians in every generation, from plainchant in the earliest monasteries to contemporary composers, from setting the words to music. For this reason, we are more than the passive heirs of a mysterious gift from the past. Composers and artists will be setting these words to new forms of music far into the future, and choirs, just like the ones at Utrecht, will still be singing them, long after we are gone.

Reading the Psalms is like walking among ruins—past a sheared column, over a hearthstone bearing the indentation of footsteps, down into a crypt where you inhale the odor of damp stone and run your hands along the mortar, dip your finger into the masons' marks and come into contact with the anonymous artisans who built so well. It is then, with the masons, with the psalmists, that we find ourselves belonging to a chain of meaning that has kept faith, all along, with beauty.

This chain begins with the Jewish elders who collated the various versions of the 150 Psalms then in circulation and set them in sequence in the Hebrew Bible, then to the Greek scribes who transcribed the Hebrew, then to the early Christian and medieval copyists who rendered them in Latin, then to the first typesetters who put them into European vernaculars, and down to the committee of English clergy, working under the authority of their "dreaded sovereign," who started all over again, reviewing the Greek, Hebrew, and Latin texts in order, in 1611, to give English speakers the majestic rhythm of the King James Version.

Besides rooting us in deep time, the Psalms also have enabled men and women in pain, throughout the ages, to grasp the commonality of their experience. Psalm 137—"By the rivers of Babylon, there we sat down, yea, we wept, when we remembered Zion"—reminds modern Jews of their kinship with their ancestors in the Babylonian captivity. But it also speaks to the suffering of the peoples of Africa, sent to work the plantations in the American colonies and the Caribbean. The Psalms are a source of the spirituals sung by enslaved and then by freed people who created the mighty gospel tradition of the Black American church. In Psalm 137, the injunction sacred to the Jewish people—"If I forget thee, O Jerusalem, may my right hand wither, may my tongue cleave to my palate"—is an admonition for anyone who has tasted the bitterness of exile. The psalm also understands the enduring anger of those who have been driven from their homeland. Its text begins with lament and ends with rage, directed at the Babylonian tyrants. "Happy shall he be that rewardeth thee as thou hast served us," the psalmist says, and then he issues the terrifying curse: "Happy shall he be that taketh and dasheth thy little ones against the stones." The authority of the Psalms lies in their capacity to express not only grief and loss but also annihilating rage.

The Psalms tell us that the makers of this tradition were men and women just like us. They knew what it was to suffer exile and loss, to fear death and dying. The worst of despair, as they knew only too well, is to feel alone. The consolation they offer is the certainty that others have felt exactly as we have done and that we are not alone, in our rage and despair, and our longing for better days.

Consolation depends on this recognition. To console someone is to say, over and over: I know, I know. We share what we have suffered so others will know they are not alone. It is the most essential and difficult exercise of solidarity that ever falls to us. This is the duty that the Psalms counsel us to shoulder, in ancient but recognizable images. They tell us how to do so by urging us to be truthful. We cannot console if we are not truthful. Among the truths they counsel is to admit what it is to feel petrifying fear:

I am poured out like water and all my bones are out of joint.

The psalmists knew desolation:

My heart is smitten and withered like grass; so that
    I forget to eat my bread.

And they understood our solitude:

I watch and am as a sparrow alone upon the house top.

The psalmists knew too the unbearable experience of waiting in vain for solace. They pay attention to the pain of cries unheard, of desperation unanswered:

How long wilt thou forget, O Lord? Forever? How long wilt thou hide thy face from me?

The psalmists do not doubt that God exists—and this makes their anguish different from ours—but there is solace in their doubt-filled waiting for a sign of his grace and mercy. The psalmists' doubts can free us from spiritual nostalgia, from the feeling that there is a world of certainty we can never recover. The Psalms help us to understand that there is no human era, even one where faith in God is adamantine, in which doubt and anguish at his inscrutability were not present.

Doubt, the psalmists say, over and over, is intrinsic to belief. It is fanciful to believe that faith delivers certainty. As a wise friend of mine says, doubt is to certainty as shadow is to light. Doubting, the psalms say, tests faith and deepens it. A life of faith is *supposed* to feel like a test of human endurance, and if we find faith drying up inside us, the psalms tell us not to fear despair. From knowing despair, the psalms teach us, we come to know what hope actually is, and it is the memory of despair that can make us fight so hard to live in hope. Our weeping, the psalmist says, may endure for a night, "but joy cometh in the morning."

This duality of hope and despair is intrinsic to the structure of the Psalms. Their recurrent pattern is lamentation followed by affirmation, so that all consolation—through faith in God's power and mercy—is earned, as it were, through an unsparing focus on what it actually is that we seek consolation for. A psalm that begins in near despair—"My days are like a shadow that declineth"—concludes with an affirmation of divine order and human continuity through time: "But thou art the same, and thy years shall have no end."

Like Job, the psalmists engage in a constant dialogue with God, asking him to explain the intolerable gap between the world as it is and the world as they wish it to be. The psalmists do more than wait for justice. They question why it never seems to arrive: "How long will ye judge unjustly and accept the persons of the wicked?" And the psalmists actually dare to offer God a vision of justice as the standard he should follow:

"Defend the poor and fatherless: do justice to the afflicted and needy." Like Job, the psalmists dare to assert that humans know what justice is. Why does God seem not to understand? The Psalms hauntingly express a paradox about our situation: for all our sins and failings, we can still imagine, with perfect clarity, what a just world would look like. Yet for reasons best known to himself, this all-powerful God of ours withholds this perfect world from our grasp. The consolation that the psalmists offer is that one day the Messiah will appear on earth to usher in the perfect world. Until then, we wait and hope and pray, yearning for justice here on earth. It is not until the Greek city-states of the fifth century BC that men begin to imagine a new kind of activity—they call it politics—which grasps that the work of justice cannot be left to the gods. It must be the work of men.

It becomes possible, at last, to understand those tears of recognition in a concert hall in Utrecht, to see why, in a modern world of unbelief, ancient texts like the book of Job and the Psalms still retain the power to console. It is their extraordinary capacity to give words to our own doubts, our maddening sense of the inscrutability of the world, the absence of justice, the cruelty of fate, and our longing for a world where our experience finds validation and meaning. The very fact that they have been saved across thousands of years, recited, copied out, rescued from the flames, affirms that we are not alone in our search to give meaning to the world and to our existence. We do not have to believe in God to believe this, but we do need faith in human beings and the chain of meanings we have inherited.

Two

Waiting for the Messiah

Paul's Epistles

The man who created a new language of Christian consolation from the Jewish prophetic tradition came from an artisan's family in a provincial town on the social and geographical margins of the Roman world. He was, by his own description, a young Jewish zealot from a family of sail and tent makers in the Greek-speaking port town of Tarsus, the Roman administrative capital of a region called Cilicia, located in what is now southeastern Turkey. By zealot, a word he used with pride, he meant someone who lived his life believing in the coming of a Messiah, as prophesied in Isaiah, Jeremiah, and Psalms. He was a Pharisee, a member of a Jewish sect that practiced strict observance of the Jewish law in the midst of a pagan Roman trading city. For a fiery young man in his twenties, temptation was always near, and his commitment to God and the Torah was tested in the brothels and bars all around him, as well as in the arguments about politics and religion that flowed between shopkeepers and artisans crowded into the markets and alleyways of Tarsus.

Named Saul at birth, he was an unprepossessing figure with

a quick temper and an unbridled tongue, and he came of age at exactly the moment another zealot, a carpenter's son, began preaching in the Judaean hills that he was the Messiah promised by the prophets of Israel.

Jewish leaders in Jerusalem might have ignored Jesus of Nazareth's ministry to the poor or his presumptuous claim that he was the Messiah, since there had been many such trouble-makers in the past; but they could not stand by quietly when he strode into the Temple, the seat of their power, overthrew the tables of the money changers, and accused the religious authorities of allowing the holy place to become a den of thieves. Enraged, the Jewish leaders of Jerusalem handed him over to the Roman occupation authorities. Some Roman governors might have chosen to let such rabble-rousers go. What business was it of Rome to settle Jewish quarrels? But this one was proclaiming that he had arrived in Jerusalem to overthrow all earthly authorities and usher in God's kingdom. This was rebellion and sedition, and for this the carpenter's son was crucified.

Usually such a display of brutality would have brought the locals to their senses, but this heresy, unlike so many others, refused to die out. The preacher's disciples scattered, then slowly regrouped, spreading the claim that their crucified leader had in fact reappeared in the flesh, proving that he was, as he had said, the Messiah and that those who believed in him could live in hopeful expectation of his Second Coming. Early Christian communities began to form within the Jewish world, holding goods in common, practicing charity, building a structure of rituals—the bread and the wine in imitation of the Last Supper—and a rudimentary organization. At every moment, they believed they were preparing for the end of time prophesied in Samuel, Daniel, Isaiah, and Deuteronomy.

About two years after Jesus's crucifixion, around AD 33,

members of a Greek-speaking synagogue in Jerusalem dragged one of their congregation, a man named Stephen, before the Sanhedrin, the Jewish court in Jerusalem, charging him with preaching that followers of Jesus would destroy the synagogue and alter the laws handed down by Moses. Saul went to the trial, where he heard Stephen's speech in his own defense.

Stephen argued that it was not he who had blasphemed against Moses, but those who accused him. Did they not remember how the people of Israel had prevented Moses from reaching the promised land? Were they not doing exactly the same thing, persecuting those who were more faithful to God's command than they were? Had they forgotten that it was Moses who had prophesied that God would send them a prophet? Instead of realizing this prophet was Jesus, they had handed him over for crucifixion. You are just like your fathers! Stephen exclaimed. Was there ever a prophet your fathers did not persecute?

Stephen's speech threw the court into an uproar. Men covered their ears so they would not have to listen to the blasphemy; others seized him and dragged him from the court to a place outside the city walls. There they tied his hands behind his back, formed a circle around him, and began pelting him with stones. One of the onlookers who followed the crowd out of the city gates to watch the stoning was Saul.

It was an experience he would never forget: watching a man die like that, hopelessly seeking to protect himself from the blows, staggering, bloodied, in a cloud of dust, amid shouts of hatred, then falling to his knees, stunned, half-dead. Saul would have seen it all, with the bloodthirsty chanting and mockery filling his ears. Stephen's friends came too, helpless to intervene, and they recorded that Stephen cried out, "Lord Jesus, receive my spirit." Some even claimed that his last words were, "Lord, lay not this sin to their charge," before he fell for the final time.

Saul's first reaction to this traumatic moment was radical denial. He enlisted among the Pharisee enforcers who hounded the believers who listened to such rebels. He administered the thirty-nine lashes customarily inflicted on those who broke Jewish law. He rode to Damascus to rout out the sect there. It was on the road between Jerusalem and Damascus, with the memory of Stephen's death in his mind, the looks of fear and hatred in the eyes of those whom he had whipped pressing on his soul, that he heard a voice like the one that had come to Job in the whirlwind, this time issuing out of a blinding light from heaven:

"Saul, Saul, why do you persecute me?"

He fell from his horse and lay stunned, as the voice of Jesus told him to go to the house of a Christian believer in Damascus and await further instructions.

Saul's collapse on the road to Damascus was an experience of mental anguish so convulsive that it translated into physical breakdown. It left him blind and helpless, able only to stagger into Damascus on the arms of his associates and take shelter in the dark. Now he had to face himself alone. What if everything he had ever believed was wrong? What if those he had persecuted had been right? What if Israel's God had sent the Messiah and, instead of hailing him and rallying to his cause, Saul had been persecuting those who had seen the truth? In the days he lived in darkness in a believer's house in Damascus, his mental world collapsed.

But when his sight and his wits returned, his recovery was swift and his conversion complete. Moving from the old faith to the new, he believed, would be seamless. In his new faith, as in the old, there was only one God, the God of Israel. In both his old life and the new, he could keep the Jewish laws and win followers to the new faith from among the Pharisees, the worshippers of the Greco-Roman gods, and the adherents of the Stoics and Epicureans. Though he believed now that Jesus was the chosen one, he also understood that his coming had been predicted by the Jewish prophets. The decisive new element was that the Messiah promised everlasting life to those who believed. Once Saul recovered in Damascus, he went into the desert to purify himself; when he returned to Jerusalem, he was a changed man, no longer Saul, now named Paul.

Paul's own conversion experience convinced him that, if God so ordered, each of us could become a new person, literally from one day to the next. "Listen I tell you a mystery. We will not all sleep, but we will all be changed—in a flash, in the twinkling of an eye." A human being was not chained forever by habits, compulsion, addictions, and needs. A person could be reborn anew, redeemed and granted a better life. The classical Stoics and Epicureans held out no such hope: you could discipline your nature, control your impulses, but you could not become a new person. Paul made it his life's work to persuade everyone he met that God could change their lives in the here and now, to prepare them for eternity.

At this point, in AD 34 or 35, there was no Bible, no testaments of Matthew, Mark, Luke, or John, no Acts of the Apostles, no priests and bishops, no ecclesiastical organization, nothing but an oral tradition kept by a small band of Jesus's disciples, Judean fishermen, tax collectors, and country people who spoke mostly Aramaic. Compared to them, Paul was a cosmopolitan—he hailed from a Mediterranean seaport, he spoke Greek fluently, and he was the only one among them already familiar with the trade routes by land and sea that linked the empire together. The original apostles, led by Peter, were suspicious of him at first, but he plunged into the synagogues of Jerusalem and began preaching, using his own conversion story as evidence of God's power. By his own admission, he was not much of a speaker, and he was not a charismatic presence, but he possessed a vulnerability and charm that drew people to him. "For I am the least of the apostles," he told the Christian community in Corinth, "and do not even deserve to be called an apostle, because I persecuted the church of God." But I am what I am, he said, and besides, I worked harder than all the other disciples.

He may have worked harder than they, but Jesus's original apostles remained suspicious. They had known Jesus. He had not. They had prayed with Jesus in the garden of Gethsemane, and he had not. But he overcame their doubts by making himself indispensable.

He understood that a sect with only an oral tradition to guide it would not survive. An oral tradition lacks a steadying, central authority: without such an authority, their group risked fragmenting into feuding sects that would be crushed between the twin hostilities of the Jewish and Roman authorities. Somehow, if the faith was to survive, it would have to generate a creed, written down to guide the faithful.

Paul's letters to the communities that he visited provided such guidance. They are practical documents, seeking to encourage, to chastise, to reverse backsliding, to clarify ethical and theological disputes. Sometimes he used his letters to slap down factional fights and challenges to his authority. Still, if that were all they offered, they might not have left a trace, but this sail maker's son made his Epistles the foundation stones of an orthodoxy that survives to the present day.

He turned Christianity from a Jewish sect into a universal faith open to all. The other disciples, Peter especially, were wary of the Gentiles. Paul thought differently. He came from a port, where Jews and Gentiles, pagan worshippers, Epicureans and Stoics all competed in the marketplace for the allegiance and commerce of their neighbors. Paul believed that the Messiah had come to save all men. It was Paul who was to declare, in his letter to the Galatians, the truly revolutionary message:

> There is neither Jew nor Greek, there is neither bond nor free; there is neither male nor female, for ye are all one in Christ Jesus.

The consolation offered in the Old Testament—of Job and the Psalms—had been written by and for the chosen people alone. The consolations of Stoic and Epicurean philosophy—of Cicero and Seneca, Epicurus and Epictetus—to which we will return, were written for the Greek and Roman elites. Paul believed that the Messiah's imminent coming would bring salvation for all. Paul created a language of consolation that was the first and most powerful language of human equality ever created, the one that, mostly unacknowledged, underpins the secular, revolutionary, socialist, humanist, and liberal languages of equality that came afterward.

In the end times, once the kingdom of heaven had come down to earth, all human beings might be equal, Paul knew, but in the here and now, believers must make accommodations to reality. His doctrine affirmed the equality of slave and free but counseled against slaves rising against their masters; he affirmed that while women and men were equal in Christ, women must obey their husbands. As for the powers that be, Paul never disputed Roman authority. He indeed insisted on being accorded the rights of a Roman citizen. Render unto Caesar, his master had preached, and he was faithful to that injunction.

Until the Messiah ushered in a new world of revolutionary equality, Paul taught, believers had to learn patience and endurance. He had to learn it too. Suffering, he told his followers in

Rome, teaches perseverance. "And perseverance produces character and character produces hope." A man learned to console himself, he was telling them, by accepting a large share of tribulation. Over the course of thirty years or more as an unmarried itinerant preacher traversing the lonely roads of the eastern Roman Empire, he adapted his message of good news to the sorrows and anxieties of the humble men and women to whom he ministered, people who wanted to believe that the Messiah was coming but also needed to be consoled for the harshness of their daily existence.

Where the Epicurean codes of the Roman world taught that the only sensible course in life was to seek pleasure and avoid suffering, the new faith made suffering the core of human experience and the most shocking image of that suffering—a crucifixion—its abiding symbol.

It was Paul's idea to model his discipleship on Christ's own via dolorosa. Suffering both tested faith and proved its resilience. Paul, who had used the lash himself on Jewish backsliders, now made a point of confessing that he also had been beaten:

> Five times I have received at the hands of the Jews the forty lashes less one. Three times I have been beaten with rods; once I was stoned. Three times I have been shipwrecked; a night and a day have I been adrift at sea; on frequent journeys, in danger from rivers, danger from robbers, danger from my own people, danger from Gentiles, danger in the city, danger in the wilderness, danger at sea, danger from false brethren; in toil and hardship, through many a sleepless night, in hunger and thirst, often without food, in cold and exposure. And, apart from other things, there is the daily pressure upon of me of my anxiety for all the churches.

In telling of his own humiliations, Paul was teaching believers to ennoble suffering itself, to understand that, as Jesus had suffered on the cross before he returned in glory, so must they suffer, in expectation of salvation.

He drew on the Hebrew Bible for inspiration and authority. He recast Abraham's willingness to obey God, even to the length of sacrificing his son Isaac, as authorization for his doctrine of choosing to suffer as the ultimate proof of faith. For once Isaac was spared, Abraham had been rewarded with God's ultimate blessing:

> I will surely bless you and make your descendants as numerous as the stars in the sky and as the sand on the seashore. Your descendants will take possession of the cities of their enemies and through your offspring all nations on earth will be blessed because you have obeyed me.

"All nations on earth": there it was, the warrant Paul needed to spread the news of the Messiah's coming to all peoples.

A decade or so after Jesus's crucifixion, Paul settled in Thessalonica, a Greco-Roman capital city on the Via Egnatia, the imperial highway to the east, filled with devotees of pagan gods as well as Roman administrators and servants. He remained there for two years, plying his trade as a sail maker, while building a congregation who would meet in the house of one of the faithful. He arrived promising them that the Second Coming, the end-time, was imminent.

By the time he left for Athens two years later, several of his congregants had died, and the rest wondered whether their departed friends would be saved and how long they would have to wait for their own salvation. When Paul got word that his Thessalonians were backsliding, he dispatched his trusted assistant Timothy to them, with a letter he hoped would restore them to the right path. Paul told them that Jesus's imminent return might steal upon them as suddenly, and shockingly, as a woman going into labor. But when that travail came, they should prepare themselves for the end of time and the dawn of paradise:

> For the Lord himself will come down from heaven, with a shout, with the voice of the archangel and with the trumpet call of God, and the dead in Christ will rise first. After that, we who are still alive and are left will be caught up together with them in the clouds to meet the Lord in the air. And so we will be with the Lord forever.

Wherefore, he told the Thessalonians, "comfort one another with these words." No more influential idea of consolation was ever devised. Instead of aging and decay, instead of fear and loss, a climactic moment would come when time would be abolished and believers would live beyond loss and pain in an eternal present. This yearning had begun with the Old Testament prophets, but it was Paul who turned it into an everyday longing, first of hundreds, then of thousands, then of millions of believers along the shores of the eastern Mediterranean in the first century after Christ.

Paul fervently believed that he would live to see the Messiah, and he preached to his congregations that the blessed arrival was imminent. But when the Messiah did not come, when the hard missionary work stretched from years into decades, he began recrafting the ecstatic message to console those who had already waited long enough, who had lost loved ones and were wondering whether the promise was still true. As a practical political leader trying to hold doubting communities of faith together around the Mediterranean, Paul found himself obliged to craft a rhetoric of hope that would console believers for a deliverance that never seemed to come.

Paul also understood a paradox: that hope becomes believable only if those who have hope acknowledge how difficult it is to put doubt and despair to rest. Paul's Epistles quote Job and the Psalms in many places, as if he had learned that words console only if they serve as a mirror in which would-be believers see their own doubts reflected.

Paul was persuasive because he never hid the price he had paid for believing his own good news. After being imprisoned and narrowly escaping death on a missionary trip to Asia Minor, he told the community of Corinth that he returned to them "in weakness, with great fear and trembling," so low in spirits that he needed their comfort so he could comfort others. This confession of his own dejection and heartbreak helped him to secure and hold the trust of his fellow believers. In his fragility, they saw an image of their own.

After the first ecstatic energies released by his conversion, after the early years in Thessalonica when he discovered his own gifts as an organizer, theologian, and spiritual leader, the road of faith became rougher and harder for Paul to travel with every passing year. Synagogues threw him into the street. Jewish mobs chased him out of cities. Governors tossed him into jail. Communities that he thought were firmly committed to the Lord lost their faith or were seduced by rival preachers. He was imprisoned at Ephesus and Philippi, and in letters written from prison, he called himself, disconsolately, an "ambassador in chains." When he left Ephesus, in about AD 55, after more than twenty years crisscrossing the Mediterranean, he told the faithful there that he was going to Jerusalem, though he feared he would be called before the Sanhedrin, as Stephen had been, and he doubted—and they wept to hear it—that he would ever see them again. He warned the Ephesians that "savage wolves will come among you and will not spare the flock." It was up to them to hold fast. He could help them no further.

In Jerusalem, when he once again told his story of how he had witnessed the martyrdom of Stephen, how he had persecuted the faithful and had been saved on the road to Damascus, Jews rioted in the city—demanding his death—and he was taken before the Sanhedrin. In the courtroom, a zealot struck him in the face and Paul exploded in fury. Turning to the judges, he cried, "You sit here to judge me, according to the law, yet you yourself violate the law by commanding that I be struck." His words were an uncanny echo of Stephen's in the same courtroom. The Sanhedrin sent him to be flogged by the Romans, but when the soldiers stripped him and tied him down, he shouted that he was a Roman citizen and they relented, dispatching him to Caesarea, where he remained in prison for two years. He kept demanding to be brought before Caesar for trial and the Romans eventually agreed, shipping him off, in the hands of a sympathetic centurion, for trial in Rome. When he arrived, he appeared before the leadership of the Jewish community in the city, still wearing chains, insisting that he had never done anything against his own people. "Our salvation," he told the Jews of Rome, "is nearer now than when we first believed. The night is nearly over; the day is almost here."

The book of Acts records tersely that "some were convinced by what he said but others would not believe." The historical record trails away at this point, with Paul awaiting trial and preaching to skeptical Jews. He would have been in his early sixties at this point, an old man by the standard of his times. The historian Tacitus tells us that when Rome burned in AD 62, the tyrant Nero blamed the Christians for the fires, and thousands were routed out and killed. It is thought Paul was one of them, but we do not know.

We do know what tormented him most, what he needed consolation for at the end of his life: the enduring enmity of

his own people. In the letter he wrote to the Romans, he had
made a stark confession:

> I speak the truth in Christ—I am not lying, my conscience
> confirms it in the Holy Spirit—I have great sorrow and
> unceasing anguish in my heart. For I could wish that I
> myself were cursed and cut off from Christ for the sake of
> my brothers, those of my own race, the people of Israel.
> Theirs is the adoption as sons; theirs the divine glory, the
> covenants, the receiving of the law, the temple worship
> and the promises. Theirs are the patriarchs, and from them
> is traced the human ancestry of Christ, who is God over all,
> forever praised!

He had made it his life's work to be an apostle to the Gentiles, but his deepest disappointment had been his failure to
"somehow arouse my own people . . . and save some of them."
Some of them . . . the phrase suggests how truly discouraging it
had been.

He had thought that the promise in Genesis and the Psalms
was for all men, and that his own people would enlist in the
propagation of a universal faith, based as it was on their scriptures. The faith of the Jews rested on the belief that they were
God's chosen people and that the covenant made with Abraham was reserved for them and them alone. To be faithful was
to observe Jewish law. But Paul had seen Gentiles, men and
women who did not know the law or even the ancient scriptures but who lived a godly life. From them, he had learned
that "a man is justified by faith apart from observing the law."

He had created a new faith in which men, he proclaimed,
were saved not by their works, by their performance of ritual obligations, but by God's all-forgiving grace. From his
own moment on the road to Damascus, he believed that when

you were blessed with this grace, it was all the validation you would ever need.

Yet one has to ask how Paul himself endured the utter opposition of his own people and his forced estrangement from his own tribe. He quoted, in rueful recognition, the despairing words of the prophet Isaiah: "I have labored in vain. I have spent my strength for nothing at all."

Paul was honest enough to confess—and this honesty gave his faith its power of attraction to succeeding generations—that he remained, throughout his life, a man torn between the demands of a new faith and the deep hold of the one he had left behind. In his letter to the faithful in Rome, he cries:

> I do not understand what I do. For what I want to do I do not do, but what I hate I do. . . . What a wretched man I am! Who will rescue me from this body that is subject to death?

This is the Paul whose anguish speaks across time to those who believe and those who do not, a Paul whose faith endured not in spite of but because of adversity.

Paul clung to the hope that the Messiah would come, but day by day he found solace at hand—in the ordinary routines of missionary work, in the friendships he had made, in his recollections of those he had brought to faith, in their tears as he departed Ephesus, and in their sorrow as he left them behind. His love for them was never abstract. He remembered them in all their singularity, these men and women who sheltered him, plied the same trade, journeyed the same roads, endured the same prisons. The names of these faithful recur throughout his letters: men and women, rich and poor, real people in all their individuality: Phoebe and Priscilla, Andronicus and Urbanus, Titus, Barnabas, Timothy. He takes care to single them out, to thank them for their fellowship and their comfort. With all of them, he had created a bond that distance and persecution, arguments and quarrels could not break. In the long hard road from Damascus, he had learned something that had not been in the ancient scriptures. He had learned, in fact, the lesson that faith alone might not be consolation enough. It was the living, and their love, who gave him hope:

> If I have faith that can move mountains but have not love, I am nothing. If I give all I possess to the poor and surrender my body to the flames but have not love, I gain nothing. Love is patient, love is kind. It does not envy. It does not boast, it is not proud. It is not rude, it is not self-seeking, it is not easily angered, it keeps no record of wrongs. Love does not delight in evil but rejoices with the truth. It always protects, always trusts, always hopes, always perseveres.

It is possible, given the kind of scorching honesty he lived by, to read this as a veiled confession. He truly had faith to move mountains, but faith had not been enough. It was the love he had been shown, by these strangers who became his companions and friends, a love that he had perhaps failed to reciprocate, during his decades of ceaseless labor, that he now knew was the light to live by:

> But where there are prophecies, they shall cease; where there are tongues, they will be stilled. Where there is knowledge it will pass away.

Not even the ancient prophecies—of Isaiah, of Daniel, of Abraham—were now enough to console him with the certainty that he had lived a life in obedience to God's command:

For we know in part and we prophesy in part, but when perfection comes, the imperfect disappears. . . . Now we see but a poor reflection in the mirror; then we shall see face to face. Now I know in part; then I shall know fully, even as I am fully known.

As an old man at the end of a long road, Paul knew that the Messiah might not be coming in his lifetime. He knew that he had served to the limit of his strength; and he knew that the proof of what he had managed to achieve lay in the love of those he was about to leave behind. In their love—real, intense, enduring—he had been given the only sign that humans can ever have of what God's love might be like:

And now these three remain: faith, hope and love. But the greatest of these is love.

Three

Cicero's Tears

Letters on the Death of His Daughter

The early Christian communities of the Mediterranean world lived among elite pagans schooled in Epicurean and Stoic ideas of how to sustain hope in the face of discouragement and misfortune. Unlike Paul's Christians, neither Stoics nor Epicureans made universal claims: their philosophies were written for and by a Roman male elite. Unlike the new faith, Roman philosophy did not take suffering as a proof of divine favor, but as a misfortune to be mastered with self-discipline. Stoics taught that a wise man should learn to endure suffering, while Epicureans believed men should avoid pain as best they could and live for pleasure. The purpose of life, for an Epicurean, was to live well. Consolation was delivered not by salvation but by social approval. The pagan philosophers did not suppose that men could be consoled, as the Christians were, by a vision of the universe as meaningful and of time as having a purpose or direction. Some Epicureans, Lucretius in particular, strongly suspected the universe had no order other than random chance. In the face of tragic loss and the prospect of death, the Roman philosophers counseled a manly code of self-control. If a man could control his reactions to loss, consolation would come in the respect and admiration of his male peers.

When Paul began his preaching, these ideas were long entrenched as the conventional wisdom of the Roman upper and middle classes. The leading Roman politician of the late Roman republic, Marcus Tullius Cicero, who lived from 106 to 43 BC, prided himself on his mastery of this Stoic code and fancied himself a philosopher of consolation. His book *Consolatio* has vanished, but his *Tusculan Disputations* have survived, and they are a brilliant dialogue on the Stoic creed.

When his beloved daughter died, without warning, in 45 BC, Cicero had to apply Stoicism to stanch a deep wound in his own life. Not for the first time in our story, words met their match in life's pain, and philosophical writings about suffering proved unable to console even the man who had written them.

We know Cicero's daughter—as we know most women in the ancient world—only through what a man (in this case an adoring father) said of her. Little Tullia, he called her in his letters, dearest to his heart. She looked just like her father, he said, though what she inherited from him—he with his long nose, cruel eyes, rounded head, downward turn of the lips, and cutting voice crafted for declamation and malicious jokes—is anybody's guess. He praised her womanly modesty, but he did not think to leave more than a trace of the singular person she was. As a writer who could recall verbatim the utterances of colleagues and philosophers, he left but one instance of words his daughter spoke. When she was still a child, he reported, she had demanded that he ask his friend Atticus to bring her a present on his next visit and had insisted that her father pledge that his friend keep the promise. Atticus had a young daughter too, and the two men exchanged letters in which they appreciated the comedy of fathers being ordered around by their daughters.

Cicero loved her, no doubt, but she was a chattel. He had married her off to three prominent husbands: the first died, the second divorced her, and the third was a wastrel named Dolabella. Tullia was pregnant for the first time—at the age of thirty-two—and her third marriage was heading for collapse. The father insisted that the marriage had been not his idea but his wife's, foisted upon him when he was away governing a province in the east. And now another divorce was imminent with all the whispering that would follow, not to mention the risk that Dolabella would default on the rest of the marriage payment he owed Cicero. There was also the delicate question, hanging in the air, as to whether the errant son-in-law might consider himself free to betray his father-in-law to Caesar, the dictator whose ascent to power was crushing the republican form of government Cicero had spent his life defending.

His daughter had been there to witness the worst and best moments of Cicero's illustrious career. He remembered how she had fainted with anxiety and fear when the Senate sent him into exile in 58 BC. When the Senate voted to recall him the following year, it was she, not her mother, who made the journey south from Rome to the dock in Brundisium to greet the boat carrying him back from Athens. It was she who traveled in the litter that carried him through cheering crowds in town after town as he made his triumphant progress back to Rome.

While the courts and the Senate of Rome were the sites where he displayed his scathing oratory, his sneering asides, his magisterial command of the Latin tongue, intercut with show-off references in Greek, she was the audience for his private confessions of folly. After more than thirty years of marriage, the sixty-year-old Cicero had divorced his formidable wife, Terentia, and married his eighteen-year-old ward, Publilia. What had possessed him? Was it lust? Publilia's inheritance? Who knew? Afterward, he regretted the decision, and from

Tullia he sought forgiveness and forbearance. It was with Tullia, not Publilia, that he spent what private time his public duties allowed. In January and February 45 BC, as father and daughter awaited the term of her confinement, she would have had confessions of her own, painful for him to hear, of Dolabella's betrayals and the breakdown of her marriage. Father and daughter were drawn closer as they shared the disarray of their disintegrating personal lives.

Cicero's private worries were joined to public ones. He had lined up on Pompey's side in the civil war that had ended with the battle of Pharsalus in 48 BC, only to realize, almost immediately, that he had backed a loser. While he had made it up with Julius Caesar, who had emerged victorious, he had been unable to prevent Caesar from taking dictatorial powers, sidelining the Senate and putting in jeopardy Cicero's lifework.

For Cicero, the republic meant much more than the cursus honorum of posts—quaestor, aedile, consul—that he had climbed by age forty; more than the courts, where he had won fame with his oratory; more than the Senate, where his speeches convicting the Catiline conspirators in 62 BC were widely credited with saving Rome. The republic was the frame that gave Cicero's life its meaning. To be a republican meant to practice the virtues of the Roman citizen: to be public-spirited, to sacrifice one's life, if need be, for the defense of the republic, and to be stoic in the endurance of pain. Republicanism was a male code, honored in the breach as much as in the observance, but central to it was contempt for womanly weakness, for tears. A woman might grieve, rend her garments, cover her face with a veil, but a man must accept the blows of fate and the approach of death with philosophical calm and self-control. Roman citizens who bore the burden and the glory of defending the republic were supposed to endure the perils of both public and private life with stoic reserve.

Cicero had adhered to this version of consolation in his letters, all written to men, all offering *consolatio* for the reverses of fortune customary in politics but endemic in a time of civil war: proscription, confiscation of estates, revenge killings, and score settling, as well as the less mortal but still wounding misfortunes of slander and gossip. Created for these experiences of Roman politics, *consolatio* was also intended for private grief: loss of parents, children, wives, favored slaves, and other servants.

Cicero became the master of this manly and moralizing discourse. As he wrote in 46 BC to a male friend who had suffered some reversal:

There is a form of consolation, extremely commonplace I grant you, which we ought always to have on our lips and in our hearts—to remember that we are human beings, born under a law which renders our life a target for all the slings and arrows of fortune, and that it is not for us to refuse to live under the conditions of our birth, nor to resent so impatiently the misfortunes we can by no process of forethought avoid, but, by recalling to mind what has befallen others, to induce the reflection that what has happened to ourselves is nothing new.

Consolatio was a secular code; the gods played only a vestigial role. Men were supposed to sacrifice animals to the gods, just as women of a superior rank were chosen to guard the precincts of the temple of the vestal virgins. Both understood that while fate was in the hands of the gods, they watched from on high, aloof and indifferent to human tragedy. But this could be borne and endured, in a republican understanding of the world, just so long as the republic continued to provide a frame of meaning for a man's life. The brute terror that sent people asking, in the Psalms or in Job, why God had visited horror on mankind was held at bay by faith in Rome and the empire's astounding expansion and extent. As long as the republic endured and Rome remained preeminent among the nations, a man's life could make sense; but now, with Caesar in full control by 45 BC and the Senate reduced to a nonentity, Cicero believed his republic was in its death throes.

This was the larger context in which the most famous Roman of his day was asked to endure the disaster that struck him in February of that year, when he learned that his grandson—called Lentulus—had been born, struggling but alive, but his daughter, despite all the efforts of the best midwives and physicians, had died delivering him.

The blow was catastrophic. So distraught was he that there is no mention of her funeral or cremation in any of his letters. He appears to have left her body as well as her child in the hands of Dolabella's household slaves and fled south from Rome, to his estate of Astura in the Bay of Antium. There he shut himself away, could not bear company, suffered sleepless nights, and by day wandered in the woods of his estate, alone, disheveled, and weeping. This went on for six weeks, through the rest of February and early March. When his oldest friend, Atticus, asked after him, Cicero confessed that womanly tears were his enemy. "I fight against them as much as I can: but as yet I am not equal to the struggle."

As his grieving became public knowledge, it began to polarize opinion back in Rome. His friends were surprised that this most articulate and domineering of men could be so undone. His collapse gave his enemies the opportunity to brand him as an effeminate hypocrite, unable to practice the stoic self-control he had preached.

Cicero was trapped. He had perfected *consolatio* and now he was inconsolable. Words were useless. He realized, too late, how much he had loved his daughter. He understood, again too late, that he had been deranged to divorce his wife, confessing to a friend that thoughts of her were "wounds I cannot touch without deep groans." The frame that gave meaning to his life had collapsed.

At this moment, in March of 45 BC, Servius Sulpicius, an old schoolmate who had studied oratory with Cicero, wrote him a letter of condolence from Athens, where he was serving as governor. He began by confessing that had he been present at Cicero's side, he would have needed comforting himself, not just for private griefs but for the desperate state of the republic, now firmly under the control of the dictator Julius Caesar. It was this—the parlous state of the republic, not the death of a child—that they should lament. What, he dared ask his old friend, are you crying for?

> Why is it that a private grief should agitate you so deeply? Think how fortune has hitherto dealt with us. Reflect that we have had snatched from us what ought to be no less dear to human beings than their children—country, honor, rank, every political distinction. What additional wound to your feelings could be inflicted by this particular loss? Or where is the heart that should not by this time have lost all sensibility and learned to regard everything else as of minor importance? Is it on her account, pray, that you sorrow?

Why weep for Tullia? he asked. What possible life could she have lived? Her husbands had either died or betrayed her. She would miss out on the entirety of a woman's hopes: to see her son grow to achieve power and preeminence. Each of the opportunities available to a woman, Sulpicius said, "had been withdrawn before it was fulfilled." She had lived to share in the joy of her father's brilliant career. Should that not be enough for her?

He wrote that he had recently passed through Corinth and Megara, once prosperous towns and now desolate ruins, "lying prostrate and demolished before one's very eyes." If this was the fate of all human achievement, he went on, all men should take heed of their own finitude. Why, again he asked, should Cicero be so grieved by the death "of one weak woman"?

He warned Cicero not to let his enemies believe that he was crushed by the loss of a daughter. Make them believe you are grieving for the republic, he advised. Do not imitate those physicians who fail to practice the healing art on themselves, and remember, he concluded with a dark warning, your grief makes you vulnerable. If you wish to have a future in politics, put away womanly sorrow:

> We have seen you on many occasions bear good fortune with a noble dignity which greatly enhanced your fame: now is the time for you to convince us that you are able to bear bad fortune equally well.

Cicero replied that he took comfort in his friend's "partnership in my sickness of soul" and admitted that it was "dishonorable not to bear my affliction in the way in which you think it ought to be borne." Still, he wasn't up to it. He felt "crushed and hardly able to fight my grief." In the republic of the past, he went on, "private grief was mitigated by high positions" of service to the state. But now the republic was an empty shell, and his public life was bereft of meaning:

> It was no pleasure to me to do anything in the courts; as for the senate-house, I could not bear the sight of it.

In times past, he went on, whenever he suffered reverses in his public life,

> I always had a sanctuary to flee to and a haven of rest; I had one whose sweet converse could help me to drop the burden of all my anxieties and sorrows.

Now, he said, desolately,

> I absent myself both from my home and from the courts, since neither can the sorrow the state causes me any longer be consoled by my home life nor the sorrow of my home by the state.

Consolation was possible only when the public life of the republic gave his existence meaning. Now, he concluded, "in a period during which we must adapt ourselves unreservedly to the inclination of one man," there was no consolation to be had.

When word of Cicero's continued grieving got out in Rome, his male friends lost patience. His behavior was not merely a display of weakness. It also threatened to undermine the code itself. Brutus reproached him for failing to display the stern self-control of a Cato. A historian whom Cicero had once begged, shamelessly, to be praised in his latest work now wrote him a partly jocular, partly needling request to pull himself together:

> Come now! Shall you be the only man not to see what is obvious—you who with your keen wits penetrate the deepest secrets? You, the only man not to perceive your daily lamentations are doing you no good?

When Atticus, his oldest friend, gently urged him to put his grief behind him and resume his duties, Cicero would have

none of it. "All consolation," he said, "is defeated by pain." And
then he added, as if some spark of hope had just been kindled,

> I have, however, done something no one ever did before
> me. I have consoled myself through writing. I will send
> you the book, if the clerks have copied it. I can tell you
> that there is no consolation like it.

In a sudden rebirth of activity, he ransacked his library
shelves, looking for inspiration anew, ordered his freed slave
and amanuensis Tiro to find the ancient Greek sources, and
began to write an entire book whose title was expressive of his
mood: *Consolatio*.

Only a fragment of it remains. In this surviving portion,
Cicero speculates feverishly on the nature of the soul, whether it
was "moist or airy or fiery," how entwined the soul must be with
"the memory, mind or thought," and how these capacities must
be the work of the gods. "Whatever it is that thinks, knows,
lives and grows"—his Tullia—"must be heavenly, divine and
therefore eternal." He began pestering his friend Atticus to buy
him some land where he could erect a shrine to her. Though
this came to nothing, as far as we can tell, he was deadly serious,
aware that he was making amends for failing to understand how
deeply he had needed her.

Atticus chided him about his obsession with a shrine for his
daughter and begged him to show more composure, since Rome
was beginning to talk. Cicero replied with some bitterness,

> You exhort me and say others want me to hide the depth
> of my grief. Can I do so better than by spending all my
> days in writing? Though I do it, not to hide, but rather to
> soften and to heal my feelings, still, if I do myself but little
> good, I certainly keep up appearances.

A father who had just lost his daughter might have sought comfort in the company of his infant grandson, but apart from urging Atticus to ensure that the little creature had all the care a household could provide, Cicero never went to Rome to see him. Within months, the child too was dead.

It was as if the code he lived by—manly reserve, composure, devotion to public affairs—had closed off all routes to healing except one: to regain his public stature as the sage of the republic, which was now being crushed by Caesar's tyranny. At first this path too seemed closed to him, as he confessed to Atticus:

> You call me back to my old way of life. Well, I have long been bewailing the loss of the republic, and that was what I was doing, though less strongly; for I had one harbor of refuge. Now I positively cannot follow my old way of life and employment; nor do I think I ought to care what others think about that . . .

But he knew this role was the only one left to him. True consolation as opposed to temporary comfort, he finally accepted, meant becoming Cicero once again, the scourge of tyrants and upholder of republican values. Slowly, doggedly, alone with himself in his villa, he wrote himself back into that identity. By May, after three months of frantic self-torment and solitude at Astura, he felt strong enough to say to Atticus,

> If those who think my spirit is crushed and broken anew knew the amount and the nature of the literary work I am doing, I fancy, if they are human, they would hold me guiltless. There is nothing to blame me for, if I have so far recovered as to have my mind free to engage in difficult writing, and even something to praise me for. . . . I am doing everything I can to cast off my sorrow.

By July, he had understood that grief may resist all comfort, but eventually it succumbs to time itself:

There are many roads to consolation, but this is the straightest: let reason bring what time is sure to bring about.

In late summer, he was ready to return to his estate at Tusculum, haunted though it was by memories of Tullia and Terentia and the family life that once was his. There, in imitation of the Greek academies at Athens, he had constructed arcades, where he placed sofas for guests to recline and discourse on philosophical subjects, and he began to write the *Tusculan Disputations*, a series of dialogues in which he played all the parts, ruminating on the nature of death, grief, and pain. Philosophy, the Greeks had taught him, existed to teach men not to fear death. Having felt the sting of death, he was ready now to write his own philosophy of consolation.

He read voraciously for these Tusculan discourses, chiefly in the ancient tragedians, Euripides, Aeschylus, and Sophocles, those great artists of irrecoverable folly and human delusion. He found that his admiration had deepened for the Spartans, for their virtuous contempt for pain and their willingness to die for their city, and he returned, little by little, to the austere verities of a code that only months earlier, in the depths of his grief, had seemed to demand too much of him. In the *Disputations*, he writes, as if to remind himself,

For the name virtue comes from *vir*, a man, and courage is the peculiar distinction of a man: and this virtue has two principal duties, to despise death and pain. We must then exert these if we would be men of virtue, or rather, if we would be men.

The soft parts of the soul, he now believed, led to "lamentations and womanish tears," and these soft parts of a man's soul should be kept under strict confinement, "like our servants, in safe custody, and almost with chains."

In the late summer of 45 BC, he wrote an essay, "On Grief." He now looked back at the torment of sorrow he had lived through in February and March as a mad illness. He had been grieving not for her—since she could suffer no more—but for himself. The madness had been nothing other than cowardice in the face of his own death. In a series of syllogisms, logical perhaps but tense with pent-up feeling, Cicero declared to the world, but most of all to himself,

> A wise man is never affected with grief: for all wise men are brave; therefore, a wise man is never subject to grief.

Cicero had submitted himself once again to the Stoic code that had been beyond him only months before. His problem now, he thought, if he was to resume life as the Cicero of old, was to match wisdom with bravery.

The demands of returning to public life in Rome required a continuously convincing performance of Stoic heroism. He vowed to Atticus,

> When I come to Rome, they shall have nothing to find fault with in my looks or my conversation. The cheerfulness with which I used to temper the sadness of the times, I have lost forever: but there shall be no lack of courage and firmness in my bearing or my words.

Once castigated for political opportunism, he now understood that surviving his daughter's death required him to choose

one path and stick to it. Following that path was made easier
by the unfolding political disaster around him. Caesar's dicta-
torship left him with only one choice: to resist tyranny to the
death if necessary.

As he wrote to a confidant in 44 BC, he would rather perish
in a noble cause—the defense of the republic—than live under
despotic rule:

> Undoubtedly my courage, weakened as it was perhaps by
> the uncertainty of the issue, has been wonderfully fortified
> by the loss of all hope . . .

Upon his return to Rome that year, he plunged into the
struggle against Caesar. While he did not join the assassination
plot—Brutus and Cassius kept him out—he was present at the
bloody spectacle in the Senate chamber on the ides of March
when the conspirators' knives brought the dictator down.
When Mark Antony raised his sword against the Senate and
sought to take Caesar's place, Cicero launched a wave of ferocious rhetorical attacks—he called his speeches his Philippics,
after Demosthenes's attacks upon the tyrant Philip of Mace-
don. When his friends urged him to be more cautious, Cicero
became still more reckless, reprising one last time the role that
had created his reputation as the republic's great defender. It
was as if Cicero—having confronted his own fear of death in
the loss of his daughter—now felt able, for the first time in his
calculating life, to throw caution to the winds.

For a brief time, it seemed as if he had put himself on the
winning side. But when Antony and Octavian, Caesar's heir,
united and combined forces with Lepidus in late 43 BC, Cicero
knew he was finished. The victors had him proscribed—which
meant that anyone could hunt him down and kill him for a

bounty. He fled south to his estate, briefly considered escaping to Greece by sea, and then thought better of it. No more running now. It was time to face his fate. As the killers closed in, Plutarch tells us, Cicero ordered the servants bearing his litter to set him down and calmly awaited their arrival. He even knew one of the assassins, having argued his case in court. It was too late and too undignified to plead for mercy, to use his famous eloquence in one last attempt to dodge the blow. Squalid, unkempt, "his face wasted by anxiety," in Plutarch's words, but with his gaze steadfast, he inclined his head so that it lay defenseless and uncovered before his assassins' blades. They sawed it from his body and cut off his hands, and sent them back to Rome, where they were displayed as final proof that the republic's last defender and the dictatorial party's most feared opponent was no more. It was said that Antony's wife had been so enraged by Cicero's attacks on her husband that she tore Cicero's tongue out of his decapitated head and pierced it with needles.

Thanks to the legend that Plutarch and others created, Cicero's death linked together Stoic self-command and republican virtue in an association that was to last for a further thousand years. A century later, in AD 55, Seneca died by slow and agonized exsanguination in submission to Nero, whom he had tutored as a young man, advised as a ruler, and come to despise as a tyrant. His death helped consolidate the pattern that Socrates had begun and Cicero had embellished: that a man could secure immortality by the defiance he showed a tyrant and the equanimity with which he faced death.

Those who lived closer in time, those who regarded themselves as heirs of the codes by which Cicero lived, were less sentimental about his legacy. Livy, Rome's greatest historian, who was a young man when Cicero died, concluded that Cicero had faced four great burdens in his life: exile, proscription, the death of his daughter, and his own death. He had faced only his own death "as a man." The masculine code was unforgiving, especially toward the one who had done most to give it expression. Indeed, of all the legacies that this particular father bequeathed to the story of consolation, the one that remains most enduring is in the way men learned to repress their emotions. Right up to the fathers of the American Revolution, men were raised to believe that a public life of republican virtue required a private life of stoic self-command. It is from Cicero and Roman Stoicism that men learned, for a thousand years and more, that they must refuse the comfort of tears, that they deserve the consolation that comes from the approval of their male peers only if they remain dry-eyed and composed through all their trials. Such consolation came at a high price, not least for its own author.

Four

Facing the Barbarians

Marcus Aurelius's Meditations

In the later years of his reign, between AD 165 and 180, in the encampments in which he lived while fighting the barbarian tribes, Marcus Aurelius began to write notes to himself at night. In medieval times, these became known as his *Meditations*, but in the earliest manuscripts, they are labeled in Greek *ta eis he'auton*, "things to oneself." Cicero had sought consolation in the performance of a Stoic code for the sake of a watching audience, but Marcus Aurelius, striving to master fear and loneliness in the solitude of darkness, found consolation in confession.

NIGHT WOULD HAVE FALLEN ON the armed encampment next to the dark river by the time he could find time to write for himself. After a day of inspections, parleys with barbarian chiefs who had come to pay him tribute, consulting with his generals about the disposition of his legions, the aging emperor—curt, reserved, always remote—was at last alone.

He would have liked to unburden his heart, but to whom could he confess his feelings? His wife was dead, and in any case his memories of her were not tender. Rumors had reached him from Rome that she had betrayed him. He chose not to credit these stories, but he knew that she had a connection with one of his best generals and that after his victory in the Parthian wars that general had indeed conspired to dethrone him. After the general's capture in the East, his head had been delivered to the emperor, rotting in a box. If he could not trust a man of that quality, whom could he trust? His slave concubine? Well, one did not confide in concubines. His teachers? As a young man, he had confided in them, especially Cornelius Fronto, in witty letters, but they were dead. In any case, he could not trust Fronto, who had always laid the flattery on with a trowel. Here he was, twenty-three hard days of travel from the eternal city, in a fortified camp on the Danube frontier, with the brown viscous river in front of him. Out there in the darkness the barbarians were waiting, and the peace he had imposed on them was fragile. Attacks were bound to resume. He could see their flickering campfire lights.

His son Commodus was in Rome, as far away from the front line as he could be. There could be no confiding in him. He was already calculating his chances of succession on the rumors that reached Rome of his father's weakness, his insomnia, his difficulties taking food, his obvious aging. Commodus knew his time would soon be at hand. As for the old man, he could hardly begrudge his son's impatience. Between the ages of twenty and forty, he himself had waited for power, patiently serving at the side of Antoninus Pius, the father who had adopted him as a son and heir; he had accommodated his adoptive father's moods, executed his instructions, sometimes grinding his teeth with impatience. Soon enough, the whole thankless burden would pass to his son. He had once doted on that boy and now ugly rumors reached his ears: dissipation—that could be forgiven— and, harder to forgive, wildness and a sadistic streak. He was not deceived about what might happen upon his death, but he had secured his succession. His duty was done.

Busts of him—the long face fringed with beard, the curly hair, the diffident and distant look in his eyes—were on display in the public squares of his empire. He was an object of veneration, but he knew he was not loved. He knew his generals and courtiers mocked him behind his back as "the schoolmaster" for his punctiliousness, his way of correcting their speech. He imagined them whispering at his deathbed: "At last we can breathe freely again."

How could his men love a man who did not love their pleasures? The mob cheered him at the forum because they had to, but he found the spectacle—the slaughter of animals, the bloody gladiatorial combats—wearying in their endless repetition of the death struggle, and though he ordered the games for the distraction of his people, he preferred not to appear if he could avoid it. His asceticism, which started early and came naturally, was a constant reproach to those around him. He did not drink—well, he couldn't now—because he couldn't hold anything down. As for women, that was long past. But his attitude toward carnal love had not endeared him to his people either. He once remarked that coitus was nothing more than a brief convulsion followed by the ejection of some mucus. Those around him had looked at each other with disbelief. His repulsion for the physical and his otherworldliness did not draw people to him. He also was indifferent to wealth, as only men can be who have never known anything else. So how could they love him? How could they even imagine what it was to be him, chosen at age twenty to be the emperor, ascending to the throne at forty, and now, after fifteen years of ultimate power, still the unchallenged master of the known world?

He found it ironic to reflect on how little actual control,

even with all that power, he exercised over his own destiny. What had the fates done to him? At the height of the empire's prosperity, within five years of his accession in AD 160, a plague had struck his people. Borne from the East by soldiers returning from the Parthian wars, it had swept away a third of his imperial subjects. And then the barbarians, unthinkably, unimaginably, had broken through at the very top of the Italian peninsula, sacking a city. Suddenly the road to Rome lay open. He, who had never worn a helmet or carried a shield or strapped on leggings, had to steel himself to become a warrior emperor. At first, the Romans mocked him behind his back as a weak-chested hypochondriac, but he had made himself a master of battles. He had been fighting to drive the barbarians back ever since, in a war that kept him away from Rome for more than a decade, marooned in the swampy, forested lands on the Danube frontier. Here he was—raised for study and debate, for refined conversation in villas with a view of the sea, fourteen years into a brutal campaign of violence against the Marcommani and the Quadi, pushing them back across the Danube, killing their women and children, burning their camps.

In Sirmium, Aquincum, Vindobona, and Carnuntum, the garrison towns of the Danube campaign, the routine was the same: a long winter of preparations followed by a summer of fighting, then the counting of the dead, the arrival of new recruits, the march of legionnaires in the parade grounds, the unending rhythm of a relentless campaign of suppression. He had defeated these barbarians many times, pacified them with agreements and truces, only to find them returning where he least expected, crossing the river to raid, kill, and take captives. After years of this, he had decided to end their incursions at any cost and to make peace even if it meant creating a desert. He returned in force and burned and destroyed, over and over. The barbarians had been cowed. They had retreated across the Danube. There were parades in Rome. Statues were raised, bas-reliefs were cut in marble, showing the barbarians on their knees clutching the flanks of his horse, begging for mercy. Here he was back again, this time making plans to turn the conquered regions into Roman provinces.

What he had seen in those campaigns had dried out his heart. In the night, alone at his desk, he confessed his horror at it all:

> If you have ever seen a dismembered hand or foot, or a head cut off, lying somewhere, apart from the rest of the trunk, then you have an image of what a man makes of himself.

Horror, but also weariness and disgust. At the baths in these encampments, they cleared out the legionnaires before he entered to perform his ablutions, but still he found it a repellent experience to be close to other human beings, all that "oil, sweat, dirt, greasy water, all disgusting." When he rode past burning villages, the stench of bodies, the dismembered corpses, all the smells stayed in the folds of his tunic. When he reviewed legions, passing close down the rows, he could not escape the foul odor of their bodies. He was expected—all eyes were upon him—to display exhilaration and resolve, and the performance made him long to say what he really felt, but to whom could an emperor confide?

Only one person: himself. So he began to write at night, when he could not sleep, thoughts at random as they came to him, not in Latin but in Greek—on rolls of papyrus, with ink made from oil stained with charcoal. If his thoughts stalled, he revived them by reading the works he had ordered sent from Rome: Epictetus, Cicero, of course, and Seneca, Lucretius too. But if there had ever been a time when he had thought of composing a work of philosophy, that time was long past. No treatise now, no clever disputations with the dead. He was old and exhausted, and it was time, at last, to talk to himself.

He'd leave talk of the campaigns just ended to the chroniclers and historians. His days were filled with dictating dispatches to Rome, so he had no desire to reprise that dreary story yet again. If he were to discourse on the politics in Rome, prying eyes might discover his candid thoughts, copy them down, and take them back to Rome, where distorted versions would spread like the plague itself.

No, this writing was for his eyes alone. He would write when he couldn't sleep, and he would keep the scrolls close by, locked away and guarded. He would use the writing as a confessional, to gain such mastery over himself as he could, to express what he could not say to anyone lest it damage his authority and be used against him. It would be his consolation, the only one that was his to control—consolation as confession, as a reckoning with himself—to relieve loneliness, to take away the edge of fear, to give him the will, if not the hope, to carry on.

He began conventionally enough, recollecting all of those— his adoptive father, his tutor, his teachers—who had made him what he had become. It must have been agreeable, in the lonely camp by the great river, to remember these departed shades. In the portrait he drew of his adoptive father, the emperor Antoninus Pius, he painted his own idealized self-image:

> The qualities I admired in my father were his lenience, his firm refusal to be diverted from any decision he had deliberately reached, his complete indifference to meretricious honors; his industry, perseverance and willingness to listen to any project for the common good; the unvarying insistence that rewards must depend on merit; the expert's

sense of when to tighten the reins and when to relax them; and the efforts he made to suppress pederasty.

Ah yes, pederasty. Just like his adoptive father, Marcus Aurelius was conservative, puritanical, revolted by the flesh— even as he admitted, without any sense of contradiction, to a passing fancy for a boy he called Theodotus, only to praise himself for avoiding the pleasures commonly enjoyed by young Roman noblemen.

He liked to think of himself as a construction, carefully put together after years spent watching how Antoninus had assembled his own persona, and then maintained it in the face of the unrelenting scrutiny of courtiers, slaves, hangers-on, and the frightening Roman mob. What he admired in Antoninus was the way his performance came to feel so natural, as if the mask had become the man himself. Yet only a moment later, after fondly recalling Antoninus's performance, Marcus confessed that "the natural life"—by which he meant a life lived in obedience to "true inwardness"—had eluded him. How could it not? His whole life had been an imperial performance.

The show began at daybreak. The moment he opened his eyes, a servant or a guard would appear to await orders. He braced himself for the day ahead:

Begin each day by telling yourself: Today I shall be meeting with interference, ingratitude, insolence, disloyalty, ill will and selfishness.

To get through the day, he had to act as if these insolent and treacherous courtiers—his officers and generals—were his brothers, fellow creatures, similarly endowed with reason and "a share of the divine." It was easy to say all this, but his temper was short, and he knew his occasional rages lowered him in their eyes and in his own. The gulf between his desire to play the Stoic and his constant sense of petty irritation with those around him led him to ask himself, as if for the first time, who was he, really?

A little flesh, a little breath, and a Reason to rule all—that is myself.

And what was this Reason? Now at age fifty-five, in chronic intestinal pain, he could feel that he was, without exaggeration, "on the threshold of death." How could Reason help him? He knew only too well that Reason was a "slave," "twitching puppet-wise at every pull of self-interest." So how could he regain mastery of himself? How could he keep the performance going?

The wisdom of Seneca, Cicero, and Epictetus could not help him either. Cicero took consolation from others' admiration of his performance of Stoic virtue, but what consolation was that for an emperor whose entire existence was a performance? It was time to understand himself in a larger frame than philosophy, to see himself under the eye of Fate, to understand "that your time has a limit to it," and to use the time that remained to "advance your enlightenment" before it was too late. Approach each action, he told himself, "as if it were your last."

It was time to stop measuring life by success at public rituals in the eyes of the court, the hangers-on, the barbarian chiefs. For this was the trap of a life lived as a performance: you forgot whom the play was for.

His thoughts turned recurrently to death, to the "swiftness with which all things vanish away, their bodies in the world of space and their remembrance in the world of time." To a man whose vocation was to build monuments, establish provinces, subdue barbarians, enlarge the boundaries of empire, and leave behind busts of himself and marbled inscriptions testifying to his greatness, the mocking impermanence of things was terrifying. In the life of man, he wrote,

> His time is but a moment, his being an incessant flux, his senses a dim rushlight, his body a prey of worms, his soul an unquiet eddy, his fortune dark, and his fame doubtful.

The river that flowed in front of his encampment at night seemed to him a metaphor for time itself. "All that is of the body is as coursing waters, all that is of the soul as dreams and vapors." Here in the land of the barbarians, his campaigns had taught him that life itself was "warfare" and his time on earth a "brief sojourning in an alien land." Astonishingly for a man who had as good reason as anyone alive to believe he would never be forgotten, he took no consolation in the thought of being known to posterity. Who would remember him anyway? "After repute, oblivion."

Along with the feeling that time was running out, he felt his own powers—of cunning, resolve, and insight—were wasting away. "We must press on in haste; not simply because every hour brings us nearer to death, but because even before then our powers of perception and comprehension begin to deteriorate." And then, as if the bread left on his night table led to an unexpected thought that now he let rise to the surface, he remarked that the cracks in the loaf, "though not intended in the baking have a rightness of their own and sharpen the appetite." He also let his thoughts pause over some olives the slaves had left for him on his writing table. He noticed that they split open to show their ripeness, and he remarked how "the very imminence of decay adds peculiar beauty to the fruit." This was a new register in a relentless, punctilious perfectionist's coming to terms with his own mortality.

He was reassuring himself in the face of his own decay and the sudden suspicion that for all his preeminence and fame he would be soon forgotten:

> This mortal life is a little thing, lived in a little corner of the earth; and little too is the longest fame to come— dependent as it is on a succession of fast perishing little men who have no knowledge even of their own selves, much less of one long dead and gone.

The vainest of human hopes, but the one that gave most men consolation, was *kleos*—glory and renown—as the Greeks had called it. Antoninus was still remembered. His bust remained on plinths throughout the empire. The words of Cicero and Seneca were still taught to children. Why should he, emperor of all, not seek the consolation of fame? He sternly told himself to put this hope behind him:

> The man whose heart is palpitating for fame after death does not reflect that out of all those who remember him everyone will himself soon be dead also, and in course of time, the next generation after that, until in the end, after flaring and sinking by turns, the final spark of memory is quenched.

What remained, he asked himself, from the time of the emperor Vespasian, a hundred years earlier—"men and women busy marrying, bringing up children, sickening, dying, fighting, feasting, chaffering, farming, flattering, bragging, scheming, calling down curses, grumbling at fate, loving, hoarding, coveting thrones and dignities." It was chilling to think that not a trace of that teeming life had survived.

If one could not live in hope of being remembered, he told

himself, then all that one could do was practice virtue in the present. What should inspire a man was "the just thought, the unselfish act, the tongue that utters no falsehood."

Yet he struggled to follow his own injunctions. There were mornings, he confessed, when the demands of the day were too much, and he just wanted to stay in bed. The peace of mind he sought by writing kept slipping away:

> O the consolation of being able to thrust aside and cast into oblivion every tiresome intrusive impression and in a trice be utterly at peace!

His anxieties had a way of deepening in the watches of the night. Alone, he had seen himself, fleetingly and frighteningly, as a man like any other. There turned out to be little enough comfort in that. It was better to remember that he was also an emperor. Inevitably for someone used to holding forth in public and expecting an audience to hang on his every word, he began piling injunction upon injunction, striving for the memorable and quotable line. "Fate is at your elbow," he would say, then catch himself and remember what this writing was for:

> Mislead yourself no longer; you will never read these note-books again now, nor the annals of bygone Romans and Greeks, nor that choice selection of writing you have put by for your old age. Press on, then, to the finish; cast away vain hopes.

Little by little, though he could not see this clearly, his intimate writing intended only for himself turned into little speeches to impress and edify others and, though he kept deny-ing it, to win the attention of posterity. He had turned to these scrolls at night to console himself. Now he used them to produce aphorisms—sententious and empty—for public consumption:

The man of ambition thinks to find his good in the operations of others, the man of pleasure in his own sensations; but the man of understanding in his own actions.

On and on in this vein: didactic lessons written as if for himself but actually for others, drawing him back inexorably to the very role in which he had felt imprisoned and which he sought to escape by writing only for himself. Ironically, these passages, the least honest and authentic in the text, are what were to be remembered as the wisdom of Marcus Aurelius. In reality, it is the passages that portray an emperor alone with himself, at the end of his tether, that are the most compelling—and the most consoling for us to read.

In the end, he could master his weariness of life only by professing imperial disdain for life itself and for his tiresome fellow human beings. Existence, he wrote sourly, was

An empty pageant, a stage play; flocks of sheep, herds of cattle; a tussle of spearmen; a bone flung among a pack of curs; a crumb tossed into a pond of fish; ants, loaded and laboring; mice, scared and scampering; puppets, jerking on their strings—that is life.

The disdain gave him refuge from the courtiers, and the imperial role gave him reassurance. "I was born to be their leader," he reminded himself, "as the ram is made to lead the flock or the bull the herd." Scorn and superiority gave him the sense that he was high on a mountaintop, above the lesser mortals, looking down on "the buffoonery, quarreling, timidity, slothfulness and servility" that surrounded him.

Hurrying back to the reassurance provided by his own role, however, could not protect him from darker thoughts. The scrolls he covered in Greek weave unsteadily between cold assurance and agonizing doubt. He could not get those severed limbs he'd seen on the field of battle out of his mind. They seemed to be a metaphor for his own inner dissociation, for the feeling of being severed from his real self. "Yet here is a beautiful thought," he told himself, somewhat desperately:

It still lies in your own power to reunite yourself. No other part of creation has been so favored by God with permission to come together again, after once being sundered and divided.

A man could make himself whole again, put the sundered pieces back together, true enough. If only he knew how:

O soul of mine . . . when will you be content with your present state, happy in all about you, persuaded that all things are yours, that all comes from the gods, and that all is and shall be well with you?

The paradox his writing laid bare was that such comfort as he could find, such consolation as there could be, did not come from confession, from being alone with himself, but from the role, the duties, the burdens he bore. These pages of self-examination—unique in the ancient world, or at least the only ones that descend to us—conclude wistfully. He imagines himself as an actor on the stage, fully inhabiting his role, only to be told brusquely that his time was up. "But I have played no more than three of the five acts," he heard himself plead. Just so, a voice tells him, "in your drama of life, three acts are all the play."

He was fifty-nine when he died of the plague, or so it seems, in one of those spartan military encampments at Sirmium—about forty kilometers from the modern city of Belgrade. Anyone who so obsessively tried to persuade himself that he would leave no trace to posterity must have pined for the opposite. He secured immortality not thanks to the monuments, decrees, bridges, roads, or conquests that his contemporaries remembered, but thanks rather to a secret activity no one knew about—the "things to oneself," the dozen scrolls that as a dying man he must have bundled up and consigned to his most trusted adjutant to be borne back to Rome with his body, to remain unknown for centuries and then be recopied by scribes in monasteries in the ruins of his empire and, through copying, be given a new purpose he was not alive to see: consoling others for the perplexities and anguish not even an emperor knew how to master.

We identify his *Meditations* today as one of the great expositions of Stoicism, but like Paul's Epistles or Cicero's *Tusculan Disputations*, what makes them endure is not the doctrine but the doubts that doctrine could not still. What enables them to afford consolation to later generations is their unrivaled candor about the loneliness, discouragement, fear, and loss that make us seek consolation in the first place. For it *is* consoling to know that not even an emperor can get through the night, alone with his thoughts. That is something we can share with him.

Five

The Consolations of Philosophy

Boethius and Dante

For the Romans of the fifth century of the Christian era, the unthinkable collapse of the empire arrived in stages. Catastrophes—like the sack of Rome in 411—were followed by decades of decay, with the imperial administration shrinking, territories surrendered to alien tribes, buildings left to crumble, viaducts going unrepaired and leaking away their supply of water to the cities, and the people, once fed by the bounty of Rome, left to starve. To this day, we wonder how Romans managed to comprehend the unwinding of their world. At times it proceeded so slowly they could not see it; at other times, when change engulfed single lifetimes, it must have seemed apocalyptic. At all times, but especially when history no longer seems comprehensible, people cling to illusions of continuity, particularly those manufactured by their rulers. While the Roman republic died with Cicero's death in 43 BC, Augustus, the new princeps, took pains to retain the old republican institutions such as the Senate and to pay lip service to the freedom of the city of Rome. In reality, these republican institutions were reduced to a shell. Imperial rule, violent and capricious, governed Rome for centuries, behind the crumbling façade of the republic. By AD 500, only the simulacrum of freedom remained.

Through this long declension, men were able to go on believing they had staved off the worst. As the emperor Marcus Aurelius lay dying in Sirmium in AD 180, he went to his grave believing that his years of frontier war had guaranteed the security of the empire. Soon the futility of his struggle became apparent. The barbarians kept advancing, and before their repeated assaults, the empire settled into a pattern of slow but inexorable retreat. In AD 378, a Roman emperor perished at Adrianople in a disastrous and total defeat, and a century later the tribal chieftains Marcus Aurelius thought he had subdued became rulers of his empire.

By AD 500, the Ostrogothic king Theoderic, a descendant of those warrior leaders, sat on the throne of the Western Empire in Ravenna. He had made himself the master of Italy, Gaul, and Spain, and his only equal in power was the Eastern emperor in Constantinople. He had seized the throne by knifing an Ostrogothic rival at a banquet, but he was shrewd enough to realize that he could not hold on to it through violence alone. It was vital to clothe his rule in the regalia, institutional forms, and Latin script of Rome. He ordered his robes to be dyed imperial purple. He issued coins that looked like the imperial models. He rebuilt Roman baths and refurbished Rome itself and planted brass plates with his name in the foundations so the people would give him credit. He restarted the circuses and games in the Forum and he accorded deference to the Senate, even though Cicero's once great assembly was now a shadow of its former self. He also adopted the new faith of Christianity, albeit in an Arian form.

Theoderic ruled an Italy still dominated by a landed Roman aristocracy whose latifundia provided them with food and rent, grand villas, well-furnished libraries, and legions of slaves. These aristocrats continued to pursue the cursus honorum of Cicero's time even though their posts were denuded of real power. The Romans told themselves that although a barbarian was on the throne, they held on to real authority—of law, tradition, respect, and lineage. Theoderic knew that some of the Roman elite viewed him as a usurper and heretic, while others served him only to secure restoration of their ancient glories. But he needed their experience and their administrative capacity, since he wrote neither Latin nor Greek. Instead of signing documents, he stamped them with a metal stencil that planted the Latin word *legi*—"I have read it"—on official papers. Romans whispered that their new ruler was "without training in letters and of dull comprehension."

Of all the Roman aristocrats who enlisted in the service of the barbarian king, none was grander than Anicius Manlius Severinus Boethius, a member of the gens Anicia, an ancient Roman family that in centuries past had provided consuls, two emperors, and a pope to the empire. Boethius's own father had been consul, and after his death the orphaned Boethius was adopted by Quintus Aurelius Memmius Symmachus, consul, prefect of Rome, and head of the Senate. The boy received the best possible classical education and was quickly recognized as a prodigy, mastering Greek and Latin and then astronomy, mathematics, and music.

By early adulthood, Boethius was part of an inner circle of Roman aristocrats—including his kinsman Cassiodorus, the king's leading scribe, as well as Ennodius, one of his bishops—serving the barbarian king in Ravenna. Of this trio of Romans, Boethius soon established himself as primus inter pares. It was he who designed a water clock and sundial as a gift from Theoderic to the Burgundian king, and he who, thanks to his talent for music, was asked by the barbarian king to choose the lyre and the lyre player to send to Clovis, king of the Franks. Boethius was also asked to report to the king on the state of the monarch's coinage, and by the age of thirty he was awarded the honorific post of consul, just like his father.

But his heart was in his studies. Whenever he could, he repaired to his library in Rome, to resume the life of the patrician scholar modeled for him by Cicero and Seneca. He set himself the task of translating all of Aristotle and Plato into Latin and, in doing so, to guarantee the survival of philosophical learning for future ages. In the end, he managed only a fraction of these translations, for he was continuously called back into the service of the king.

He might have imagined his public life as a fulfillment of Plato's ideal that rulers should be guided by philosophers. He might even have dreamed that one day, he himself might become the philosopher-king. Whatever his motives were, he certainly knew success. By 522, Boethius was *magister officiorum*, master of the king's household, effectively his prime minister and head of the civil service.

Understanding what happened next requires entering the mental world of the Roman aristocrats: remembering their pride, their patrician superiority, and also their shame at their subjugation to the barbarian kings. The barbarians treated these Roman aristocrats as servants of their whims. They mocked Boethius's cleverness and gave him thankless tasks, while he had to watch, helpless, as they plundered Italy, enriched themselves, neglected to feed the people of the provinces who depended on the grain supplies of Rome, and above all treated the Senate and its traditions with contempt.

These barbarians were also heretics. The Ostrogothic people had embraced a heresy—Arianism—which Boethius once dissected in a letter to a close friend. Applying the philosophical knife to the faith of his king was dangerous, but he took the risk, since the very promise of Christian salvation would be null and void if Arianism were true. Arianism rejected the doctrine of the trinity, of God as Father, Son, and Holy Spirit. For Arians, Jesus was a divine creature created by God to fulfill a mission on earth. They denied that he could have been a man like any other, prey to suffering, hunger, and sexual longings. These doctrinal differences mattered, for, as Boethius wrote to his friend, Deacon John, if Jesus was not a man just like us,

> Then the human race has not been saved, the birth of Christ has brought us no salvation, the writings of all the prophets have but beguiled the people that believed in them, contempt is poured upon the authority of the whole Old Testament which promised to the world salvation by the birth of Christ.

Theoderic was aware that Boethius and other Roman Christians would have regarded his Arian theology as a threat, and he took a prudent path forward, according equal tolerance to the Arian and what was already called the Catholic faith. But he could not allow Catholic Christians to take their faith into politics, for he feared they might conspire with the Eastern emperor to reunite the two halves of the empire under the authority of Constantinople. Theoderic knew only too well that certain of the Roman aristocracy harbored such ambitions. The calculated respect he displayed toward the city of Rome and the Senate indicates he knew his hold on the Romans was fragile. For decades he managed their resentments skillfully. But after thirty years in power his grip began to slip. In 518 his designated successor died; his network of alliances with other barbarian kings began to disintegrate; he feared that the Eastern emperor might ally with the Roman senators and bring about his downfall. He took measures to keep the Romans under control: forbidding them to wear swords, promoting his own brand of Christianity, tearing down Catholic shrines, and watching for any sign that the Roman Senate was in secret negotiations with Constantinople.

In 523, Theoderic's courtiers produced letters, probably forged, revealing a plot by Roman senators to invite the emperor in Constantinople to depose Theoderic. In the council chamber, when a courtier leveled this accusation at one of the senators, Boethius leapt to his defense and in the king's presence proclaimed, "If you are accusing them, you are accusing me." Of course, he said, we defend the prerogatives of the Senate and the freedom of Rome. What else do you expect? We are Romans. But we were not plotting against you.

Boethius's outburst was one of those sudden impulses that had been years in the making, but if he thought other Romans would follow his lead he was mistaken. His words were met with stunned silence. His kinsman Cassiodorus looked away. Theoderic ordered his guards to seize Boethius and confined him in a baptistery in Pavia. Then he banished him to a remote estate outside the city and kept him under close guard to await his fate. Theoderic ordered a cowed Senate in Rome to condemn Boethius to death for treason. If there ever had been a plot, it dissolved in the face of Theoderic's anger.

We know little of Boethius's conditions of confinement, including whether his wife, Rusticiana, or his two sons were able to visit him. This most bookish of men would have longed for a library, but there is no evidence that he was allowed books, so all the words needed to calm a man shattered by political defeat and the prospect of execution had to be coaxed out of the shadows of his own distracted and desperate mind.

Imprisonment under sentence of death was a crushing blow.

Whatever the physical hardships he endured, it was the long-ing for a lost life that tormented him. "In all adversity of for-tune," he confessed, "the most wretched kind is once to have been happy."

Psychic suffering plus hard rations caused him to waste away and his hair to turn white. Once a healthy, indeed lusty, man in his forties, Boethius now looked down at his own body with shame. He was, he confessed, "a worn-out bone-bag hung with flesh."

As he waited for execution, he conjured up the memory pal-ace of his erudition to come to terms with his predicament. He was the heir of the entire Greek philosophical tradition, as well as the Roman tradition of *consolatio* going back to Cicero; he was also a Christian, familiar with Paul's Epistles and the Psalms. In one man, the rich tributaries of the classical and Christian traditions flowed together. In his hour of extremity, to which tradition would he turn?

He could have embraced his destiny as a Christian martyr. Since Saint Stephen, it was considered glorious to die in the faith and to inspire others to do the same. Across the Medi-terranean world, there were shrines to Christian saints before which humble people lit candles or left food and other offerings. There is little doubt that Boethius saw himself as a Christian, but there was the delicate question of which kind of Christian he was. The dispute with the Arians made this a minefield. He may have entertained hopes of surviving the wrath of the king and securing a pardon. If so, it would not be wise to proclaim his non-Arian Christianity too loudly. Whatever the reason, the text he wrote in confinement is silent about whether he was any kind of Christian at all.

There is at least one plausible explanation for this silence. From his point of view, he was not in prison because he had criticized Theoderic's faith, but because he had challenged the king's political authority. Boethius was adamant that he was what we would call a political prisoner. His political defiance is perfectly explicit:

> . . . the fact is I did desire the safety of the Senate and will never cease to.
> . . . As for the forged letters cited as evidence that I had hoped for the freedom of Rome . . . there is no freedom left to hope for. If only there were!

It would have been easy to cast himself as a citizen martyr and to depict Theoderic as a latter-day Octavian or Nero. But he did not take this path either. Cicero and Seneca could only tell him to endure his fate like a man and a Roman. He knew their *consolatio* by heart: not to lament the loss of fame, fortune, or wealth, since these were transitory and inconsequential. While in prison, he made use of this Stoic rhetoric to rid himself of the baggage of life. What Stoic texts could not explain was why a just and merciful God should have permitted the rank injustice of his fate. Like Job, he had a quarrel with God. You can almost hear him shouting at the walls of his cell when he cries out, "it is nothing short of monstrous that God should look on while every criminal is allowed to achieve his purpose against the innocent."

Finally, Boethius turned neither to the Stoics nor to the Christians, but to the Greeks, Plato above all, especially the *Timaeus* and the *Phaedrus*—which he had translated and knew by heart. These held out to him a language with which to understand his situation. The Greeks taught him to think of himself as a victim of pitiless fate, bound and tied to "Fortune's ever turning wheel."

Greek philosophy's role, as Boethius understood it, was to reconcile man with Ananke, Fate. Boethius followed in this path when he called the text he wrote in Latin *Consolatio Philoso-phiae* and settled on the model of the Platonic dialogue. The dialogue captured the dialectical process of his own mind, the ebb and flow of assertion and refutation, question and answer, through which the mind, in discussion with another, slowly grasps the truth.

It was Plato who taught Boethius, in effect, that if he was to escape the labyrinth of his own depression, he needed a kindred soul to talk to. But who was this soul to be? He sought inspiration in one of the oldest literary associations of all. Sophia, the Greek word for wisdom, was also a woman's name. When, in an act of creative inspiration, he created "Philosophia" as his soul mate, the words began to flow. He could split himself in two: the doubting, fearing, lonely "bag of bones" awaiting death, and lady Philosophy, the mordant embodiment of his own rationality. He imagined her as a caustic woman his own age dressed in clothes of an imperishable material, "like statues covered in dust." Her robes were decorated with the sign of theta, the symbol of wisdom, but her garment had been torn, pieces of its hem ripped off by marauding philosophical disputants in their futile competitions for preeminence. In her right hand, she carried books of philosophy, and in her left, a scepter symbolizing knowledge. She was a magnificently real invention—one imagines Boethius wrote certain features of his own wife Rusticiana into her character—as she briskly shooed away the muses, "those hysterical sluts" with whom he had been fruitlessly dallying in feeble attempts at poetry. Poetry, she said dismissively, "habituate[s] men to their sickness of mind instead of curing them." She was the one who had the cure. She sat beside him on the bed and wiped away his tears. She knew what the problem really was, she told him. Despair had torn away the moorings of his reason. She would restore him to reason through sympathetic dialogue. Yet as Boethius gave their dialogue shape, the struggle for consolation turned into a dialectical inner battle between fear and reason, never securely won.

Over and over, Lady Philosophy applies the medicine of sober reason, like one of Job's comforters, counseling acceptance of fate and stoic indifference to hardship. Over and over, the prisoner can't help gnawing away at the injustice of his fate and the apparent indifference of God. Boethius's *Consolation*, like the Psalms and the book of Job, is an unflinching portrait of a radical crisis of belief, afflicting a man who now actively wondered whether it wouldn't be easier to bear his lot if he drove the idea of God from his mind and accepted that the world was ruled by chance.

> I am utterly amazed that . . . punishments for crime oppress good people, and that evil people snatch away the rewards owed to virtues. And in fact, I would be less amazed at this were I to believe that all things are confused together by chance occurrences happening at random. But as it is now, the God who is the helmsman makes my incomprehension that much greater.

Consolation is faithful to the drama of any internal struggle—and also captures its bleak comedy. No sooner has he announced that he forgives his enemies—their wickedness is just a sickness they cannot help—than he begins to rage, once again, at the injustice they have done him. Lady Philosophy in turn loses patience with his repetitive self-dramatizing. Cheer up, she tells him briskly. Stop moaning. The prisoner, for his part, tires of her relentless good cheer. "So soon as your words stop sounding in our ears," he confesses, "the mind is weighed down again by its deep-seated melancholy." Instead of all this philosophy, he longs to hear a little music or poetry.

The *Consolation* has had a long afterlife with readers—including Dante, Queen Elizabeth I, and Thomas More—because of the surpassing literary skill with which Boethius depicted what it feels like to suffer a radical crisis, to stare at your own body and feel your teeth chattering with fear, to struggle to get control over the inner chaos of anguish and dread.

But while the *Consolation* has certainly consoled others, the question remains as to whether it succeeded in consoling the man who wrote it. The evidence is ambiguous. Some have said the text is incomplete, as if Boethius were taken away before he could finish it. The concluding sentences offer not exalted reassurance but only subdued injunctions to honesty, virtue, and prayer:

> Hope is not placed in God in vain and prayers are not made in vain, for if they are the right kind, they cannot but be efficacious. Avoid vice, therefore, and cultivate virtue; lift up your mind to the right kind of hope and put forth humble prayers on high. A great necessity is laid upon you, if you will be honest with yourself, a great necessity to be good, since you live in the sight of a judge who sees all things.

Dutiful passages like this enabled the Church to appropriate a work that made not a single reference to the promise of Christian resurrection. When the Eastern emperor Justinian conquered the Ostrogothic kingdom in 536 and installed himself in Ravenna, the Catholic Church's appropriation of Boethius as a martyr saint began. In this it was aided by Justinian, who launched an ideological campaign against Theoderic's most notorious crime. In the mosaic portrait of the new monarch, set in the ceiling of the presbytery of San Vitale in Ravenna, some scholars believe Boethius himself is portrayed standing just behind the emperor's shoulder. The new regime also circulated an apocryphal tale according to which Theoderic died tormented by regret at Boethius's death. The story went around that when a large sea fish was served to him on a platter, something about the fish's glassy stare reminded him of the man he had ordered executed and caused him to recoil in terror.

Yet the posthumous restoration of Boethius to the bosom of the imperial church is full of ironies. He could be appropriated only if the faithful ignored certain passages in the *Consolation* itself, where Boethius goes so far as to query the entire point of prayer. If Fortuna has us all tied to her wheel, why pray at all?

> It is pointless, therefore, to hope for anything or pray to escape anything. What can a man hope for, or pray to escape, when an inflexible bond binds all that can be wished for?

A stubborn litany of doubt flows like an incantation throughout the *Consolation* and lends it dramatic force. The book's recurring image of the wheel of fortune expressed desperation at the futility of human striving. Beginning in the Renaissance, figures like Machiavelli would argue that human reason could bend Fortuna to its will, but these consoling ideas were alien to Boethius:

> For if you are trying to stop her wheel from turning, you are of all men the most obtuse.

If God was watching, there was nothing a man could do to catch his attention:

> He looks out from the watch tower of Providence, sees what suits each person, and applies to him whatever He

knows is suitable. This, then, is the outstanding wonder of the order of Fate, a knowing God acts, and ignorant men look on with wonder at his actions.

These are not consoling thoughts, so much as resigned ones. But it may miss the point to ask whether Boethius found hope in Christian salvation or in Platonic argument. What consoled him, as it had Marcus Aurelius, was the writing itself, the intense inner communion that enabled him to feel, at times, that he was rising above the prison house. "Human souls are of necessity more free," Boethius wrote, "when they continue in the contemplation of the mind of God and less free when they descend to bodies and less still when they are imprisoned in earthly flesh and blood."

He did try imagining himself accepting death, "for often, when there are reasons which force death upon a creature, Nature turns away in horror, but the will accepts it." But he was candid enough to add that his body still recoiled. He confessed, touchingly, that he was like Orpheus trying to leave the underworld without looking back, but like the lyre player, he could not help a glance back at the life he was about to leave behind. These are not the thoughts of a man at peace with fate.

The historian Edward Gibbon, completing his *Decline and Fall* in the 1760s, spent time in Ravenna, wondering whether Boethius had been consoled by what he had written. The *Consolation*, he concluded, was too vague, too abstruse to have consoled its author. Boethius's sense of misfortune might have been "diverted by the labor of thought," but he did not write himself into a state of philosophical calm. Rather, "he must already have possessed the intrepid calmness which he affected to seek." In the end, his anguish was brought to a close only by "the ministers of death" who killed him. Consolation was a performance, Gibbon concluded, that had won the admiration of succeeding generations but was unlikely to have calmed its author.

If the writing did give Boethius consolation, it was a solace constructed, phrase by painful phrase, in documentation of his own struggle. In this exercise, he gained some sovereignty over his inner world and, in doing so, the capacity to come to terms with his prison house. We can read him thinking ahead to the dire moment that awaited him. Some people, he mused, "are excessively afraid of suffering" and discover, on the contrary, that they can endure it. Others, he said, are full of scorn for suffering "they cannot in fact bear." He had learned he was one of those. He had come to understand, he wrote, that Fate brings men to "self-discovery through hardship." And what, beyond this bleak counsel of endurance, did he look forward to? Posterity, he hoped, would remember him. Thanks to anonymous acts of virtue by jailers, servants, his wife and sons perhaps, possibly that errant kinsman Cassiodorus, Boethius's manuscript was found and kept hidden from the Ostrogoths, so it could reach the copyists and librarians in Constantinople and Rome, and from them, us.

WE DO NOT KNOW HOW long Boethius had to await the final ordeal. We do not know even whether he finished the book. We do know how he died, since someone—a faithful but appalled witness—passed on the story or pieced the terrible truth together from the state of the body once it was released for burial. The men Gibbon called the "ministers of death" had duly arrived and, without ceremony or trial, tied him up, strangled him with a cord until his eyes stood out from their sockets, and then clubbed him to death.

IN BOETHIUS'S CONSOLATION, FOUR GREAT Western traditions that have consoled men for injustice and misfortune—the Greeks Plato and Aristotle; the Romans Cicero and Seneca; the Hebrew prophets in the Psalms and Job; and the Christian fathers Paul and Augustine—were all brought together in a supreme act of imagination by a man awaiting death. The work is a monument to one man's heroic memory, but also to his faith in a certain idea—that philosophical reasoning has the power to enable us to bear suffering, injustice, and death. To this day, we cannot be sure whether he managed to sustain his own faith in reason's healing powers.

His great heir, eight hundred years later, was the poet Dante. Dante knew Boethius intimately because he spent the last five years of his own life in exile in Ravenna, banished from his native Florence. He composed the third part of the *Divine Comedy*, the *Paradiso*, amid the remains of Boethius's world—the small fifth-century brick basilica of Galla Placidia, with its mosaic-filled vaults, and the soaring cathedrals of San Vitale and Sant'Apollinare Nuovo. These awe-inspiring monuments could only have helped inspire the composition of an ecstatic vision of paradise that Dante was writing at the very peak of his creative powers. Everywhere he looked, in every holy place, the walls were ablaze with sparkling gold, green, and blue mosaics, proclaiming a Christianity without a crucifixion, without suffering and despair, only the promise of paradise and the serene intercession of the saints.

We know from Dante's *Convivio*, a philosophical tract he wrote between 1304 and 1307, that as a political exile himself he identified strongly with Boethius. He studied his works carefully, most of all the *Consolation*, since it was in reflecting on Boethius's creation of Lady Philosophia that Dante, enraptured since childhood by Beatrice, began to grasp how he could create a similar work, formally organized as a search for enlightenment, from hell through purgatory to paradise, under the guidance of a wise woman. Boethius's Philosophia was reincarnated, seven centuries later, as Beatrice, Dante's guide to the ecstatic regions of paradise.

As Dante describes his journey with Beatrice into the divine regions, he constantly stresses that words fail him—they cannot convey what he sees dimly in the empyrean regions of heaven. Dante wants us to understand the limits of language and the need for a faith that goes beyond language. Dante's phrase *trapassar del segno*—"going beyond the limits"—may also be his reflection on Boethius's failure to find consolation in the face of death. Only faith beyond words, beyond reason, Dante wants us to understand, can truly console human beings.

Reason might be imperfect, incapable of consoling men for what they fear most, but the ambition of reason, Boethius's sheer daring, earns Dante's deep respect. It is Dante who created the unforgettable image of "passing the limits" in the new story he invented of Ulysses persuading his crew to sail beyond the Gates of Hercules, into the dark ocean in search of new lands, only to drown in the attempt. Ulysses pays for his hubris, but there is no mistaking the poet's admiration. It is even possible that the story of Ulysses was Dante's way of confronting his own guilt for the hubris of his poetic ambition. Like Ulysses, he had passed beyond the limits prescribed for human reason—and language—when he dared imagine paradise.

When Dante reaches heaven in company with Beatrice, he sees Boethius there, in the empyrean region, among the wisest thinkers of the Christian tradition—Thomas Aquinas, Isidore of Seville, Albertus Magnus, Peter Lombard, Siger of Brabant, and others. In placing Boethius among this learned company in a Christian heaven, Dante recuperates philosophy for the Christian faith, and asserts, in effect, that consolation is possible only if philosophy is in the service of faith. But there is a tenderness in his evocation of Boethius. Dante lets us know that he paid a personal pilgrimage to Boethius's actual resting place, a humble seventh-century brick church in a quiet square in the northern Italian town of Pavia. The church, which survives to this day, has a beautiful name—San Pietro in Ciel d'Oro—Saint Peter of the Golden Sky—though the once gold ceiling has long since flaked away and the church itself is often empty and closed. Boethius's tomb is in a crypt below the high altar, where, it so happens, the remains of Saint Augustine are on display inside a magnificent marble catafalque. When you descend into the crypt below Augustine's tomb, as Dante must have done, you can see in the crepuscular light the casket of San Boecio, along with a few bleached white bones that are kept illuminated and are, it is supposed, his only mortal remains.

In the *Paradiso*, Dante pauses to remember Boethius, as if to confer on him the consolation of peace that the prisoner himself may never have known:

> *The body he was hounded out of*
> *Lies below in Ciel d'Oro—here*
> *Peace ends his exile and murder.*

Six

The Painting of Time

El Greco's The Burial of the Count of Orgaz

In Santo Tomé, a medieval church in a narrow street in Toledo, Spain, a painting called *The Burial of the Count of Orgaz* occupies the entire alcove of a side chapel just inside the entrance. All day people from around the world pay to line up and see it.

The Count of Orgaz was a pious medieval Spanish nobleman, buried in 1323 in a tomb that lies directly below the painting itself. Two hundred and sixty years later, in the 1580s, Santo Tomé's parish priest commissioned a local painter, known as "the Greek," to depict the count's burial and the legend that had grown up around it. It was said that as Count Orgaz was lowered into his grave, Saint Augustine and Saint Stephen appeared from heaven and assisted the mourners in burying him, a sign of divine gratitude for the count's benefactions to the Augustinian friars in the city and to the Church itself. The saints' appearance—and the painting to commemorate the event—had the force of an injunction to the gentlemen of the city: do as he did, live as he lived.

In the foreground of the painting, Saint Stephen and Saint Augustine, clad in gloriously shining gold vestments and

wearing bishop's miters, are bending down to tenderly lower
the body of the count into his tomb. The count's face has the
pale, expressionless pallor of the dead, and his steel armor
gleams darkly in the candlelight. Supervising the scene is the
parish priest who had commissioned the painting. Just behind
the two saints stand more than a dozen Toledan gentlemen in
black garb with white lace collars: lawyers, courtiers, and academics, the prominent men of the 1580s. Between two pairs
of shoulders in the crowd stands the artist himself, an angu-
lar man in his forties, his jaw outlined by a sharply trimmed
brown beard, his piercing black eyes staring back at us.

An angel flutters above the Toledan gentlemen, reaching
down to guide the count's spirit up to heaven. The count's soul
is a swirling mass of vapor, which the angel is lifting toward
the gray-blue clouds above. Among the clouds we see other
spirits rising to the heavens, where Mary and Saint John, the
Old Testament prophets, Jesus and his disciples, and a most
helpful earthly intercessor, the contemporary monarch of
Spain, Philip II, all wait to receive Count Orgaz's soul. Since
there is no image of hell or damnation to be seen, the painting's
message is clear: he is heading straight to paradise. Like Dante's *Paradiso*, El Greco's painting portrays the joyful certainty
of salvation and the immense consolation that such a vision can
bring to the faithful.

This vast, magnificent painting is also a depiction of time,
as understood through a certain kind of ecstatic Christian faith,
current among the notables and priesthood in what was then
a leading city of Catholic Counter-Reformation Spain. What
looks, at first sight, like a chaotic jumbling of past, present,
and future is in fact an organized vision of time itself, in which
past, present, and future are treated as if they were all happening at once. Orgaz himself is wearing the shining steel armor
of the sixteenth century, not the medieval versions current in

his own time. Saint Augustine, who died at the end of the Roman Empire, and Saint Stephen, who was stoned to death in AD 34, are dressed as contemporary sixteenth-century Catholic bishops. The Toledan crowd gathered for the interment are depicted as contemporaries of the count, though his actual burial had occurred more than two hundred years earlier. These depictions are not anachronisms. All these layers of time, from the Roman Empire to the present, are shown occurring in the never-ending present, as if the painter wished to declare that if one has faith enough, the faithful can inhabit a moment where past, present, and future are experienced as simultaneous. The painting underlines this point by portraying the Toledan gentlemen watching the miracle of Augustine and Stephen's appearance entirely unastonished, as if they were attending a regular Sunday morning mass, and the collapse of time were the most natural thing in the world. The picture depicts how faith brings communities together in acceptance of the supernatural, the intercession of the saints, and the prospect of heaven above. Saint Stephen, the early Roman martyr; Augustine, the late Roman philosopher from Carthage; the medieval count from Toledo; and the modern Toledan gentry all share the same present beneath a heaven that beckons them upward with the promise of paradise.

This painting depicts what Toledans believed or thought they should believe: that they were joined together as Christian brothers in defense of an embattled faith; that the way to heaven was through charity to the living; that the saints would intercede on their behalf and that angels would lift their souls to heaven; and that the living, the dead, and the yet to be born were all linked together under God's care.

Yet their faith was also under immense strain. The ones who believed it most, or had to be seen to believe it most, were the conversos, the descendants of Jewish faith who had been forced

to abandon their religion during the time of Jewish persecutions initiated under Ferdinand and Isabella, after they joined
the kingdoms of Castile and Aragon to create the Spanish monarchy in 1492. The conversos lived under permanent suspicion.
They had to prove the "purity of their blood" and display rigor-
ous conformity to the doctrines of the Church. Conversos stand
among the Toledan gentry in the picture, and conversos were
among those who footed the bill for the painting. So, in the
moment when this painting is completed, Toledo is tense with
suspicion of those who might not be as faithful as they seem,
frantic with the desire of converts to prove, all appearances to
the contrary, that they truly belong, all of this policed by the
local branch of the Inquisition. On top of this, just twenty years
before, the Catholic king had moved his capital from Toledo to
Madrid, and a city that had been the center of the faith and of
an empire was beginning to understand the inexorability of its
own decline.

Only two years after the painting's unveiling in 1586, a
great disaster befell this world—the defeat of the Spanish
Armada off the shores of England. The year 1588 marked the
beginning of the slow decline of the Spanish Empire. But these
gentlemen of Toledo do not yet know this. They are safe from
the knowledge, encapsulated inside the ecstatic moment when
Saint Augustine and Saint Stephen intercede for one of their
own and lower him gently into the earth.

SO THERE IS FEAR, AS it were, just off the edge of the canvas.
Of all that it is, the painting is also an exercise in collective
reassurance. It is a declaration of faith: this is what we share,
here in Toledo. Thanks to our Catholic faith, we believe that
nothing from the past is ever lost, the present remains rooted

and connected to the past, and the future beckons with a call to paradise.

No wonder the painting proved so popular in its own time. The crowds from around the world that now gather before the image were first from Toledo itself. They came to point out and recognize their friends and neighbors, the grand gentlemen in black they saw parading in the street, depicted standing together in a reverent semicircle. They came to look at the astonishing images of souls in upward flight—was this what heaven looked like? And they could identify figures both historical and biblical: there was Lazarus, there his Royal Highness, the king of Spain himself, who even though he had relocated his court far away in the Escorial would surely not forget his subjects in the capital he had abandoned.

The Burial of the Count of Orgaz consoled a community for losses, reassured them of the benevolence of almighty powers, but also resumed, in a single image, the entire language of Christian consolation—the one we have traced from Paul to Boethius and from Boethius to Dante. Except here paradise is so close, just above the heads of the Toledan gentlemen, and the saints are right there, among the crowd. Here too, as in the basilica of Galla Placidia and the churches of San Vitale and Sant'Apollinare Nuovo in Ravenna, the darker and more threatening side of the Christian message is entirely absent. There is no sign of the crucifixion, no sign that there is a hell waiting for sinners. In the iconography of the Spanish Counter-Reformation, there is an abundance of this darker reality, but not here, not in this image that radiates confident hope and pictures the living, the dead, and the unborn all delivered from the tyranny of time and the pain of loss.

What the painting helps us to understand is that the recurrent subject of consolation is time itself—the fact that it goes one way and cannot be stopped, cannot be slowed down, cannot be reversed; that our losses cannot be made good; that the future is unknowable, the past is irrecoverable, and time for us ends in death, while it goes on for others as if we never existed. The painter's deeper intention was to depict consolation as the dream of an escape together from the downward funnel of time. The painting's ecstatic feeling is just the other side of despair, in its recognition that this escape from time can be imagined only through art but cannot be lived or experienced.

The painting speaks to a longing that doesn't ebb just because the Christian doctrine that once sustained it has lost much of its power. The proof is in the crowds from all over the world who come and linger in front of it. We wish that time should not slip so irrecoverably into forgetting, that the present should not be so fleeting, that the future should not be so shrouded and so unknown. This is what we seek consolation for. We would like to be these Toledan gentry, unastonished, quite at home with the suspension of time, beneath the awesome canopy of heaven, in the year of our lord 1586. We too would like not to know what kind of trouble is coming our way.

And what of the painter himself? We know that the painting began as a job of work, commissioned by the parish priest, done to a contract that stipulated what he had to put in it, according to the rules set down by the Council of Trent. The painter took the commission and made it into an expression of the faith he brought with him. He was a recent émigré from Greece, an icon painter who was already master of the flat, hieratic, expressionless Byzantine style, perfected a thousand years before in the mosaics of the churches in Ravenna. He had left his native Crete and traveled to Venice to study with Tintoretto, and then to Rome, where he had seen the Sistine Chapel and its vision of heaven, and made enemies by saying he wasn't impressed. He was now settled and established with a young family in the city. The artist transformed a standard commission into a personal statement not only of his own faith but also of his hope for the future itself, by painting his son into the picture.

The boy must have stood in the studio day after day watching his own likeness take shape, silently witnessing his father's attempt to express his longing for continuity and its consolations. The boy is holding a torch next to Saint Augustine and Saint Stephen. He is about eight, dressed in a lace collar and short trousers, with his eyes staring back at the painter, as if the painter wishes to say, you, Jorge Manuel, my son, are my future, you will inherit this image of what I believe, you will carry it forward and believe as I, Doménikos Theotokópoulos, known in the city as The Greek, an icon painter from the island of Crete, have believed. I have settled here with these Toledans since 1577 and I will die here, in 1614, revered as the greatest painter in the city.

As time would have it, El Greco would be forgotten for centuries, finally remembered when new generations arose who thought his elongated, yearning figures were not strange or incompetently painted, but actually among the truest depictions ever of the human longing to escape, to be taken up into heaven, and to enjoy the blessing of timelessness.

Seven

The Body's Wisdom

Michel de Montaigne's Last Essays

In the same years that El Greco was painting *The Burial of the Count of Orgaz* in Toledo, Michel de Montaigne was writing the third volume of his *Essays* in retirement in his château near Bordeaux. In El Greco's hands, consolation took the form of a triumphant vision of the communion of saints, interceding on behalf of the noble count and carrying his soul up to heaven. Seven hundred and fifty kilometers away, in Montaigne's solitary tower, consolation assumed a very different form. When he reviewed what consoled him, Montaigne made almost no mention of the saints, salvation, or paradise. He sought solace elsewhere, in a sometimes amused, sometimes anguished process of inner reconciliation with his age, his times, and the course of his life. In his writing, consolation left the realm of faith altogether and returned to the frame it had once taken in Cicero, Seneca, Virgil, and Plato. But he did not remain there. He discarded the consolations of philosophy and found solace instead in the pleasures, rhythms, and resilience of the human body itself. In doing so, he moved the search for consolation away from the mind to the feeling, second by second, that life was worth living simply because you could feel its rhythms coursing through your veins.

This passionate vindication of life itself and its bodily pleasures occurred precisely when Montaigne was dealing with intimations of mortality, with the decline of his body, and with the sour comedy of old age. He was fifty-six, still vigorous, still happiest riding through the country on his horse, but also struggling with kidney stones, whose passage hurt so much that he thought he would die.

He had reviewed and discarded a host of consolations available to a man of his place in society. It was conventional for an aging nobleman, for example, to take enjoyment in his estate, his gardens, vines, and houses. Montaigne's father had been that kind of gentleman, but the son ruefully concluded these joys were not for him. It wasn't that he was indifferent to the attractions of home. The château had been his birthplace after all, and memory had its comforts, but the rustic arts urged upon gentlemen since the time of Virgil did not do much for him. Unlike his neighbors, he was uneasy with the stewardship of his estate. He suspected his servants stole from him a little but could not work himself up to do anything about it. He did not know much about vines or crops and lacked his father's practical touch. When he had an old wall repaired, he remarked sadly that he did it more to give his dead father pleasure than himself.

He was a Gascon, with an intense attachment to its dialect, its traditions of plain speaking, and its local institutions, but absent from his reflections is any pleasure in belonging, in connection to a place. To a man actually living in his ancestral home, roots seemed to count for relatively little. Instead of consoling himself with the thought that at least he could die at home, in the company of his servants and family, he found himself asking whether it wouldn't be better to die on the road, alone. Even in some dark country inn, he imagined, you could always find a servant whom you could pay to massage your feet.

Many find, in old age, that marriage and family are a source of comfort. Montaigne had been married for twenty-five years to Françoise de La Chassaigne, but of this woman who shared the same house and had her own bedroom elsewhere, below his tower, there is no mention at all. Of marriage itself, he remarked, "the result is what is observed of cages: the birds outside despair of getting in, and those inside are equally anxious to get out." He was distinctly cool to his own daughter, Eleanor, wishing only that some man would marry her and take her off his hands. As for the idea of grandchildren as a comfort in old age, Montaigne was dismissive: "I have never thought that to be without children was a want that should make life less complete and contented."

A man in his fifties, old by the standards of his time, might have drawn contented recollection from the offices he had held, the public roles he had performed, the services he had rendered to his city or his region. Montaigne had been mayor of Bordeaux twice; unkind voices whispered he hadn't accomplished much, and Montaigne admitted they might be right, but leaving no trace at least meant you had done no harm.

He had served as an advocate in provincial law courts but had come away only with a sense of how idiotic and cruel the law could be. He had risen to advise the Catholic king of France himself and had been in the delegations that visited his Protestant rival Henri of Navarre. Yet for all his efforts as a go-between, the religious wars, which had begun when he was barely thirty, now seemed certain to continue long after he was gone. He had always been led to believe, by his reading of the Roman classics and by the admonitions of his father, that a public life was a gentleman's true vocation. But what, he now wondered, had his public life been worth?

Altogether, he was in a melancholy mood. He spent most of his time in the tower, where his bedroom and his library were. This circular library was his throne room; from where he sat, he could see the portrait of a nubile Venus, Latin inscriptions carved into the beams ("Nothing human is alien to me"—Terence), a window that gave onto the stable yard and the gardens and the fields beyond. It was all familiar, but not necessarily comforting.

It was his unkind fate, he realized, to have lived in an age of iron. Thirty years in the very midst of a civil war had not shaken his faith, but the wars had made him loathe religious fanatics and their conviction that mere ideas, mere doctrines could license murder and pillage. For a man whose most treasured possessions were on the shelves of his library, the wars shook the foundation of a scholar's life: faith in ideas themselves. The destruction in the villages nearby, the narrow-eyed hatred that came over colleagues he had once called friends, made him ask what ideas, generalizations, abstractions—the harvest men took from all these books—were good for if they destroyed countries and plunged brothers and sisters into murderous strife.

Fanaticism had all but destroyed the tissue of sociability that had once allowed families of different faiths to live together. His château was a Catholic household in the middle of a Protestant region, and it had become an ever more perilous business to maintain good relations with the noblemen around. One of his neighbors had recently invaded his courtyard with a posse of men, and it took all of Montaigne's charm and cunning to persuade them to leave the place unmolested. Recently when he was out riding, he had been set upon by masked highwaymen who held him captive for hours in a forest, while they ransacked his saddlebags and his money box. Montaigne persuaded them to spare his life by reassuring them of the good relations he had managed to maintain with the local Protestant warlords. It rankled him to live under their precarious mercy.

He had lived nearly twenty years amid unrelenting law-lessness: brigands on the roads, massacres nearby, troops pillaging and raping in nearby villages, and if his house had escaped unscathed it was by purest chance. Bordeaux had been taken by one side, then the other. He had seen terrible sights: pigs gorging on corpses left behind from some skirmish; cruelty he could scarcely believe; men watching others suffer for the sheer pleasure of it.

While he had learned to look upon his own time as one might watch a tragedy at the theater, a spectator of his country's calamities, he had also known real terror. "I have gone to bed a thousand times in my own home, imagining that some-one would betray me and slaughter me that very night."

In 1586, he had been forced to leave his house with his family and servants and take to the roads for six months to escape the plague. He and his family had to live on the inconstant charity of friends and neighbors, only to be driven out onto the roads again by fear, to "shift their abode," he said bitterly, as soon as one of his group "began to feel pain in the end of his finger." Why? Because "all illnesses are taken for the plague."

He had learned lessons about mortality by watching common people, infected with plague, prepare themselves to die. They left their vines untended and died in the fields, some even digging their own graves and lying in them to await the end. Instead of being horrified, he drew comfort from their resolution, from the way "each man universally gave up caring for his own life."

When he looked at these peasants dying peacefully, he thought Seneca had been wrong to "meditate upon exile, torture, wars, diseases . . . so that you may not be a novice to any misfortune." We were all novices, Montaigne concluded, when it came to misfortune. Cicero had also been wrong to believe that "the whole life of a philosopher is a meditation on death." Death was the end of life, but not its goal. Common people understood this better than philosophers. In a quietly wise sentence, Montaigne observed, "Life should be an aim unto itself, a purpose unto itself: its rightful study is to regulate, conduct and suffer itself."

In the midst of this dispiriting turmoil, he had discovered that there was consolation to be had simply in living and creating, in seeking to fashion and understand what his life had meant, and in wagering that someone in the future would find comfort in what he had learned at such cost. He had already published two editions of the *Essays*, but it was only with the third volume, composed between 1585 and 1588, that he began to realize and take delight in the sheer novelty of what he was trying to do: to make himself—his moods, his flights of fancy, his memories, his remembered learning—the subject of the book. The essays were expeditions into the depths of his own heart, for the sheer pleasure of it—and as he began to think, his own heart could lay bare the human soul in general. "Each man," he wrote, "bears the entire form of a man's estate." If he wrote about himself alone, he might, he thought, capture a truth or two about the whole human condition.

He was too honest, however, not to understand that he had to struggle against his own illusions. There was bravado and perhaps some self-deception when he told himself, "If I had to live over again, I would live as I have lived. I have neither tears for the past nor fears for the future." In fact, he had plenty of tears for the past, and he often felt a kind of disgust at his own useless scribbling. It seemed, he thought, a symptom of an unruly age. "The desolation of this state coincides with the desolation of my age." Men committed themselves to paper only to air their fanatical opinions or to persuade themselves that they were innocent bystanders. He cheered himself up as best he could, but there were days when "I abandon myself in despair, and let myself slip toward the precipice, and as they say, throw the handle after the ax."

He observed how small things could overwhelm his precarious detachment:

> My soul easily achieves detachment from a distance, but . . . a rein fixed badly on my horses, a stirrup leather slapping against my leg, will keep me in a bad humor a whole day.

He was keenly aware that his own good cheer was an artful pose to keep dark thoughts at bay, and so consolation might well stray from truth. In his honesty about this question, he did more than expose his own contradictions. He changed the way everyone who reads him has thought about consolation ever since.

In an essay called "Of Diversion," written for the third volume of his *Essays*, he asked whether to console someone was simply to distract them. He remembered how he had once tried to console a noble lady who was truly mourning, unlike most women, he said tartly, whose "mourning is put on and perfunctory." He understood, he said, the deep sense in which any effort at consolation was, at bottom, an attempt to delude and "cover up the trouble." Though he was one of the most famously learned men of his time, with a library filled with the entire classical literature on consolation, he decided in the face of this noblewoman's grief that, in a moment of real extremity, it was better to give up on the consolations of philosophy altogether. Something else, something more intimate, more tactile, less wordy, was needed. Montaigne simply talked to the grieving noblewoman, deflecting her from the path of grief and toward inconsequential subjects, imperceptibly stealing away painful thoughts and keeping her in good spirits while they were together. This was consolation, he thought, and it was indistinguishable from deception. It was also fruitless, he confessed, since those who took up his place after he had left found her sliding back into deep grief once again. As he admitted, "I had not laid the ax to the roots."

On further reflection, he concluded, "we rarely make the soul meet the troubles head on." Few of us could ever approximate the composure of a Socrates who, facing death, sought "no consolation outside the thing itself." Most of us, Montaigne thought, had a limited capacity for facing reality. We take flight from the present with fantastic hopes of future glory or, better still, vengeance upon our enemies:

> the hope of a better life stays and supports us, or the hope of our children's worth or the future glory of our name, or flight from the ills of this life or the vengeance that threatens those who cause our death.

To be consoled, he now thought, was to be diverted and ultimately to forget. Time, he wrote, was the "sovereign physician of our passions." His beloved friend Étienne de la Boétie, nobleman, poet, and political polemicist, had died twenty-five years before, in an ordeal that went on for ten whole days and which Montaigne witnessed by his friend's bedside, moved and horrified. Looking up from his desk in the tower, Montaigne still remembered Étienne, but the love and delight of his youth were ebbing away. Even love, he concluded, was powerless in the face of death and time.

Fear of death, he thought, could be conjured away with philosophy, but lofty reflections lost all power to console, he knew only too well, when the body felt death's actual grip. In Montaigne's case, death's grip—kidney stones—gave him pain so intense he wished he could die. "I saw death nonchalantly when I saw it universally, as the end of life. I dominate it in the mass; in detail it harasses me." He could be reconciled to death in the abstract as long as he did not start imagining what it would be like to be actually dead: the tears of his servants, the last touch of a hand, and afterward the distribution of his old clothes. It was these anticipated details, not the fact of death itself, that made him feel "disconsolate and sorry for himself."

A false consolation if ever there was one, Montaigne went on, was to imagine the pleasant things that people would say about us after our deaths.

> I renounce any favorable testimonials that anyone may want to give me not because I shall deserve them but because I shall be dead.

Our deaths were ours alone. We had to understand that no one could truly share death with us. There were strict limits to human empathy:

> No matter how great a man's wisdom, he can never grasp, through his judgment alone, the cause of another's grief in all its intensity.

If empathy was limited, human solidarity too had its limits. Étienne de la Boétie on his deathbed had frittered away his final hours consoling his distraught wife and his friends. Montaigne reflected, "I have enough to do to console myself without having to console others." Dying, he thought, "is not a role for society; it is an act for one single character."

As a young man, he had entertained the belief that his soul—and the instruction it derived from philosophy—was his master. With age, with the kidney stone, with fatigue, it was "the body's turn to guide my mind to reform." Up in the tower with his books, he confessed it had been twenty years since he had really been able to spend an hour with a book. Now he found himself wishing instead that he could "play at cobnut" or spin a top. Sexual reveries returned—the walls of his study were decorated with pictures that some considered shocking— and he found himself thinking that the pleasures of the body had offered him more joy and more true diversion from fear of death than anything he had ever read.

His time in the tower was consumed with haunted memories of his lusty youth and more recent recollections of a noblewoman in her twenties, Marie de Gournay, who had befriended him on his last visit to Paris and who had vowed to devote herself to his *Essays* and his memory. Though he never saw her again, she proved as good as her word, issuing the first posthumous edition in 1595.

Age and sexual longing made him begin to appreciate that body and soul were bound together. It was an error of philosophy to "tear apart a living man," even to try to claim that reason could comfort a man for the agonies of pain or hold him back from the impetuous pleasures of the flesh. He was beset by memories of Marie de Gournay, who had told him in Paris that she considered him her second father. He knew of his own neediness, remarking of old people like himself, "we demand more when we bring less." But he knew that he had to stand aside and let others, younger and more virile, take his place. He wanted love, even in old age, but he recoiled at the thought of a young woman taking pity on him. He would "much rather not live at all than live on alms."

In his final essay, "Of Experience," Montaigne put his books aside and reflected instead on what life had taught him. His various themes—the increasing distrust of book knowledge and philosophy, the ever franker affection for nature and the body, the warmhearted awareness of human ignorance, especially his own—all found their summation. Now he praised habit, idiosyncrasy, doing things your own way, with a keen sense of how consoling it was in life to have rhythms, routines, daily practices, provided they were your own. These were the reassuring constancies of his life:

> I cannot, without effort, sleep by day, or eat between meals, or breakfast, or go to bed without a long interval of about three full hours after supper, or make a child except before going to sleep, or make one standing up, or endure my sweat, or quench my thirst with pure water or pure wine, or remain bareheaded for long, or have my hair cut after dinner; and I would feel as uncomfortable without my gloves as without my shirt, or without washing when I leave the table or get up in the morning, or without canopy and curtains for my bed, as I would be without really necessary things.

This was a hymn of praise to the ordinary, to the routine expectations and pleasures of bodily existence. Every book in his library told him these were transitory and fleeting forms of solace, but he was no longer listening to his classical muses.

In his final essay, he chronicled his favorite meals and how he liked his bed made up. "I like to sleep hard and alone, even without a woman, in the royal style, rather well covered up." He derived pleasure from scratching his itches; he enjoyed his

bowel movements and did not like to be interrupted in his
evacuations, adding with a cheeky bow to his superiors, "Both
kings and philosophers defecate, and ladies too." By some
strange logic only he could understand, thinking about these
humble functions suddenly brought to mind something that
Étienne de la Boétie had exclaimed, during his fatal illness,

"Is it so great a thing to be alive?"

To which Montaigne now replied, it was indeed a great
thing to be alive—but only if you accepted it all: the pleasure,
pain, the excrement, the miseries and joys of the humble human
body.

We must learn to endure, Montaigne now believed, what
we cannot avoid. Even the kidney stone, that curse of his final
years, he now looked upon as the natural wastage that the
body eventually suffers. When passing a stone, he sweated and
writhed, passed black urine, endured strange convulsions, but
he took pleasure when friends congratulated him for his stoic
self-command. Besides, illness cured him of any frantic desire
to hold on to life. "You do not die of being sick," he wrote,
"you die of being alive," and illness teaches you, he concluded,
when your body stops hurting, to love life all the more.

In a time when zealots on both sides of the civil war had
waged a fanatical war against lusts and bodily temptation, he
now aligned himself with "the pursuit of pleasure." The world
does the opposite, he noted wryly, "and thinks nothing is ben-
eficial that is not painful." If we wished to be reconciled to life,
he was telling his readers in this ultimate summing up, we
should seek pleasure, seek ease. He was at war with those zealots, but he was also in combat with the guilt and self-denial
inside himself:

We are great fools. He has spent his life in leisure, we say.
I have done nothing today. What, have you not lived? This

is not only the fundamental but the most illustrious of
your occupations.

The "most barbarous of our maladies," he concluded, "was
to despise our being." We spoiled our lives, he went on, with
joyless moralizing and self-regarding high-mindedness:

> Philosophy is very childish, when she gets up on her hind
> legs and preaches to us . . . that sensual pleasure is a brut-
> ish thing unworthy of being enjoyed by the wise man;
> that the only pleasure he derives from the enjoyment of a
> beautiful young wife is the pleasure of his consciousness of
> doing the right thing.

Let us not, he concluded, suppose that the reason for living lies in any reasons we could give for it. It lies in the body,
in the second-by-second cascade of sensations, feelings, needs,
pleasures, pains that give us the consciousness, sufficient unto
itself, of being alive. Provided we never lose this feeling, we
would have no need for consolation at all. We should not live,
he said, by trying to stand on stilts. His final words said it all:

> The most beautiful lives, to my mind, are those that con-
> form to the common human pattern, with order, but with-
> out miracle and without eccentricity. Now old age needs
> to be treated a little more tenderly. Let us commend it to
> that god, the protector of health and wisdom, but let it be
> gay and sociable wisdom.

Gay and sociable wisdom, the last words of his final essay,
pointed the way forward to a modern sensibility about consolation that turns its back on trying to understand the ways of
God and instead gives attention, all of it, to the demands of

ordinary life and the people around us. At the end of his life, Montaigne had moved beyond faith, disgusted by the violence and cruelty of religious fanatics on both sides. Instead of trusting to God's salvation or even his mercy, he trusted instead— and taught everyone who came after the same lesson—to the deepest attachments we have, our love of life itself.

Eight

The Unsent Letter

David Hume's My Own Life

In 1734, a twenty-three-year-old Scottish gentleman, alone and desperate, stopped in London on his way to Bristol. There he wrote a letter to a doctor who specialized in nervous disorders, seeking an appointment. He told the doctor that he had been struck down by depression at nineteen, and it was still so severe that he had given up living at home in the Scottish country-side with his widowed mother, given up the law, renounced his great love, philosophical study—in order to go to work for a merchant in Bristol. There, he said with touching bravado, he hoped to "toss about the world, from one Pole to the other till I leave this Distemper behind."

At age eighteen, he confessed, his mind had been flooded with sudden intimations of a "new scene of thought," a stream of ideas that he embraced "with an ardor natural to young men." What so excited him was the intuition that the classical authorities—Cicero, Seneca, Plutarch—had not grasped what human nature truly was. What was needed, he realized, was a new science of man, modeled on Isaac Newton's achievement in the natural sciences. He had set himself this challenge, but after being swept away by intellectual excitement, suddenly "all my ardor seem'd in a moment to be extinguish'd and I could no longer raise my mind to that pitch which formerly gave me such excessive pleasure."

Doubt turned into despair and despair into depression. He told the doctor that he had fought the disabling affliction as best he could. Every day, he rode alone through the countryside around the family estate of Ninewells, hoping vigorous exercise would shake his depression loose; he continued to be a dutiful son and brother, but he couldn't resume philosophical work. Reading, when he could do it, made matters worse. He was continually obsessed with thoughts of "Death and Poverty and Shame and Pain and all the other calamities of life." His mind flailed about like an arm striking out and missing its aim. He now understood those religious mystics who wrote about being abandoned by God. Too much study of philosophy was going to drive him mad, unless he chose a path of "business and diversion." So, he concluded his letter to the doctor, he was taking the coach to Bristol to apprentice himself as a clerk to a slave and sugar merchant.

We only have the letter—unsigned and undated—and we have no evidence that it was ever sent. What we know is that David Hume kept the unsent letter in his papers for the rest of his life.

He lasted only a few months in Bristol, apparently fired for correcting the diction in his master's business correspondence, and left, disgruntled and unhappy, but convinced this time that philosophy was his destiny. With a meager family allowance to support him, he moved to France, where he chose to live in modest seclusion in La Flèche, in the Loire valley, near a Jesuit seminary that had once included Descartes as a pupil. There, in a quiet room with a view of gardens and a river for walks nearby, the young man sat down, and for the next four years, between 1734 and 1738, he wrote the book that in his anguish he thought he would never be able to write: *A Treatise of Human Nature*. He was only twenty-seven when he finished it. It took every ounce of his courage.

The radical skepticism he applied to settled belief was breathtaking. He questioned the nature of causality itself, arguing that it was not an actual relation between things, just a conventional belief induced by observation of a constant conjunction between cause and effect. Having rethought causality, he took a hatchet to the idea that humans possessed a soul, arguing that we all died with our bodies. Then he turned to personal identity. When he asked himself what his "self" was, what his "personal identity" consisted in, he found it impossible to fix upon any clear idea at all. When I am asleep, he said, my "self" vanishes, and when I am dead, he concluded, I am nothing, a "perfect non-entity." Hume concluded that the pillars on which Western reason had rested—causation, identity, the soul—were nothing more than fictions.

This was no Olympian exercise in rational skepticism but an anguished process of self-discovery. Thinking these thoughts, he said, had been like putting out to sea in a leaky, weather-beaten vessel and trying to sail the globe. He was constantly in despair at the limitations of his own faculties, but he struggled on alone, feeling he was, as he put it, "a strange uncouth monster" locked inside his brain, unable to rejoin the human race.

He feared what people would make of his ideas and worried that he would attract the enmity of "all metaphysicians, logicians, mathematicians, even theologians." Would they hate him for challenging their doctrines? Worse, could he be sure "that in leaving all establish'd opinions I am following truth?"

Reason, as he saw it, was not the master of the passions, as the Stoic philosophers believed it could be, but rather their slave. But if this were true, it undermined his own ambition to ground his thought in an experimental science of human nature. For what confidence could be placed in chains of reasoning based on thought experiments if, when examined carefully, our thoughts were nothing but a confusion of wishes and desires, fantasies and imaginings?

He had bet on his own reason and it had driven him to the edge. He had discovered that there were questions to which no possible answer could be given: "Where am I or what? From what causes do I derive my existence, and to what condition shall I return?" These standard metaphysical conundrums had tormented him precisely because they were unanswerable. Trying to answer them had driven him into the "most deplorable condition imaginable, inviron'd with the deepest darkness." There were no philosophical routes out of this maze. Reason was incapable of dispelling these clouds or curing "this philosophical melancholy and delirium."

In words that echoed Michel de Montaigne's essay "Of Diversion"—we know Hume had read him—the young man came to a similar conclusion: philosophy offered no consolation, but human company did:

> I dine, I play a game of back-gammon, I converse, and make merry with my friends; And when after three- or four-hours' amusement, I wou'd return to these speculations, they appear so cold, and strain'd, and ridiculous, that I cannot find in my heart to enter into them any further.

In seeking diversion in the company of others, Hume was acknowledging how much he needed others to escape the maze of his own mind and how little reason actually contributed to consolation of any kind. We need human society in order to escape ourselves, to see ourselves as others do, to compare our understanding with theirs, to share a common world of feeling. What gives consolation, Hume concluded, is the social world: its games, rituals, honors, and rewards. After five years of illness and four years of solitude, he realized that he could not make sense of life or bear it except in company with others. Like Montaigne, he concluded that it was an arrogant error for classical philosophers, such as Cicero or Marcus Aurelius, to despise the "vanity of human wishes," and to counsel indifference toward the ordinary comforts and distractions of their fellow men and women. The only way to bear life was, like the rest of their fellow creatures, to live it, side by side with them:

> Here then I find myself absolutely and necessarily determin'd to live, and talk, and act like other people in the common affairs of life.

Why then, he wondered, do philosophy at all? At times he had wanted to toss all his books and papers into the fire. But then, he said, he would go for a walk by the river, and little by little the incorrigible ambitions, the ones he had set out in the letter to the unnamed doctor, would return: of contributing "to the instruction of mankind and of acquiring a name by my inventions and discoveries." He had tried to banish these ambitions when he went to Bristol, only to learn he would have been "a loser in point of pleasure"; and this, he concluded, was "the origin of my philosophy," the sheer pleasure of doing it and the desire for recognition that he hoped would follow.

Philosophy, he reasoned, had to make peace with the rituals of social life and understand their comfort. It had to become a civic discourse, a secular guide to the perplexed, and it posed no dangers, Hume wrote sardonically, since "the errors in religion are dangerous; those in philosophy only ridiculous." Philosophy could become a useful guide to error and an enemy to superstition, he concluded, provided it was humble and skeptical about its own claims. It should avoid the use of the phrases "tis evident, tis certain, tis undeniable." As he finished the last words of his *Treatise*, he admitted that he had been overfond of those phrases himself, but now he knew what price he had paid trying to answer questions that had no answer, and he knew, henceforth, that his philosophizing would sing the praises of the humble consolations of social life.

This view about consolation translated, in his later work, into a deep skepticism toward the idea, propagated from every pulpit in England, that social order could hold together only if the church preached resignation to the poor and excluded. The new science of man that took shape in Hume's *Essays*, Adam Smith's *Theory of Moral Sentiments*, and Adam Ferguson's *An Essay on the History of Civil Society* rebelled at the idea that order depended on the consolations of an afterlife. They explained the facts of social cooperation and social order entirely without depending on shared fear of God's punishment or hope of his eternal rewards.

In these founding texts of classical economic theory, they argued that social order was maintained by each individual's search for the satisfaction of their needs and cooperation with others in the division of labor. It is to Hume, Smith, and Ferguson, these sociable philosophers of eighteenth-century Scotland, these pioneers of the new discipline of "political economy," that we owe the first fully elaborated account of the operations of a market society. As they understood it, a market society was secular, held together not by common faith but by the invisible hand of social cooperation and economic exchange.

Hume never forgot what it had cost him to think himself free of religious belief and the stoic indifference to material things. He never forgot what it had been like to be impecunious and alone. The misery of mental illness had taught him that you could not think yourself into reconciliation with life.

Solitude had taught him what it was to need human beings for comfort and diversion. The confidence he had gained in the pursuit of the "science of human nature" made him increasingly hostile to religion. His circle of friends, Smith for example, were as skeptical as he, but they studiously avoided giving offense. But for all his carefully constructed persona of debonair detachment, Hume was ferocious on the subject of faith, concentrating his scorn on its role as false comforter.

In *The Natural History of Religion*, published in 1757, he argued that it was a false consolation to think that prayer and faith would give answers as to the purpose of life, any more than philosophy itself. Hume is the single thinker most responsible for philosophy's abandonment of metaphysics and theodicy, all its grand attempts to make sense of the world as a divinely created order, or even as any kind of order at all. Philosophy's role, Hume thought, should be commensurate with the very limited power of human reason and should confine itself to epistemology, to causation, to the meaning of concepts and our understanding of the external world. It should abandon the ground of consolation altogether.

In the *Dialogues Concerning Natural Religion*, which he wrote in 1759 and continued to revise until his death, he argued that since man had invented God to explain and endure the injustice and harshness of life, there was no consolation in such illusions. It was far better to enjoy life than to waste effort trying to explain why it was as it was. Nor did he see any comfort in nature itself. Establishment divines, who published tracts denouncing his views, all insisted from their pulpits that God revealed himself in the beauty and order of nature. The poet Alexander Pope had praised the design and purpose that Newton's physics and optics had revealed in the physical universe. There might be a design in nature, Hume conceded, but it was not a design that bore any relation to human intentions. In the savagery of natural competition, Hume saw not divine intention at work, but only the relentless unfolding of the life force itself. In a paragraph of burning intensity that he added to the *Dialogues* at the very end of his life, he wrote of

> a blind Nature, impregnated by a great vivifying principle, and pouring forth from her Lap, without Discernment or parental Care, her maim'd and abortive Children.

When he inserted these lines in 1776, one of the last of his inveterate corrections, he was already dying of a "disorder in my bowels" that had become "mortal and incurable." He told a friend that tinkering with his own manuscripts as he lay dying was rather like the Greeks, during the siege of Constantinople by the Turks, occupying "themselves entirely in Disputes concerning the Procession of the Holy Ghost." But habits were habits, and if they took his mind off his malady so much the better.

James Boswell came to visit him in his apartments in St Andrew Square in Edinburgh and found him "lean, ghastly, and quite of an earthy appearance, dressed in a suit of grey cloth with white metal buttons and a scratch wig." Boswell was curious to know "if he persisted in disbelieving in a future state even when he had death before his eyes." Hume replied briskly that he had no more uneasiness imagining the afterlife than imagining the "before-life" preceding his birth. If there were an afterlife, he mused, he could give as good an account of himself as any man.

His friend Adam Smith also came to visit and hoped his old friend would recover. Hume was briskly dismissive, saying that he looked forward to a speedy dissolution. He then told Smith that he had been rereading one of his old favorites, Lucian's *Dialogues of the Dead*, and mentioned the excuses the dying had offered to Charon, the boatman, to persuade him to

spare them the final voyage across the river Styx. Hume thought
the only excuse he would offer would be a request for more time
to correct the editions of his works, but he doubted that Charon
would grant his wish. Perhaps, he told Smith, he should ask
Charon for a little time to see mankind delivered from superstition, but he could guess Charon's answer: "That won't happen
these two hundred years. Into the boat this instant, you lazy
loitering rogue."

The two men laughed at this—and later Smith was to tell
the story in his published account of Hume's death and in so
doing to provoke a more furious reaction from the divines, he
ruefully admitted, than anything he had received for his *Wealth
of Nations*, published in 1776, the year of Hume's death.

Hume's equanimity in the face of his own death was a
scandal to the divines, to Boswell, and to his friend Samuel
Johnson, who insisted that Hume was merely playacting, per-
forming a good death on the model of Socrates. When he was
off the stage, Johnson held, Hume had to be as terrified as the
rest of us. Johnson genuinely thought it was impossible to die
without the consolation of Christian faith. He himself was terrified of dying, fearful that he might be damned for his sins and
sent to hell. He recoiled in horror at the thought of a secular
death, one in which a man accepted that his soul died with his
body and that the material body returned, in time, to the dust
of which it was composed.

Johnson was wrong about Hume. Those who were at his
bedside in the last months testified that he suffered pain with
calm and forbearance and never wavered in his genial determination to die as he had lived, without the comforts of faith. The
question is not whether he brought off the performance—he
did—but how he managed it. His death became a historical
marker, a sign that a new way of dying, and hence a new way
of thinking about consolation, was making its way into the

world. What gave him the equanimity with which he faced his final days?

The answer to this question may lie in the last document he wrote, *My Own Life*, composed in a single day on April 18, 1776, in his neat, cursive hand, with its characteristic swirling *g*'s and *y*'s. It was not a confessional autobiography like Augustine's or Rousseau's, and it was highly selective, casting into silence, for example, Hume's bitter quarrel with Rousseau. It was a narrative of validation, a proud affirmation of what he had achieved, meant not for his eyes alone but for posterity. It described a secular pilgrim's progress of obstacles overcome, of a life given meaning and shape by the pursuit of fame as an author. He chronicled the challenges he had faced, especially the initial reaction to his *Treatise*. When it appeared, it "fell dead-born from the press," without even exciting, he said ironically, the "murmur of the zealots." Faced with the failure of the *Treatise*, he had recast it in more accessible form as *An Enquiry Concerning Human Understanding*, only to find it ignored once again. Partisan political reaction to his *History of England* so discouraged him that he thought of giving up writing altogether. Only the publication of his *Natural History of Religion*, and the "petulance, arrogance and scurrility" that it provoked, "gave me some consolation for the otherwise indifferent reception of my performance." He discovered that he thrived on adverse reactions. Little by little, the books sold better, and he was able to achieve independence of the arbitrary favors of patrons and the rich. In Paris in the 1760s, he even knew fame amid the company of "modest women." He became known as *le bon David*, and fashionable society hostesses, like the Comtesse de Boufflers, fell for the Scottish burr with which he inflected his French.

Hume looked back on the glory years in Paris with contentment but without nostalgia. More important to him was telling posterity that he had earned a thousand pounds in a good year. He took pride in the "sufficiency" and "ease" that thirty years of hard work had earned him. The test of a good life, Hume was telling us, was whether you had been true to your ambitions and fashioned a path for yourself. This attitude to life was of a piece with his attitude to death. Much earlier in his life, he had written an essay on suicide in which he insisted, with real passion, that religious authorities had no right to deny a man the choice of his own death. Death, like life, had meaning to the degree that we shaped it to our own ends, that we "owned" it. His essay on suicide was a passionate defense of human freedom, and it was marked by a profound sympathy, earned from his own years of depression, for those who could reach a point where they found life no longer worth living.

He took the same fearless and matter-of-fact approach to death. He knew that his affliction was "mortal" and "incurable," but he still loved reading as much as ever, enjoyed the company of his friends, and had never suffered any abatement of his spirits. "It is difficult to be more detached from life than I am at present," he wrote. He even referred to himself in the past tense: "I am, or rather was, for that is the style I must now use." He concluded *My Own Life* by confessing that "this funeral oration of myself" might display some vanity but his claims for himself could easily be verified.

He wrote this valediction in one day, with few corrections, in a continuous flow that suggested he had known what he wanted to say for a long time. Once it was done, he put his affairs in order. He disposed of his fortune to his nephew, assured himself that his books would be published in new editions and that the *Dialogues Concerning Natural Religion* would appear in print. He ordered papers burned and servants paid. He said goodbye to all his friends and went to meet his end, with calm composure. Among the papers that he chose not to destroy was the letter to the doctor, left unsent forty-two years before. Like another famous unsent letter, the one Beethoven wrote to his immortal beloved, Hume kept it as a reminder of the price he had paid to become the man he was. It allowed him to show himself, and us, that he had chosen a life and had lived it to the full, that he had realized the dreams of the anguished twenty-three-year-old he had once been. He had crafted a new form of consolation: autobiography as a narrative of self-realization.

Nine

The Consolations of History

Condorcet's A Sketch for a Historical Picture of the Progress of the Human Mind

On July 8, 1793, two medical men knocked on the door of their former lodging house in Gravediggers' Street—the rue des Fossoyeurs—near Saint-Sulpice in Paris. With them was a middle-aged man in an agitated state. The two men asked the lady of the house, Madame Vernet, to take him in. Madame Vernet knew that he had to be a fugitive. Marie Rose Vernet was a childless widow, originally from Châteauneuf in Provence, who rented out rooms to medical students. When her two former lodgers implored her to give him shelter, she asked only: "Is he virtuous?" They assured her he was. "Then let him come," she said. When he offered payment, she refused and was to refuse his money for the rest of his stay. He was to be her guest for nine months. It was not until later that she learned his real name: Marie-Jean-Antoine-Nicolas de Caritat, marquis de Condorcet, deputy of the National Convention, former recording secretary of the Royal Academy of Sciences, mathematician, scholar, politician, and now an outlaw, proscribed by the Jacobins, his estates confiscated and his life at risk of the guillotine. He had once been the leading intellectual figure of the moderate revolutionaries and now was a man of fifty at the end of his tether.

Since the intoxicating summer of 1789 when the Bastille had fallen, Condorcet and his wife, Sophie, a spirited aristocrat twenty years his junior, had been at the center of the revolutionary fervor in the city. She was a famous beauty and the hostess of a sparkling salon. He was the most famous mathematician in France, the recording secretary of his country's most elite scientific institution, an intimate friend of Voltaire, and a prolific pamphleteer on every progressive cause of his time. While he was a shy and nervous man, with little speaking ability, whom a society hostess had once rebuked for biting his lips and chewing his fingernails in public, the revolution offered him the grandest possible stage on which to display his talents.

In the first months, on fire with revolutionary enthusiasm, Condorcet had even been seen in the streets of Paris wearing the new uniform of the National Guard, though he chose to wear it with an umbrella rather than a sword. Men like him, armed with the new disciplines of calculus, probability, and political economy, believed they could build a republic on the foundations of science and free France from the lackadaisical incompetence that had doomed the ancien régime. He knew the régime's faults from the inside, having been an adviser of its reforming ministers Turgot and Necker, and having witnessed their attempts to bring the debt-ridden public finances of the monarchy under control.

The house where he and Sophie lived, in Auteuil, on the outskirts of Paris, became the gathering place of the moderate revolutionaries. Reform-minded aristocrats and new men like the Abbé Sieyès, author of the epochal pamphlet *What Is the Third Estate?*, met to plan, to socialize, and to entertain the illusion that they actually controlled the precipitous unfolding of events. Condorcet served on committees that drafted the

first program for a system of national education. For him and
for Sieyès the revolution offered the opportunity to liberate a
whole people from superstition and ignorance. As a founding
member of the *Société des amis des Noirs*, he drafted legislation
outlawing slavery in French colonies. Under Sophie's influence,
he wrote a pamphlet arguing that women should have the same
rights of citizenship as men, though when he went on to draft
the French constitution in 1792 he omitted to grant them
the vote. In a revolution struggling to master the new logic of
democracy, he put probability theory to work, devising proce-
dures to ensure that when matters were decided by majority
vote, the results, arrived at through successive ballots, would
be optimal. He wrote articles, sometimes daily, for the newspapers that sprang up all over Paris; his natural allies, men
like the Abbé Sieyès and the journalist Jean-Baptiste-Antoine
Suard, believed that the revolution was a historical opportunity to reconcile popular sovereignty with executive power and
to anchor a new polity in a charter of rights that would protect
citizens from tyranny.

At first, he supported establishing a constitutional monarchy, but when the king and his family tried to flee in 1791 and
were stopped at Varennes, he and his wife, along with close
friends like Tom Paine, believed the monarchy should be abolished and France should become a republic. He even supported
laws to suppress titles and family names like his own—the
marquis de Condorcet became Citizen Caritat. He wrote articles justifying extraordinary suspensions of the rule of law in
times of revolutionary emergency.

This leftward movement cost him many of his aristocratic
friends. The royalist scientific societies in Saint Petersburg and
Potsdam stripped him of his honorary memberships. Unde-
terred, he plunged into revolutionary politics, securing election
as a deputy to the National Assembly and later to the National

Convention, appointed to draft a new republican constitution. When the king was put on trial in December 1792, he voted to convict the monarch of high treason but voted against sending him to death, since the revolution, he argued, should not execute even its enemies.

With the revolution threatened from without by allied armies and from within by fratricidal division, his vote to spare the king's life gave the Jacobins their opportunity to strike him down. They voted against his draft of a new republican constitution, and in June 1793 the people of Paris stormed the convention, forcing terrified deputies to authorize the arrest of his allies the Girondin moderates. At this moment, Condorcet could have chosen silence and withdrawal. Allies like the Abbé Sieyès and Jean-Baptiste Suard chose to keep their heads down. Drawn on perhaps by the illusion that his eminence made him untouchable, Condorcet wrote an article that same month denouncing the new Jacobin constitution for delivering the country to the despotism of Robespierre and Saint-Just. The Jacobins pounced. His houses were sealed. He was forced to flee, and his enemies thought that he had gone abroad into exile.

Instead, for nine months he took refuge with Madame Vernet in the heart of revolutionary Paris. He and the Provençal landlady were an unlikely couple, but they soon became so close that he took to calling her his "second mother." This may have been to allay the suspicions of his devoted wife, but it was also admitting to the need for maternal consolation, rooted deep in his childhood. His father, a military officer from an old but minor noble family, had died when he was an infant. His "first mother" had been a pious widow who had dressed her only son in pure white girl's clothes until the age of eight in the hope that he would grow up a virtuous Catholic. Her efforts failed utterly. By the time he had graduated from a lycée in Paris, he was already moving in circles that dismissed religion as a

lamentable superstition. While still an adolescent, he was recognized as a mathematical prodigy, and he published his first
work on calculus at the age of twenty-two. Like David Hume,
Condorcet was intoxicated with his own intelligence and with
the ideal of revolutionizing the "sciences of man." This belief
in unaided human reason made him a lifelong foe of the faith
that had comforted his mother in her widowhood.

As the summer of 1793 turned to autumn and then to a
bitter winter in which food and fuel fell short in revolutionary Paris, the fugitive took his meals by the fire with Madame
Vernet and two other lodgers and then repaired to his room to
work on his papers. When he learned in October that thirty
moderate deputies in the National Convention, his comrades,
had been guillotined in the Place de la Révolution, Condorcet
came to Madame Vernet's room in tears. She took him in her
arms, and he wept helplessly. In a letter she wrote thirty years
later, she recalled him whispering, "I am an outlaw, and you
will be too." She also remembered the comfort she offered him.
Robespierre and the Committee of Public Safety could make
him an outlaw, she said, but no one could expel him from the
human race.

Condorcet's wife, Sophie, disguised as a peasant woman,
visited him whenever she could, skirting the crowds around
the guillotine. She walked all the way from a house in Auteuil
to visit her husband, bringing him changes of clothes, newspapers, and news of their four-year-old daughter, Eliza. Their
own mansion had been sequestered, and as the aristocratic wife
of a proscribed man, she was herself in danger. She was also
penniless. She survived by drawing and selling cameo portraits
of other former aristocrats. Sophie kept telling her husband not
to surrender to despair. In a note that reached her in December,
he assured her, "Do not fear that I will give in. I can hold on. I
have no regrets. They told me: you can either be an oppressor

or a victim. I chose misfortune and I will leave them to choose crime."

This mood of defiant resignation may have reassured Sophie, but he had to struggle to maintain it himself. As the winter cold gripped Gravediggers' Street and food and fuel grew scarce, he huddled by the hearth and felt certain his end was nigh. It tormented him to think that he would lose his daughter and that she would never have any memory of him. Despite the best efforts of his wife and Madame Vernet, there were moments when he felt he had been buried alive.

He had fought for a certain idea of revolution, in which science and reason, articulated by wise and public-spirited men like himself, would guide the people to a stable and prosperous republic, at one with itself and at peace with its neighbors. By 1793 this revolution had been defeated by a people's revolution, hungry, vengeful, at war with the monarchs of Europe, desperate and relentless in rooting out enemies within. The police and informers of that radical revolution were now patrolling just below his window. It was only a matter of time before they found him.

His wife, worried by his sinking mood, proposed that he resume a writing project he had started in the early 1780s but had put aside. His original idea had been to write a grand multivolume history of the extraordinary growth of science and learning, aided by new technologies like printing, and their role in emancipating mankind from tyranny and superstition. This was the Enlightenment narrative, the new fable of progress that explained the revolution and gave his own life meaning.

He was hardly alone in believing that philosophy and science had lit the spark that caused the French Revolution. The great Anglo-Irish conservative parliamentarian and orator Edmund Burke also believed it, but in his *Reflections on the Revolution in France* insisted that the "sophisters, economists and

calculators"—a description that fitted men like Condorcet and
Sieyès to perfection——had replaced reverence for tradition
with a dangerous new faith in rational politics. In Burke's jer-
emiad, rationalism and extremism were fatal kin. Men like the
Abbé Sieyès, who had once said, "to make progress the lawgiver must destroy all the errors of the past without pity," had
given license to bloodshed.

At the other end of Europe, in Königsberg, Immanuel Kant
defended the revolution with a paper called "A Renewed
Attempt to Answer the Question: Is the Human Race Continually Improving?" He argued that the French Revolution
had revealed a "moral disposition in the human race," a desire
for freedom that would lead human beings everywhere to
overthrow tyranny. Once France led the way, his own Prussia
might follow, and self-governing republics would spread across
Europe. Peace would surely follow, since self-governing peoples,
if they were rational, would never vote to send their children to
war. The revolution would deliver mankind from the degrading spectacle—here he quoted David Hume—of nations like
"drunken wretches bludgeoning each other in a china shop."
Kant held to this view even as French revolutionary armies
crossed Europe and the continent plunged into a succession
of wars that were not to end until 1815, with the defeat of the
revolution itself. Kant clung on to these hopes nonetheless, and
for a reason. The revolution had demonstrated, once and for
all, that civil freedom and self-government were attainable
dreams. This would never be forgotten.

Condorcet believed this too, but if he was to tell a story of
hope he would have to engage with the most powerful counter-
narrative of his time, Jean-Jacques Rousseau's *Discourse on the
Origin of Inequality*. Here was the dystopian alternative, written
thirty years before the revolution, in which history was inter-
preted not as a story of progress, but as a fatal decline from

primal equality in the state of nature to a modernity disfigured by property, inequality, and tyranny:

> . . . from the instant in which one man had occasion for the assistance of another, from the moment that he perceived that it could be advantageous to a single person to have provisions for two, equality disappeared, property was introduced, labour became necessary, and the vast forests of nature were changed into agreeable plains, which must be watered with the sweat of mankind, and in which the world beheld slavery and wretchedness begin to grow up and blossom with the harvest.

In refuting Rousseau, Condorcet could avail himself of Adam Smith's magisterial rebuttal of Rousseau in his *Wealth of Nations*, published in 1776. It was impossible for Condorcet not to be familiar with Smith's work. There was a deep affinity between their intellectual circles, and Sophie would go on, after Condorcet's death, to translate Smith's *Theory of Moral Sentiments*. Without ever mentioning Rousseau by name, Smith argued that philosophers who had associated the rise of capitalism with a fatal tendency toward increased inequality had failed to factor in the unique productiveness of labor in a modern economy. There might be more inequality in the modern era than in the primitive past, but thanks to the productivity of the modern economy, exemplified in the modern pin factory, there was less absolute poverty. As a result, in Smith's words, an average day laborer in England lived better than many an African king. By emphasizing the moral function of the division of labor, Smith decisively rejected Rousseau's nostalgia for an imagined egalitarian past and gave capitalist modernity the most influential endorsement it had yet received.

Whereas for Smith the debate with Rousseau had been

about the moral meaning of what Smith called "commercial society," for Condorcet what was at stake was the very purpose of the revolution. It was Rousseau's vision of history that legitimized the Jacobins' hatred of privilege and their suspicion of titled renegades like Condorcet. Robespierre justified terror against the revolution's enemies by claiming it would prevent history from slipping back into inequality and tyranny. Condorcet's work had to show, on the contrary, that history had escaped that fatal pattern.

He knew his old plan, the multivolume history, was now impossible. He had no books, no library, and most of all no time. Instead, he called the project *une esquisse*, *A Sketch for a Historical Picture of the Progress of the Human Mind*, and as he set to work with only his prodigious memory to guide him, he covered page after page in feverish haste, struggling to get it all down before they came for him. He was fleeing, as fast as his pen would carry him, from the present into the future.

The great historians of the previous generation had seen no need to turn history into a moral epic. David Hume had rejected the conventional Whig interpretation of the history of England as the triumph of liberty. Edward Gibbon had written the history of Rome as a story of how a superstitious cult had brought about the collapse of a great empire. Condorcet was too desperate for skepticism, for any view that history could brutally reverse course and damage the brightest hopes. His *Sketch* was a relentlessly hopeful apologia pro vita sua, written in the shadow of the guillotine. It was, as he frankly admitted, an exercise in consolation, a writing of history as morality play, a vindication of his revolution against the revolution that now threatened his life.

He argued that the human species was "ceaselessly renewing itself through the . . . centuries," treading a path upward toward truth and happiness. He wanted to show that his own revolutionary ardor had not been in vain. Now, in service to that wish, he produced a vision of history in which that ardor was unstoppable:

The perfectibility of man is truly indefinite, and the progress of this perfectibility, from now onwards independent of any power that might wish to halt it, has no other limit than the duration of the globe upon which nature has cast us.

These affirmations were a way of saying that while he might not live to see it, the revolution he had fought for would eventually triumph:

We shall demonstrate how nature has joined together indissolubly the progress of knowledge and that of liberty, virtue and respect for the natural rights of man.

"We shall demonstrate"; "we will show"; "it will be proven": one rhetorical promissory note followed after another, each declarative sentence more fervent than the last, as he wrote with the intensity of a man desperate to convince himself that history would absolve him. For he had much to seek absolution for: friendships abandoned, compromises made, and radical positions that had paved the way for the terror. History, he now persuaded himself, would forgive him for everything.

The human species had advanced through nine stages, he wrote, from primitive hunting and gathering, through agriculture, to commerce, all in preparation for the ultimate tenth stage, the one heralded by the revolution. At every stage, the driver of progress was the relentless ingenuity of human reason, extracting the secrets of nature and pushing back the boundaries of scarcity and ignorance. Sometimes progress stalled, but only because tyrants and priests held back the advance of knowledge and the spread of freedom. Yet now, thanks to the revolution, their power was ebbing away.

Like Hume, Condorcet reserved his most hostile passages for the church. It was the priestly hold on men's minds, and the false promise of salvation in the afterlife, that held humanity back from seeking salvation here on earth:

> These priestly castes gained control of education in order to train men to suffer more patiently the chains that had, as it were, become identified with their existence, so that they were now without even the possibility of desiring to break them.

How, he exclaimed, could anyone freely choose to blind themselves with superstition? If faith was a consolation, it could only be false. But if faith offered false hope, might that not also be true of history? He did not allow himself to think such a thought in those last feverish months at Madame Vernet's.

Fortunately, he fervently believed, the power of faith over men's minds was weakening. The decisive blow had been the invention of printing. Printing made it impossible to suppress truth or prevent its diffusion. It made progress irreversible, since what had been thought once could now not be lost. Printing also created what Condorcet called "a tribunal, independent of all coercion," a cosmopolitan civil society of free men and women whose opinions acted as a check on the power of tyrants and the superstitions of the clergy.

As he neared the end of the *Sketch*, he allowed his imagination to take flight. Like Kant, he believed that in the future all mankind would embrace republican liberty. Like Smith, he believed capitalist modernity would deliver the species from scarcity and hunger. Like the medical doctors Pinel and Cabanis, who had once lodged with Madame Vernet as medical students and had found this refuge for Condorcet, he believed that medicine would one day conquer the diseases that flesh was heir to. Men would not die before their time but live to reach their natural span. In the misery of the revolutionary winter, he dreamed of a time when science, industry, and political economy would make plenty available to all. Emancipated by knowledge, human beings would live in freedom and peace; and war, the scourge of civilization, would die away. He leaped straight into a future that would grant him all the wishes the present denied him.

As he reached the last paragraphs of the manuscript, he seemed to awaken from his reveries. His time with Madame Vernet, he concluded, had been "a refuge where his persecutors cannot pursue him." There he had lived, he said poignantly, "in an Elysium that his reason has been able to create for him." This was the Elysium of the classical poets—he kept a Latin Horace close by him—a refuge of sunlit meadows at journey's end, beyond sorrow and fear.

He was not the first man to seek escape from a threatening present through a flight into the future—certainly not the first to believe that posterity would redeem him—but he was among the first to conceive of history as a secular alternative to divine Providence, and to argue, as Hume and Gibbon would never have done, that the guiding force of historical change was the power of human reason.

He had sought the elevation of detachment, perspective, the grand horizon of history, but in the circumstances, he may have achieved only a momentary diversion. In the winter of 1794, as soon as he finished the *Sketch*, Madame Vernet noticed how restless and uneasy he had become. He returned to earth, forced to face the reality of his confinement once more. In a letter to Sophie, he told her, "I am holding onto life only by love and friendship. I've given up on glory. What madness to dream of future centuries and not to live in the present."

When the local Committee of Public Safety in Auteuil finally confiscated all of Condorcet's property in January 1794, Sophie decided she should divorce him in order to save what was left of his possessions so that they could be safely bequeathed to their daughter Eliza. Condorcet agreed for the sake of his child, but the divorce cut another remaining tie to life. When in February the Committee of Public Safety in Paris decreed that anyone sheltering a proscribed person would be sentenced to death, he began to reproach himself for placing Madame Vernet in mortal danger. In late March, after a stranger came seeking to rent an apartment and asked questions about the other lodgers, he believed his arrest was imminent. On his last nights on Gravediggers' Street, he wrote his daughter Eliza a parting letter, now marked with the tenderness of a father fearing he would never see her again. He urged her to learn a trade, engraving perhaps, so that she would be self-sufficient, and he said he hoped that she would always remain a secular republican. If they arrested her mother, Eliza should seek out his "second mother" for protection, and if all else failed, she should try to find her way to his friend Thomas Jefferson, once the American ambassador to France, and now thousands of miles away in Monticello. He burned old papers scribbled with mathematical equations and confided the manuscript of the *Esquisse* to one of the lodgers with instructions to make sure it reached his wife.

On March 25, 1794, he dressed and breakfasted as usual, asking Madame Vernet if she would mind going upstairs to fetch his snuffbox. While she busied herself with his errand, he slipped out into rue des Fossoyeurs and bade the house farewell forever. He walked twelve kilometers to the outskirts of Paris to the house of his friends Amélie and Jean-Baptiste Suard, where he hoped to take shelter. They had known each other for twenty years and had taken the same side early on in the revolution. In his twenties, he had confided the inconstant state of his love life to Amélie and they had remained friends, or so he thought. If he had hoped these old friends would take him in, he was mistaken. When he got there, a servant turned him away, saying they were in Paris. He returned at nightfall, only to be turned away again. He wandered into a quarry nearby and slept rough that night, returning the next morning. Suard let him enter but said it was too dangerous to give him refuge. Condorcet was shown the door and, in a state of exhaustion, not knowing which way to turn, he walked to a small inn and there ordered himself an omelet. How many eggs? he was asked. Twelve, he said, whereupon suspicions were aroused. By mischance the bar was a Jacobin hangout and members of the local Committee of Public Safety began plying him with questions. He claimed he was an out-of-work roofer. They turned over his hands and could see he had never done manual work in his life. They emptied his pockets and found a fine watch, as well as a small edition in Latin of the poems of Horace. Three days on the road and nights of sleeping rough had left him too weak to walk, and so they bundled him into a barrow and wheeled him to prison, where they locked him up overnight. Next morning, they found him lying facedown, dead, with blood streaming from his nose. The likely cause of death was a stroke, brought on by exposure, exhaustion, and mortal stress. He was buried in a pauper's grave.

Months later, at the Festival of the Supreme Being, organized on the Champs de Mars in Paris by the revolution's official painter Jacques-Louis David, Robespierre, then in his glory, pronounced Condorcet's epitaph with the scornful venom of a man who believed he was untouchable: "Academician

Condorcet, formerly a major mathematician in the opinion of
the literary types, and a literary type in the eyes of the mathematicians, a timid conspirator, despised by all parties." Two
months later, Robespierre himself mounted the scaffold on the
Place de la Concorde.

Madame Vernet, Sophie, and Eliza all survived the revolution. In 1826 Amélie Suard published memoirs claiming that
she and her husband hadn't turned Condorcet away but actually had left the back door of their garden open so that he could
return and shelter on the fateful night before his arrest. Amélie
Suard made the mistake of not realizing that old Madame Vernet was still alive and had her own version of events. On reading
Amélie's memoir, Madame Vernet, then in her eighties, wrote
Eliza an indignant letter. After Condorcet had vanished from her
house, she told Eliza, she found out from her tenants where he
had been headed, and walked out there herself, perhaps in hope
of finding him alive. She walked around the back and inspected
the garden gate that the Suards had said they had left open for
him. It was blocked by a clump of grass a meter high. As far
as Madame Vernet was concerned, this proved that the Suards
had never left it unlocked. They had been monsters to deny him
shelter and hypocrites to try to falsify history thirty years later.
For the old landlady, settling the score with the Suards was her
way of vindicating what might have been the noblest gesture
of her life. She had not been able to console the stranger who
knocked on her door that morning in 1793, but at least she had
had the courage to give him shelter.

After the defeat of Napoléon and the restoration of the monarchy, two of Condorcet's contemporaries, the Abbé Sieyès and
the painter Jacques-Louis David, ended up in exile together in
Brussels in 1817. David painted a portrait of his friend Sieyès,
seated in a chair against a somber background, looking back at
the painter with a withdrawn and distant gaze. It is one of the

great studies of the desolation of exile and defeat. Later in life, when he returned to Paris and a member of the younger generation asked the aging abbé what exactly he had done in the revolution, the old man said simply, *J'ai vécu*. I survived. For someone who had once hoped the revolution would usher in a new world, it was a bleak kind of consolation indeed to believe that the best you could say was that you had survived it.

Sophie published Condorcet's *Esquisse* in 1795 and lived on until the 1820s, never remarrying, to the end a fearless aristocrat of the previous century, devoted to the revolutionary ideals of her husband. In the 1840s, Eliza prepared an edition of her father's works. Thanks to them both and to the way the French Revolution came to define the politics and passions of the entire nineteenth century, Condorcet eventually achieved canonization as the martyred visionary of the hope of progress that lies at the heart of the modern progressive tradition.

Ten

The Heart of a Heartless World

Karl Marx and The Communist Manifesto

When Karl and Jenny Marx left Cologne in the summer of 1843 and moved into furnished rooms on the rue Vaneau in Paris, they believed they had arrived, at last, in the capital of revolutionary Europe. They had been thrown out of Prussia: they were renegades from their class and exiles from their country, and they embraced their expulsion. They had won their freedom. Now they would live to make others free.

It was exhilarating to arrive in Paris for the first time and to walk the streets where the tragic history of the French Revolution had played out. The house where Condorcet had hidden was a short walk away; they could picnic on the Champs de Mars where David's Festival of Reason had taken place; they could walk by the Conciergerie from which Marie Antoinette and later the Jacobin Saint-Just had been taken to be executed. In the city's libraries, the entire revolutionary heritage—Voltaire, Rousseau, Condorcet, Marat, Robespierre, Sieyès—lay on the shelves, and cheap editions of their works were stacked on the bookstalls by the Seine.

For two young revolutionaries, the excitement of being

together, in love, and in the home of world revolution must have been overwhelming. That they were in love there is no doubt: the evidence is there in the passionate poems he wrote her, her letters of desire and surrender, and then the fact that they stayed together, as a mutually devoted couple, for the rest of their lives. They had enough to start a life together. Jenny, born von Westphalen, had an inheritance from her aristocratic father, and Karl had one from his father's estate as well as loans from his widowed mother in Trier. On top of this, he had the offer of a job with a new radical journal—the *Deutsch-Französische Jahrbücher*—published by a German artisan and journalist, Arnold Ruge.

In the Parisian cafés and bars, for the first time, they met working men and women, most of them German, who were utopian socialists, Christian socialists, radical democrats. The great German poet Heinrich Heine received them and was later to help the inexperienced couple to soothe their fractious first-born, a daughter also named Jenny. A year after their arrival, at the Café de la Régence, they would meet the young German mill owner's son Friedrich Engels, who would become part of their family for the rest of their lives.

They threw themselves into the conspiratorial world of radical workingmen's politics. Even though the cafés were rife with police spies, fellow travelers, and adventurers, Jenny and Karl did meet a few dedicated, rough-hewn artisans. These were deeply impressive, even romantic characters. They were men who had done prison time or been exiled for their beliefs, and their stout earnestness and nobility of character led Marx to say that when he gazed at their "work-worn" faces for the first time he knew what it meant to believe in the brotherhood of man.

Each sect, each tiny group had its own vision of the radiant tomorrow. You could be a follower of Cabet, Lamennais,

Proudhon, or Weitling. Which variety of socialism would it be? Utopian, Christian, communist? The young German's response was to read all the manifestos, all the pamphlets, ferociously criticizing even the most inconsequential squib—his friends teased him for his habit of bringing up heavy artillery to smash a windowpane—while his wife kept house and discovered how absent and how absentminded her husband turned out to be.

She had found her vocation in being the wife of this fervent, relentless, tough, broad-shouldered man with a black halo of crinkly hair and a dark complexion. In later life, his children called him the Moor. Fellow radicals were impressed by his vigor, his manliness, his cold fearlessness. She would have been attracted to that too, but most of all she shared his faith and his hope, writing to a friend later with gentle self-mockery, "We therefore no longer feel any inclination for the lowlier duties of life," by which she meant cooking, sewing, cleaning. "We too want to enjoy ourselves, to do things and to experience"—and here she gaily capitalized the term—"The Happiness of Mankind."

Having completed his critique of religion years earlier, Marx was astonished, when he arrived in Paris, to find the local communists—followers of Cabet, Leroux, and Lamennais—telling him, "le Christianisme c'est le Communisme." His first piece of writing, once he had settled in at his desk, was to share his demolition of religion for the benefit of his new audience, but he also laid into the political illusions around him. The communism eagerly evoked in the smoke-filled cafés, he told Ruge, was a "dogmatic abstraction." Much of it was a crude recycling of notions taken from Babeuf's conspiracy of equals, an uprising that had failed to restore the radical Jacobin revolution back in 1796. Babeuf's doctrine had proposed the abolition of private property, but in Marx's view, communism must rise above the envious desire to level down and confiscate. Instead, the revolution must use the new wealth of capitalist society, together with the latest scientific and technological advances, to realize the full human potential of all mankind. This was the touchstone of the idealism that tied Jenny to him: a haunting yet elusive goal of human emancipation that was all-encompassing, world-historical, transcendent, and transformative.

Not everyone in their milieu shared their youthful hopefulness. Ruge, now in his forties, despaired that revolution would ever be possible in Germany or anywhere else. Marx vehemently disagreed. All that was required was a spark to light up "man's self-esteem and his sense of freedom," he wrote to Ruge. With Christianity, freedom "took up residence in the blue mists of heaven," but now the task, he wrote, was to "create a community of men that can fulfill their highest needs, a democratic state," here on earth.

A democratic state had to mean something more than the French regime of Louis Philippe. True, France had a parliament, courts, and a constitutional order, and bourgeois citizens could vote, but workingmen were still not enfranchised and women, of course, had no vote at all. As Marx was to write in the first of his contributions to Ruge's radical newspaper, "political emancipation by itself is not human emancipation." In the Paris streets, Karl and Jenny encountered men sleeping rough in doorways, wretched prostitutes, abandoned children: all the misery, poverty, and inequality that had been left untouched by a revolution of rights and property.

This suffering reinforced their radical instincts, but what did they make of the radical path taken by Robespierre and Saint-Just? Robespierre had believed that the revolution must create a collective faith in place of religion, but Marx was contemptuous: revolutions should not reproduce superstitions of their own. In a transparently just social order, what need of comforting illusions?

But this was not the only Jacobin error. "Revolutionaries should be Romans," Saint-Just had cried. For the young Marx it had been a fatal mistake to force march a modern society back to the virtue of the ancients. Austere republican virtue could not be imposed on the "economic and industrial relations" of a modern bourgeois society. The Jacobins had turned to terror to defend their revolution, but terror had been pointless: revolutions—and the violence they required—were justified only when the historical conditions were ready.

He believed the radicals he met in Paris cafés and bars were making the same mistake. He came to despise their moralizing utopianism. It was devoid of any analysis of the obstacles that had to be overcome. In place of a utopian socialism, then, he proposed a scientific socialism, rooted in a philosophy of history. There was Condorcet to build upon, though his *Sketch* had been just that, a sketch. More promising were the theoretical histories of the Scottish Enlightenment. The Scottish political economists, Adam Smith and Adam Ferguson, had developed theories of the stages that capitalism had traversed, and Marx plunged into the study of their work, believing that it would allow him to grasp the drivers of history. At twenty-five, in Paris, Marx set himself the task of creating the science that would set the proletariat free.

Yet science was not enough. It had to be clear what a revolution was actually for. It could not just be about the seizure of power. A true revolution must abolish altogether the distinction between leaders and led, do away with the need for the state's apparatus of coercion, and in its place create a genuine community of brothers and sisters. Marx's goal was to abolish politics itself, to substitute in its place the "administration of things." What need of politics, if human dividedness had been abolished, if there were no more rulers and ruled, no more classes, no more religious, national, or ethnic antagonisms? In place of domination, there would merely be the care and maintenance of the public institutions that all citizens would use for their benefit. This was a politics in service to a future beyond politics. However harshly he criticized the utopianism of fellow socialists, he was committing his life to the most radical utopia of all.

It was a utopia that was only possible to believe in if you had faith that human beings as they actually were—harassed, lonely, oppressed, selfish, and envious—could be transformed by revolutionary change. Why bother with revolution if, on the other side, you were left with men as miserably individualistic, as egotistical and divided as before? In his notes, Marx copied out a quotation from Rousseau's *Social Contract*:

> Whoever dares to undertake the founding of a people's institutions must feel himself capable of changing, so to speak, human nature, of transforming each individual, who in himself is a complete and solitary whole, into a part of a great whole from which he somehow receives his life and his being.

But how was human nature to be changed? Shortly after Marx's arrival in Paris, he was asked to write a critique of the book *The Jewish Question*, by a former teacher and associate of his, Bruno Bauer. He seized this assignment as an opportunity to work out, in effect, how to overcome such parochial identities as Judaism and to become what the revolution required: a truly free human being. Being young, he thought it would be easy. If he had emancipated himself from Jewishness, why couldn't everyone free themselves of the reactionary identities that held them captive?

What was it, after all, to be a Jew? In his view, the essence of Jewishness was huckstering. Jews lived for trade and commerce. Their God was money. Would Jews still exist if the money system were abolished, capitalism done away with, private property replaced? The answer was obvious. Jewishness would vanish "like an insipid haze" in a truly free society. Jewishness and all such divisions between human beings, all such fault lines that prevented people from recognizing each other as brothers and sisters, would disappear if the root of the problem, capitalism, was done away with.

Alexis de Tocqueville's *Democracy in America* had recently appeared, and Tocqueville's America taught Marx that "a state can be a free state without man himself being a free man." How could men be free if they were still trapped inside the coils of religious delusion, no matter how freely chosen? In a communist future, to be free was to be free of the need for religious illusion and the false consolations it offered.

Marx wrote that in the political revolution of 1789, "man was not freed from religion—he received the freedom of religion. He was not freed from property—he received the freedom of property." Marx's hostility toward the religious toleration granted to Jews and others during the French Revolution was to last for the rest of his life. In 1875, six years before his death, he condemned the German Social Democrats' Gotha Program for endorsing religious toleration. He thought they should abolish religion altogether.

His utopia was dedicated to overcoming the friction, the war of all against all, race against race, religion against religion, nation against nation, inside civil society. What others might have relished about modernity—the frantic jostling of competing peoples in the modern city—filled him with dismay:

What a spectacle! A society infinitely divided into the most diverse races which confront one another with their petty antipathies, their bad consciences and their brutal mediocrity . . .

Leaving aside Marx's ugly association of Jewishness with money, it was truly extraordinary for him to believe that a communist revolution could also free mankind from Jewishness or any other national or confessional identity. He himself had shucked off the residues of Jewish faith, as he put it, like a snake's skin.

If something as rooted as religious identity was just a snake's skin, what beneath the snake's skin was the fundamental identity of a human being? Here the young revolutionary took from Ludwig Feuerbach's *Essence of Christianity* the idea that the core of a human being was their "species being," their identity as a pure and untrammeled exemplar of the human race. This vigorous young man, deeply in love, took the relationship of a man to a woman, naked in bed together, as the moment when two beings would feel most deeply their species being. He and Jenny had made new life together—their first daughter was born during their stay in Paris—and this experience confirmed for both of them what philosophy back to Aristotle had taught, that man's essential identity was as homo faber, a species who creates, in labor and in the consummation of desire, their family, environment, culture, habitat, and history—in short, their world. The ultimate purpose of their revolution was to unleash for all men and women the liberating creativity they felt in themselves.

This was an exalted vision of revolution, but if so, why did so few working people believe in any kind of revolution at all? Why were the oppressed blind to their own misery? Marx borrowed a metaphor from Rousseau. Men could not see the chains on their feet, because the chains were enfolded in flow-ery garlands. The work of a revolutionary, Marx said in early 1844, was to "pluck the imaginary flowers on the chain not in order that man shall continue to bear that chain without fan-tasy or consolation, but so that he shall throw off the chain and pluck the living flower."

The flowers that concealed men's chains were "fantasy" and "consolation," and religion was the chief source of both. That was why, in the second major piece he wrote after arriving in Paris, he held that "the criticism of religion is the prerequisite of all criticism." To lay bare the illusions of religion was to understand why men failed to see the manacles on their feet and in their minds.

Thus far, he was merely repeating the clichés about religion that he had inherited from Condorcet and Hume. Significantly, his critique reinterpreted religious consolation not just as super-stition but also as an alienated form of human hope. Religion was not simply a veil of illusion cast over human oppression. It was not simply "the universal basis of consolation and jus-tification" for an unjust world. It was, he said, "the sigh of the oppressed creature, the heart of a heartless world, and the soul of soulless conditions." Yes, it was the "opium of the people," the drug people took to endure wage labor, childbirth, suffering, and death, but it was also "the self-consciousness and self-esteem of man who has . . . not yet won through to himself," the deformed expression of the human desire for transcendence, redemption, recovery of their own lost humanity.

These desires—to live as full human beings—could not be realized in the world as it is, which was why, for millennia, men and women had projected such desires onto paradise, to a heavenly realm where all tears would be dried and all suffering would cease. Marx was contemptuous of religious illusions, but not of the longings they expressed.

He recognized also that faith was a powerful rhetoric of justice. In the Protestant Reformation and the Peasants Revolt of 1525, which both Marx and Engels believed was the closest Germany had ever come to revolution, Martin Luther and the radical Thomas Müntzer had used scripture to voice powerful demands on behalf of the poor and excluded. In the Protestant insurrection against a corrupted medieval church, Luther had "freed mankind from external religiosity," Marx conceded, "but only by making religiosity the inner man," freeing the body from its fetters only by putting the heart in chains.

Uniquely among his radical contemporaries, he read the new language of economics through the lens of his critique of religion. Just as man projects his truest longings into hopes of an afterlife beyond pain and sorrow, so in labor men alienate their creative identities as a species in selling their labor power:

> The more the worker exerts himself in his work, the more powerful the alien, objective world becomes which he brings into being over against himself, the poorer his inner world becomes, and the less they belong to him. It is the same in religion. The more man puts into God, the less he retains within himself.

Most workers Marx met actually had little religious feeling. So religion did not explain their submission. Rather, religion was the metaphor through which Marx sought to understand why they submitted to the regime of wage labor. Just as man invents gods to console himself for the mysteries of death and suffering and then thinks these gods have created him, so in a capitalist society, a worker creates the entire world of capitalism through his labor only to believe that it is an alien, inhuman realm over which he has no control.

In a communist future, "nobody has one exclusive sphere of

activity, but each can become accomplished in any branch he wishes." It would be possible, Marx imagined, "to hunt in the morning, fish in the afternoon, rear cattle in the evening, criticize after dinner . . . without ever becoming hunter, fisherman, herdsman or critic." This was a humanism whose objective was to restore man to his true nature, by emancipating his creative capacities as maker of his world. In the manuscripts he wrote in 1844, Marx understood at last that a communist revolution should aim at nothing less than "the reintegration or return of man to himself, the supersession of man's self-estrangement."

In a triumphant passage that reads like a man surfacing from the depths, summing up all his life's experience to that point, Marx wrote,

> Communism is the positive supersession of private property as human self-estrangement and hence the true appropriation of the human essence through and for man; it is the complete restoration of man to himself as a social, i.e. human being, a restoration which has become conscious and which takes place within the entire wealth of previous periods of development. This communism as a fully developed naturalism, equals humanism and as fully developed humanism equals naturalism; it is the genuine resolution of the conflict between man and nature, and between man and man, the true resolution of the conflict between existence and being, between objectification and self-affirmation, between freedom and necessity, between individual and species. It is the solution of the riddle of history and knows itself to be the solution.

If there was a riddle to history, it was the same one that Job and the Psalms had tried to answer for millennia: why the perfect God that humans imagined could have allowed injustice in his world. Christian faith told believers to accept this paradox and live in hope of the consolations of the afterlife. Marx's revolutionary creed is at root a rebellion against this Christian vision. Armed now with a theory of history that predicted the downfall of the existing order, Marx truly believed that the history of consolation was over. A new age of freedom was about to dawn.

That a revolution was coming, he did not doubt. The Silesian weavers had risen. The winegrowers in the Rhineland were restive. In the summer of 1845, Engels took Marx to England to see firsthand the new industrial proletariat in Manchester. Paris seethed with revolutionary groups; uprisings were occurring in Italy and Switzerland. Even Marx's enemies began to take him seriously. His polemical articles against the ancien régime in Prussia earned him sufficient notoriety to get him expelled from Paris. The young couple decamped to a southern suburb of Brussels to await the revolution they believed was at hand.

When it came, when in December 1847 a tiny group of British artisans, who called themselves the League of the Just, convened a conference in London at the Red Lion pub in Soho, and asked him and Engels to prepare their rallying cry, Marx was ready. The pair helped transform the Just into the Communist League, and when Engels suggested that their appeal be called "a confession of faith," or a catechism for revolutionaries, Marx objected. Religious language had no place in scientific socialism. It should be called a manifesto.

The Communist Manifesto wrote itself, and Jenny copied out the text for the printer in her neater hand. The famous opening line—about the specter of communism haunting Europe—took a wish and conjured it into reality, since actual communists in Europe numbered barely five hundred. No one before, or even since, has ever written a more dramatic panegyric to the globalizing energies of capitalism. It is easy to understand why. Capitalism was sweeping away everything Marx loathed: the nostalgic and backward-looking politics of radical artisans, the consoling pieties of the church, the ideological obfuscations of the European monarchies, everything indeed that stood in the way of the revolutionary rise of the proletariat:

> All fixed, fast-frozen relations, with their train of ancient and venerable prejudices and opinions are swept away, all new formed ones become antiquated before they can ossify. All that is solid melts into air, all that is holy is profaned, and man is at last compelled to face his real conditions of life, and his mutual relations with a sober eye.

Suddenly history was accelerating; suddenly its direction was clear. No longer did revolutionaries have to toil away at the unmasking of illusions. Capitalism was digging its own grave, creating its own gravediggers. In the factories and workshops that Marx and Engels had seen in Manchester, members of the proletariat were being drawn together by the same relentless logic that consolidated capital, and when they discovered their common interests, they would rise and throw off their chains.

After the London publisher printed up copies of *The Communist Manifesto* in German, Jenny and Karl rushed back to Paris to share the heady early weeks of the uprising that they hoped would usher in the true revolution. Soon, feeling the revolution was imminent in Germany too, Marx went to Cologne, with other German exiles, where he edited the *Neue Rheinische Zeitung* throughout the chaotic denouement of the revolutionary year. Jenny followed with the children, signing one letter to a friend, on their errant tour, "Jenny, *Citoyenne et Vagabonde*."

Few men and women of 1848 read the *Manifesto* itself, but it gave a brilliant framing of historical inevitability to the ambient rhetoric of hope, illusion, and anger that the entire generation of 1848 was to carry to the barricades. For the first time in his life, Marx seems to have articulated the sentiments of millions, especially in Germany. Richard Wagner, for example, a court musician and conductor, a servant of the king of Saxony, frequented the artisanal clubs of Dresden and threw his lot in with the revolutionaries. It's unclear what he actually read of Marx, but his essay *Art and Revolution*, published in 1849, conjures up the same analysis and the same utopia: the critique of Christianity; the denunciation of wage labor, alienation, and commerce; the appeal to a grand human revolution that would liberate both workers and artists from slavery and usher in a new era where art would be freed from the poison of commerce.

For both Marx and Wagner, the moment of euphoria was to be brief. The rising of the Paris workers in June 1848 was crushed, and by the end of the year, Paris, Vienna, and Berlin were back in the hands of the old elites. The Communist League was disbanded, and the revolutionary tide ebbed. As Marx said while watching the rise to power of the risible Louis Napoléon Bonaparte, the history of the French Revolution was repeating itself first as tragedy, then as farce. One of the last spasms of defiance was in Dresden, where in May 1849 Richard Wagner watched from a bell tower overnight as Prussian troops approached the city to extinguish the local uprising. Wagner never forgot the sounds of that night: the mournful tolling of the bell in the tower and the sound of the Prussian sharpshooters' bullets pinging against the brickwork, while he hunkered down with a schoolteacher behind a mattress filled with straw. Wagner, like Marx, was to pay for his revolutionary enthusiasms with exile. By 1849 Wagner was in Switzerland, and Marx and his family were in London, living in penury.

Unlike Marx, the composer was to know vindication in his

lifetime, when his *Ring* cycle was performed at Bayreuth and the cult of his genius began. In place of a revolution in politics, Wagner offered the next generation a revolution in art, one that gave to opera and music the vast project of redemption and consolation that religion had once taken upon itself.

Marx settled into the long capitalist boom of the 1850s and 1860s, waiting for the revolution that never came. He and Jenny managed to live on the piecework journalism he did for the *New-York Daily Tribune*. His articles were widely read, especially among the German exiles who had escaped to America after their revolutionary hopes were crushed. The *Tribune* was a Republican and antislavery paper, and Marx was such an enthusiastic champion of both causes that he wrote a letter of congratulation to Abraham Lincoln upon his election in 1861, calling him "the single-minded son of the working class." He received a polite if distant reply thanking the faraway journalist for "the good wishes of the working men of Europe."

Marx's hopes of a European revolution briefly rose with the Paris Commune in 1871, only to be dashed with its defeat. In his last years, he and Jenny experienced the death of beloved children and the betrayal and falling by the wayside of trusted comrades, yet they endured it all, sustained by Engels's generosity and the memory of that bright hope they had kindled in Paris. He published volume one of *Capital* in 1859, and the plan of work he had elaborated for himself in Paris in the 1840s took one step toward completion. Yet he could never actually finish the masterwork, and Engels had to cobble successive volumes of *Capital* together from the notes Marx left behind.

With every new edition of *The Communist Manifesto*, Engels and Marx would write a preface, reaffirming belief in the hopes of their youth, telling readers that their faith was now gospel to workers "from Siberia to California." They pinned their hopes chiefly on the German working class but were dismayed anew by the eventual incorporation of the German labor movement into Bismarck's capitalist order.

Marx took Jenny back to Paris one more time when she was dying of cancer, and they had coffee in a café and looked about them in astonishment at the Paris that Haussmann had built on the ruins of the still-medieval Paris they had known in the 1840s. She died months after that final visit, and in his loneliness, stoic endurance was all Marx could call upon. Neither his writing, nor his undoubted stature as head of the European communist movement, nor his faith in the coming revolution was any protection against the pain of loss. He confessed to his daughter, "there is only one antidote to mental suffering and that is physical pain." He died in 1883. At Marx's graveside in Highgate Cemetery, Engels pronounced a valedictory that claimed him as the father of European revolution and the creator of a science of society to rival Darwin. Only twelve people were present to hear the address.

The young Marx cannot be held responsible for what later Marxists did to the utopian hopes he expressed in Paris in the 1840s. Indeed, the hard men who created the Marxist orthodoxy—Bebel, Kautsky, Lenin, and Stalin—hardly knew what these hopes had been. Engels and the Marx family had saved the Paris notebooks—other texts were left to "the criticism of the mice"—and they weren't published in an official edition of his work until the 1930s. It wasn't until the 1960s that a new generation discovered a humanist Marx buried beneath the disgraced detritus of official Soviet Marxism.

More than 170 years later, his vision, the one he had crafted in Paris with Jenny at his side, remains the only utopia still standing, the only attempt to systematically conceive a world beyond the universe of global capitalism. In this imagined world, we share equally in the plenty of advanced economies, without waste or environmental degradation, without the division of workers and owners, without the hatreds of class, race, or nation. In this imagined world, we live without politics, without the discord of competing visions of reality, without the antagonism of rivalrous visions of the good. We rule ourselves, free of domination. Science has extended our life spans and vanquished illness. When we die, we die in the knowledge that we have reached our natural span. Condorcet had promised in 1794, and Marx believed it too, that science and knowledge would release us from the sorrows of fate.

His utopia is a world beyond the need for consolation. It is a world in which we see life as it is and need no arguments, no reasons, nothing to comfort us for reality. The real is rational and the rational is real, Marx's teacher Hegel had once said. In such a world, we may know reversals, surprises, and disappointments, but since we are in a just world, we accept that we have gotten what we deserved. So we are at peace with fate, with our existence and our destiny as human beings.

This is what the young couple in Paris believed, and because they took on the entire heritage of Western religion it was the most consequential of all their dreams. Their vision inspired working men and women, who fought and died for it for the next 170 years. It was the most sustained attempt to transcend religion and replace its consolations with justice here on earth. The criticism directed against this utopia has always been whether it is attainable. A better question might be whether a world beyond consolation is a world that is even desirable.

Eleven

War and Consolation

Abraham Lincoln's Second Inaugural Address

When Abraham Lincoln stood on the Capitol steps on that March morning in 1865 to take the oath of office and deliver his second inaugural address, the crowd below the bunting—soldiers of both races, men and women who had come through the rain and now stood in the breaking sunlight—might have expected that his speech would celebrate the triumph of Union arms. They were, after all, within weeks of final victory, and everyone could feel the weight of the war lifting from their shoulders. But he would only say, "the progress of our arms . . . is well known to the public as to myself and it is, I trust, reasonably satisfactory and encouraging to all." If the mood of the crowd was for triumphant celebration, Lincoln did not encourage it. If the crowd wanted a call for vengeance on the beleaguered Confederate armies now fighting their last stand around Richmond, he did not indulge them. If they wanted a long speech, he did not give that to them either. His was short, barely seven minutes, so anticlimactic that it left those who heard it puzzled and bemused.

He sought instead to explain why the war had happened at

all, why such a catastrophe had befallen North and South alike. His question was directed to history and to Providence. He had long brooded upon this himself, and now he judged that it was time to say out loud what he had been thinking for years.

FOUR YEARS PREVIOUSLY, ON HIS first inauguration, with the Union at breaking point and armies massed for the beginning of war, he had closed his address to the crowd assembled at the Capitol with an emotion-laden plea:

> I am loth to close. We are not enemies, but friends. We
> must not be enemies. Though passion may have strained,
> it must not break our bonds of affection.

Friends and enemies alike had disregarded him. The attack on Fort Sumter followed soon after, and then came four years of unimaginable bloodshed and industrial slaughter. Men died with bayonets at each other's throats; freed Black men who fought for the Union were massacred wholesale at Fort Pillow; the stream at Antietam ran with blood; the fields of Gettysburg were littered with bodies. Inside the coats of the dead, the burial parties found Bibles, some with holes where they had taken bullets for their bearers.

Lincoln was a president who lived the agony of his people. He visited the regiments. He talked to the soldiers. He carried in his heart what he had seen on their young faces, sometimes buoyant innocence, sometimes the dead-eyed look of those who have survived battle at close quarters. He knew that boys could be driven insane by the noise, the blood, and the terror. Every week, mothers' letters reached him, pleading for sons imprisoned for desertion. Every decision he made to hang a deserter left its mark, and sometimes his desperation is evident:

Must I shoot the simple-minded soldier boy who des-
erts, while I must not touch a hair of a wily agitator who
induces him to desert?

He hanged some of them, spared others, every decision his
alone. He executed thirty-nine Dakota warriors in Minnesota
because they had waged war against the Union. In sentences
and in commutations, he wielded the power of death and the
power of life. These at least were decisive. Less efficacious were
his efforts to console. Every week, he wrote letters to orphans and
widows, aware that in these cases, words had reached the very
limit of their power:

I feel how weak and fruitless must be any words of mine
which should attempt to beguile you from the grief of a
loss so overwhelming. But I cannot refrain from tending
to you the consolation that may be found in the thanks of
the Republic they died to save.

Every moment of the day and night, telegrams reached him
from his generals on the battlefield, with maddeningly incomplete and sometimes desperate news. He realized that by the
time he read them, events would have moved on. With his finger
tracing the progress of battle on the maps in his office, he could
see folly unfolding without being able to do much to avert it,
though he certainly tried, reproaching George Meade for letting
Robert E. Lee escape after Gettysburg. Barely keeping his temper, he wrote, in icy terms:

Again my dear general, I do not believe you appreciate the
magnitude of the misfortune involved in Lee's escape. He
was within your easy grasp and to have closed upon him
would in connection with our other late successes, have

ended the war. As it is, the war will be prolonged indefinitely.

If war was to be waged, Lincoln gradually came to realize, it must be waged with ferocious intensity. So he encouraged Ulysses S. Grant, whose army was assembled before Richmond, to keep his hand on the enemy's throat:

Hold on with a bull-dog grip, and chew and choke, as much as possible.

In the days before Appomattox, when some slacking off might have been conceivable, he wrote Grant:

General Sheridan says, "if *the thing* is pressed, I think that Lee will surrender." Let *the thing* be pressed.

Four years of slaughter had made him implacable, tender reverie wrung out of him. "We are not enemies, but friends. We must not be enemies," he had pleaded, but no more of that. Bloodshed and horror had made him inflexible. No more parleying. No more fruitless searches for armistice or peace. Only complete and utter victory would suffice.

Through this "fiery trial," which aged and hardened him as it hardened his country, Lincoln was forced to see this savage war between brothers at its full biblical scale. The terrible grandeur of what was happening astonished him. How was it to be understood? He could see how the downward spiral had begun in politics, and how decent men, believing that everything they valued was at stake, could forget the better angels of their nature:

Blood grows hot and blood is spilled. Thought is forced from old channels into confusion. Deception breeds and thrives. Confidence dies, and universal suspicion reigns. Each man feels an impulse to kill his neighbor, lest he be first killed by him. Revenge and retaliation follow.

If this was the downward spiral that drew even honest men into its vortex, how could there ever be an upward climb out of the pit? Others might think history had an upward course, a progress and momentum all its own. The consolations available to other men—Karl Marx and the marquis de Condorcet, for example, who believed history could be shaped to vindicate men's hopes—were not available to Lincoln. He knew better than they that the direction that events actually took depended on chance, fortune, human genius, and error, all unpredictable, all unforeseeable. This did not make him a fatalist. He had a powerful historical imagination and could place the ordeal of his time within the frame of his country's history, as the gravest of its crises in all its "four score and seven years." He understood the war as a hinge of fate whose turning would determine whether "government of the people, by the people and for the people" would prevail. As the war continued, he began to understand that "in giving freedom to the slave, we assure freedom to the free," and in so doing would preserve the "last best hope of earth." This was the meaning he hoped history would reveal, but he was never certain, until the last months, that it would.

History, he believed, had given both him and his country a mission, but his experience of helplessness, waiting for telegrams, unable to know what was happening or to stop folly when he could see it clearly, brought home to him how little even a president could do to master history's unfolding:

I claim not to have controlled events but confess plainly that events have controlled me. Now at the end of three years struggle, the nation's condition is not what either party or any man devised or expected. God alone can claim it.

Eventually, in the fastness of the night while he sat in the telegraph room with a blanket over his shoulders waiting for the messenger boys to deliver him the latest dispatches, tick-tacking off the wire from the battlefield, he could not avoid reaching for a religious register to ponder the higher meaning of it all. For men and women of his generation, schooled every Sunday, this would only mean inquiring into the ways of Providence.

The standard consolation offered in every church, in every gathering, in every solemn speech, to those who had lost their sons in battle, was that they had died in a holy cause. Julia Ward Howe's "Battle Hymn of the Republic" had become the Union's marching song, with its haunting injunction, "as he died to make men holy, let us die to make men free." Lincoln had wept when he first heard it, but now he had seen the full measure of the slaughter inflicted by God's terrible swift sword. God must be on their side, everyone believed. But he began to ask, how could that possibly be true?

He knew full well that across the battle lines, the gray-coated soldiers of the Confederacy preached the same pieties. A Tennessee woman had come to see him to plead for her son taken prisoner by the Union side. She had told him that he was religious. This provoked him:

In my opinion the religion that sets men to rebel and fight against their government, because, as they think, that government does not sufficiently help some men to eat their bread on the sweat of other men's faces, is not the sort of religion upon which people can get to heaven.

God could not possibly favor the maintenance of slavery, but could Lincoln be sure God was on the side of the free? He had long pondered this question. In 1862, when fate seemed to turn against the Union after the defeat at the Second Battle of Bull Run, and Lee was closing in on Washington, Lincoln sat down and wrote a paragraph, for his eyes only:

> The will of God prevails. In great contests each party claims to act in accordance with the will of God. Both may be, and one must be wrong. God cannot be for, and against the same thing at the same time. In the present civil war, it is quite possible that God's purpose is something different from the purpose of either party—and yet the human instrumentalities working just as they do are of the best adaptation to effect His purpose. I am almost ready to say this is probably true—that God wills this contest, and wills that it shall not end yet. By his mere quiet power, on the minds of the now contestants, He could have either saved or destroyed the Union without a human contest. Yet the contest began. And having begun He could give the final victory to either side any day. Yet the contest proceeds.

As both sides of the Civil War assured themselves that God was on their side, Lincoln holds our attention because he refuses such consolation. "It is my earnest desire," he wrote to supporters in Chicago, "to know the will of Providence in this matter. And if I can learn what it is, I will do it." But he added, "these are not the days of miracles."

The president's problem was not only learning God's intention. He found it difficult to have any relation with God at all.

In an August 1863 letter he observed, in reply to a query about his opinion of Shakespeare's plays, that he loved Hamlet, but preferred King Claudius's speech "O my offence is rank" to Hamlet's "To be or not to be." In that speech, the king, alone with himself, grappling with remorse, confesses:

> *Pray can I not*
> *Though inclination be as sharp as will;*
> *My stronger guilt defeats my strong intent;*
> *And, like a man to double business bound,*
> *I stand in pause where I shall first begin,*
> *And both neglect.*

A president as morally responsible as Lincoln was, who could never rid his mind of the consequences of ordering the execution of a deserter or of a command to commit young boys to battle, might well have found his inclination to pray as sharp as ever, but a stronger guilt defeating his intent.

The times had tested his faith to its limits, and alone with himself he could see only his failures of belief. As he confessed to some Presbyterian ministers in Washington, DC,

> I sincerely wish that I was a more devoted man than I am. Sometimes in my difficulties I have been driven to the last resort to say God is still my only hope. It is still all the world to me.

If he could not pray or secure consolation, he did cling to the idea that the war had been visited on the nation by a Providence whose ways it was not in his power to discern. And this is the theme he chose for the second inaugural.

His purpose, as always, was political: not a sermon, as some hearers took it to be, not a personal excursion into his own private eschatology. Rather, it was a long-considered exercise in political argument designed to prepare American citizens for the next phase of their life together, the moment when peace would come at last, when enemies would have to join together as citizens again.

For this to be possible, he had to find some common understanding, forcing each side to come to terms with illusions both sides had shared even as they fought for visions that could never be shared. When he rose to deliver his address, he was speaking to the South still fighting for its life and to the Union armies closing in on Richmond. His aim was to find language that would reunite them, at first in common sorrow, then in shared repentance, and finally in reconciliation.

He told the audience before him, lest rancor and rage inclined them to forget the fact, that neither side had desired the war:

All dreaded it—all sought to avert it.

Both sides, he said, "deprecated war; but one of them would make war rather than let the nation survive; and the other would accept war rather than let it perish." At this, the Northern crowd applauded, and some of the Black men in the audience were heard to call out "Bless you." They liked that he did not carry charity so far as to forget who had started the killing.

Lincoln reminded his audience, lest in grief and disillusion they be tempted to forget, that slavery was "somehow" the cause of the war, the word "somehow" conveying the dark reality that men can fight and die in battle without understanding the reason why. Lincoln wanted his listeners to recognize that at the very least the war had not been fought for nothing. It had been fought to set men free, and for those who had lost sons this might be the only consolation that he could offer.

He could have defined the great cause of the war as Southern slavery and brought the whole weight of moral condemnation upon one side. Instead, he took a decisive moral turn, referring to the cause of the war as "American slavery," an original sin—an "offense" he called it—that the whole nation, North and South, must now recognize as its own.

As if that was not enough, he reminded his Northern audience that the Southern enemy "read the same Bible and pray[ed] to the same God." Only two years earlier, responding to the Tennessee woman begging for her Confederate son's life, he had said that no man could be called truly religious who used faith to justify slavery. Now he said something very different. It may seem strange, he admitted, that any man should dare to ask a just God's assistance to wring bread from the sweat of another man's brow, but—here he quoted the Gospel of Matthew, chapter 7, verse 1—"let us judge not that we be not judged." Slavery was deeply wrong, but that was not the issue. The issue was whether one side in a civil war had the right to condemn the other for believing that God was on their side.

Instinctively Lincoln understood the connections between consolation, forgiveness, and reconciliation. He understood them politically as the tasks that fell to him on taking office, in this second term: to find a way for the North to forgive the South for the war, for the South to accept its defeat, and for both to be reconciled to each other by recognizing each other's losses.

To accomplish these political tasks, he decided to describe American slavery as the original sin both sides must acknowledge as they must also recognize the Civil War as God's just punishment for that sin:

He gives to both North and South this terrible war as the woe due to those by whom the offenses come.

Reconciliation would be impossible, the "new birth of freedom" he had called for at Gettysburg would founder in

recrimination and hatred, unless both sides could bring themselves to understand the war not as a triumph for one side and
a tragic defeat for the other, but as a catastrophe for both, as the
wages of an original sin both must own.

He knew, because the same doubting and questioning was so
deep inside him, that many in the audience below him would
question how a just and merciful God could possibly have
inflicted war on both sides—Sherman's march to the sea, the
carnage at the Wilderness, the slaughter at Antietam, the whole
catalog of blood and sorrow—but he pressed home his argument to the bitter end. The war was not yet won, and while he
hoped it would end soon,

> Yet if God wills that it continue until all the wealth piled
> by the bond-man's two hundred and fifty years of unre-
> quited toil shall be sunk, and until every drop of blood
> drawn with the lash, shall be paid by another drawn with
> the sword, as was said three thousand years ago, so still it
> must be said "the judgments of the Lord are true and righ-
> teous altogether."

He quoted Psalm 19, verse 9, here to vest his argument
with scriptural authority, but never has that psalm—which
begins "The Heavens declare the glory of God and the firma-
ment showeth his handywork"—had to do such demanding
moral work. For it had to affirm the most difficult thought of
all: that this same God had willed both slavery and the war to
end it. How could this possibly be?

Everything in Lincoln's peroration turns on the word *still*.
"So still it must be said." You can almost hear him bring the full
force of his voice onto the word, so that everyone in the audience, whose own faith had been tested by sorrow, could hear
what he meant: still we must believe, still we must continue

to have faith in a just God, even if the battle continues, even if the 250-year crime of slavery cannot be repaid in full by the blood of the sword. Still we must go on believing, for the alternative—though he does not say it—is that the war was senseless, and the deaths were all in vain. A single word—*still*—has to bear the entire weight of Lincoln's faith.

His quotation from Psalm 19 is the hinge on which the speech turns. To say that the judgments of the Lord are true and righteous altogether was to declare that the ultimate meaning of the war was beyond the understanding of men and women on either side. The victorious could not read their victory as God's reward any more than the vanquished could read it as their punishment. To say this was to create the political possibility of mercy and magnanimity, for if neither side could ever know what God intended by the fiery trial, then the victor had no right to raise the sword of vengeance while the defeated had the right to claim the dignity of honorable defeat. Humility about the ultimate meaning of the war, in other words, created the space for mercy. In turn, if ultimate meanings were beyond our sight, Lincoln was saying, our duties here and now were clear. They were duties counseled by the religious and moral traditions of both sides to, in Lincoln's words, "bind up the nation's wounds, to care for him who shall have borne the battle and for the widow and his orphan"—with "malice toward none, with charity for all, with firmness in the right as God gives us to see the right."

At the reception in the White House that followed the speech, Frederick Douglass, the freed slave and abolitionist, who had been in the crowd, congratulated Lincoln on a noble effort. Lincoln was heard to say he thought it would wear better than most of his speeches, but when someone suggested it would not be popular, he agreed, saying, "Men are not flattered by being shown that there has been a difference of purpose between the Almighty and them." His purpose had been to show that there was such a difference, and by opening up a place for humility and doubt, to create the space for a politics of reconciliation.

It was not to be. His assassin was also in the crowd at the inauguration, listening to the speech, and forty-one days later Lincoln was dead. His hopes for a magnanimous reconstruction were dashed; Black men and women's hopes for freedom were betrayed; and more than 150 years later the nation's wounds from that war are still not healed.

Lincoln should be with us all these days especially since "malice toward none" has been replaced by malice toward all, as if in our ideological arrogance we have forgotten that neither God nor justice is necessarily on our side. It is often said, perhaps rightly, that the Civil War whose end he thought was in sight still continues. The freedom he thought was coming to Black Americans is still not securely in their hands. His work is not done, and the words of the second inaugural, now carved on the walls of the monument where his likeness sits brooding over Washington, DC, are less a consolation than a reproach.

It is easier to remember Lincoln as a saint than to learn from him, but we cannot draw consolation from his words unless we commit to that learning. He struggled with exactly what we struggle with: the tidal force of political malice that recurrently rises and threatens the hard-won civility on which a democracy depends. What helped him, as it might help us, was the tenacity with which he forced the best traditions he had inherited—in this case the Gospels and the Psalms—to deliver insight and perspective. He did not have a secure footing in faith, but he understood that these biblical traditions called on him to forswear vengeance and judgment and to appeal for mercy and forgiveness. These traditions can speak through us too. What consolation can there be in this? That we are not condemned to live imprisoned in the rhetoric, foolishness, and mendacity of the present. We can reach back to Lincoln, to Matthew, to the Psalms, to whatever deep wisdom we have ever been taught, and find out, once again, who we are, where we are, what we must accept, and what we must not. These traditions of ours risk becoming inconsequential and empty words on monuments unless we use them, unless we force meaning from them, as Lincoln did, and unless we continue to live by them, as he tried to do.

Twelve

Songs on the Death of Children

Gustav Mahler's Kindertotenlieder

In 1804, in Vienna, a twenty-three-year-old pianist named Dorothea von Ertmann lost her only child, a three-year-old boy, after a short illness. By her own account, she fell into a deep depression. People visited her and tried to comfort her, to no avail. She was a young woman from a wellborn family who had arrived with her husband and infant child in Vienna two years before and, thanks to her playing in private salons, had made the acquaintance of Ludwig van Beethoven. When he heard of her grief, Beethoven visited her at home, sat down at the piano, and said, according to Felix Mendelssohn's later account, that they would now talk to each other in the language of music. Beethoven improvised for an hour, during which Dorothea began to weep for the first time. When he finished, he stood up, pressed Dorothea's hand, and without saying another word departed. Dorothea recorded her own feelings in a letter shortly afterward:

> Who could describe this music! I believed I was hearing angelic choirs, celebrating the entrance of my poor child into the world of light.

Sacred music—chorales, hymns, oratorios, masses—have consoled grieving men and women for millennia. Here, a purely secular occasion—a man improvising on a piano—assumed the role once performed by religious music and ritual. Two musicians trusted to the language of music, rather than sacred words or scripture, to conjure that world of light into being. When retold by Mendelssohn and romantic composers in the nineteenth century, this became a story about music's new purpose in a secular world. The musicians who came after Beethoven had to measure up to the ambitions that he had given to music in a world turning away from the promise of heaven.

This transformation of music had been underway for some time. Handel's *Messiah*—which opens with the soaring lines of his setting of the words of the prophet Isaiah—"Comfort ye, my people"—took the Christian message of consolation and performed it, not in a church, but in a Dublin auditorium in 1744 as a benefit concert for retired musicians and singers. Mozart's *Requiem*, written in 1791 but left unfinished at his death, was first performed after he died at a benefit concert for his wife. After Beethoven, Verdi and Brahms composed requiems but used them to give utterance to secular griefs and had them performed in concert halls. In the case of Brahms's *Requiem*, the cause for grief was the death of his mother; in Verdi's *Requiem*, it was the death of his friend the writer Alessandro Manzoni. Dvořák, a devout Catholic, stayed closer to the sacred. His *Stabat Mater* of 1876 mourned the deaths of two of his children. In Wagner's *Parsifal*, the composer disregarded traditional religious forms altogether and transformed the Christian story of suffering and redemption into a modern spectacle, performed not in a religious setting but at the Bayreuth Festival Hall. *Parsifal* disgusted Wagner's former acolyte and admirer Friedrich Nietzsche, who insisted, furiously, that by setting the Christian language of consolation to music, Wagner had capitulated

to Christianity's "slave morality" and its resentment-filled resignation in the face of human suffering. The only consolation
entitled to respect, Nietzsche once said, was to believe that no
consolation was possible.

The figure who inherited and then transformed this debate
about the relation between music and consolation was the son
of a Jewish innkeeper in Iglau, a small town in Moravia in the
Czech lands. At fifteen he had escaped from an unhappy family life—his father was an irascible tyrant, his mother lame,
constantly pregnant, and victimized by her husband—to make
his future as a music student in Vienna. Arriving in the capital
city of the empire, he poured into music all the ambitions of an
outsider: a provincial, a Jew, and a poor boy from an oppressive
family. To these yearnings to escape, Gustav Mahler added the
mighty ambitions for music that his generation inherited from
his forebears.

Mahler shared Wagner's conviction that music should attempt
nothing less than to provide meaning for men and women living
after the death of the gods. They both sought to develop a musical form that would provide an experience of the transcendental
and sublime. "Music must always contain a yearning," Mahler
told an admiring female friend, "a yearning for what is beyond
the things of this world." Mahler, like Wagner, dared to demand
of his music that it provide answers to questions as old as Job's.
In one of his letters, he wrote:

> What do you live for? Why do you suffer? Is it all one vast
> terrifying joke? We have to answer these questions if we
> are to go on living.

He combined this yearning for metaphysical consolation
with an uncanny realism, a capacity to compose music that
brought to life sharp, disjointed fragments of memory from the

world of his unhappy childhood. In his First Symphony, Vienna audiences of the time were baffled to hear the lilting, swaying sound of a children's song—"Frère Jacques"—shattered by the careering horns of a village band. Later audiences have heard these moments as enactment of scenes from his childhood, when the coffin that held one of his brothers was carried past the open doorway of his father's tavern and raucous noise blared heartlessly from within. Eight brothers and sisters died in infancy, and when Ernst, the youngest, who had revered Gustav, took ill in the spring of 1875, Gustav was at his bedside distracting him by inventing tall tales. After Ernst died, Gustav left Iglau. He returned only to recite kaddish beside the grave of his father. He kept in his memory a primal scene from age five or six, when he had rushed out of the family tavern to get away from his father's shouts and his mother's tears, only to run into a village organ-grinder in the street outside, playing the old Viennese song "Ach du lieber Augustin." He described this scene to Sigmund Freud in August 1910, while they paced up and down the canals of Leiden. He had come to ask Freud for advice about the crisis in his marriage. Remembering this childhood scene, he told Freud, made him understand how, when he composed, he could not help interrupting passages of elevated sorrow with sudden notes of discordant and raucous levity. It was as if he could not keep the organ-grinders or village bands of his childhood from bursting into the concert hall. This was why, he told Freud, Viennese audiences had never liked his music. Later audiences heard this feature as precisely what was new: Mahler's fusion of deeply personal and autobiographical impulses with grand, transformative, essentially religious ambitions.

His Second Symphony, for example, written in the late 1890s, re-created Mahler's own recurrent experience of psychic despair

and recovery. The music is on a vast scale, but its impact is intimate and personal. Mahler achieved this effect by combining
words and music in a symphonic form that placed dramatic
orchestral effects at the service of the solitary intensity of the
human voice. Mahler wrote lyrics of his own for the mezzo-
soprano to express his recurrent struggles to believe in himself
and his vocation:

> O glaube
> Du wardst nicht umsonst geboren!
> Hast nicht umsonst gelebt, gelitten!
> O believe!
> You were not born for nothing!
> Have not for nothing, lived, suffered!

In seeking to express the innermost struggles of the psyche, Mahler's music committed itself to transform the ancient
liturgical ambitions of music—exultation, reverence, and
consolation—for a listening public who now lived these experiences as private dramas of their interior lives.

Mahler's music may have retained essentially religious ambitions, but his view of actual religious doctrine, especially the
Christian vision of paradise, was ironic and mocking. He was
a Jew, after all, who was not allowed to ignore his Jewishness
either, since Jews had long been barred from key posts in Viennese cultural life. In order to secure his post as director of the
Vienna opera, he had converted to Catholicism, but it had been
an instrumental move to further a career, never a conversion of
the heart, and his sense of apartness and exclusion as a Jew never
disappeared.

His most extended treatment of the Christian paradise
was in his Fourth Symphony, composed in an ecstatic burst of

creativity by a Carinthian lake in the summer of 1901. In the last movement, he set to music "The Heavenly Life," one of the poems he had found in the collection of traditional folk verse, *Des Knaben Wunderhorn* (The Boy's Marvelous Horn), compiled in 1809 by Clemens Brentano and Achim von Arnim—two members of Goethe's circle in Weimar. "The Heavenly Life" is a vision of paradise straight out of Brueghel, seen from the wide-eyed and innocent perspective of a peasant boy, an alternatively cheerful and casually brutal story of saints in heaven carving up little lambs for the saved souls to eat:

> *John lets the lambkin out*
> *And Herod the Butcher lies in wait for it.*
> *We lead a patient and innocent dear little lamb to its death.*
> *Saint Luke slaughters the oxen without any thought or concern.*
> *Wine doesn't cost a penny in the heavenly cells;*
> *The angels bake the bread.*

Mahler wrote comic and tender music to convey the sheer incongruity of these peasant visions of plenty, side by side with saints engaged in blithe animal slaughter. His music ends by conveying, in the summer afternoon stillness that falls toward the end, a clear-eyed view that this peasant paradise is an imagined artifact of another time, beyond the reach of the present.

If the paradise imagined by Arnim and Brentano's peasant boy was now beyond reach, and the only paradise humans could aspire to was here on earth, for a brief moment on a summer afternoon, how were the men and women of his time—the audience he composed for—to come to terms with death and loss, the blows for which a belief in paradise had long served as consolation?

Religious music and art had given the mater dolorosa (the

grieving mother) a privileged place in its rhetoric of comfort. The grieving father or brother was less frequently depicted, and here was a subject close to Mahler's heart. Between 1901 and 1904, he composed five songs for male voice and orchestra, based on poems that a distraught young German professor, Friedrich Rückert, had written seventy years before, on the death of two of his children from scarlet fever. Alma, Mahler's fiancée by then, thought he was tempting fate to choose such a subject, but this was a terrain, after all, that he knew only too well.

In channeling this fraught material into musical form, Mahler was able to deploy his mastery of the German lieder tradition, using musical shading to give plain words an emotional charge that they might not have been able to convey on their own. This is especially the case with the Rückert poems, which were, as poems, barely mediated expressions of the poet's grief. Mahler selected just five from several hundred, and then arranged them in a narrative sequence conveying what he imagined a father would feel as he went from disbelief, to wild grief, to regret, and finally to acceptance. The fourth song begins with disbelief:

> *I often think, they have only just gone out*
> *And now they will be coming back home*
> *The day is fine, don't be dismayed*
> *They have just gone for a long walk*

By the last song, in which Mahler gives musical form to wild emotion, the mourning father is tormented by a guilt he knows cannot bring the children back:

> *In this weather, in this storm*
> *I should never have let the children out*

I was anxious they might
Die the next day
Now anxiety is pointless
In this weather, in this storm . . .

The last song begins in wild agitation but ends in serenity.
Mahler manages to convey through the last bars, which float
away into silence, a state of emotional acceptance in which a
parent could believe that the children were at peace so that
they could leave grief behind:

They rest as if in their
Mother's house
Frightened by no storm
Sheltered by the hand of God
They rest, they rest
As if in their Mother's house.

Neither in Rückert's poems nor in Mahler's reworking of
them is there any suggestion that the children are safe in a
Christian heaven. There is only music: a gently ebbing melody
that, as someone once said, feels like the touch of your mother's
hand on your head.

The philosopher Martha Nussbaum hears the music of the
last *Kindertotenlied* very differently. It conveys, she writes, "the
sleep not of comfort but of nothingness." The music conveys
the "knowledge of the impossibility of any loving, any repara-
tive effort." Mahler means to say, she maintains, "that the world
of the heart is dead."

She seems not to hear the warmth and gentleness of the final
bars. The music does evoke the stillness of death, it is true, but
for art to be convincingly consoling it must convey the reality

of what it seeks to console *for*. The music, having conveyed the full intensity of disbelief, guilt, and grief in the four preceding songs earns its right to console in the final bars of the last song. The necessary condition of any truly consoling work is that it knows of what it speaks, and because it does, the music earns a listener's assent to its transformation of the idea of death into a vision of peace and sleep.

Mahler certainly knew of what his music spoke. He was unabashed about the autobiographical impulses at work, telling a friend "only when I experience, do I compose, only when I compose, do I experience." In the *Kindertotenlieder*, his memories of those coffins passing the door of the tavern in Iglau brought the pain of his own experience to the music. So vivid were these memories that he doubted that his songs would console anyone, confessing ruefully to a friend that he had no idea who could actually bear to hear them. All he knew was that he had put into music the truth of those memories of sorrow.

The songs turned out to be an artistic breakthrough, for he managed to create a spare symphonic song form, combining the power of words and the power of an orchestra in a compellingly personal way that proved deeply popular. Artistic success could have been enough for him, but it is also possible that the work itself allowed the composer to make peace with painful memories. This peace, unfortunately, was to be short-lived.

When he wrote the first of the *Kindertotenlieder*, he was an unmarried man of forty-one; when he wrote the last one in 1904, he had been married to Alma for three years and was the father of a daughter he adored, Marie, named in memory of his mother.

Three years later, in 1907, he left the Vienna Opera, exhausted by professional battles as chief administrator of the house and worn out by his own unremitting perfectionism as a conductor, only to suffer a blow that was to change his life forever.

In midsummer, his daughter came down with the same scarlet fever that had claimed Rückert's children. Little Marie's struggle for life was ghastly and protracted. Mahler paced outside her room until the sound of her death rattle drove him away. Alma had to assist at the tracheotomy performed to help the child breathe, and when this had no effect, she ran along the shore of the lake where they were staying, crying out her grief. The child's death was a blow from which neither they nor their marriage ever recovered.

Mahler confessed to Guido Adler, his oldest friend from his days in Iglau and now a professor of musicology in Vienna, that once he had lost his daughter, "I could not have written these songs anymore."

Music had enabled him to work through the loss of his brothers and sisters a quarter century before and it helped him to console others, but even music fell silent once the loss was his. In the death of a child music met its match.

In the aftermath of Marie's death, the work of composing, conducting orchestras, and shaping a repertoire offered him a respite from grief, but her loss changed his music. There was happiness in what he was to write afterward, but always with an undertow of sorrowful awareness that joy was fleeting and brutally revocable. Mahler never referred again to the death of his daughter, but sorrow continued to seek expression in his work, in the brooding Adagio of his Sixth Symphony composed in 1907 and in the Abschied, the final movement of *Das Lied von der Erde*, composed in 1908. Mahler set a Chinese poem of regret and farewell to music for this final song. Its verses included these lines:

> *All desire now turns to dreaming,*
> *Weary mortals make for home,*
> *To recapture in sleep*

Forgotten happiness and youth.
Birds huddle silently on their branches,
The world falls asleep.

As in the final song of the *Kindertotenlieder*, Mahler composed an ethereal, floating musical line to convey the haunting melancholy of these final verses:

Where am I going? I go into the mountains,
I seek peace for my lonely heart.
I am making for home, my resting place!
I shall never roam abroad again—
My heart is still and awaits its hour!
Everywhere the dear earth
Blossoms in spring and grows green again!
Everywhere and forever the distance shines bright and blue!
Forever . . . forever . . .

In the final bars of the Abschied, as the singer whispers "forever, forever," the music lifts the listener out of the world of pain and regret into a shimmering world of sound very slowly fading into silence. As in *Kindertotenlieder*, as in the final bars of his Ninth Symphony, Mahler brings the listener and the music to the very edge of silence, as if to mark the place where music's consoling work has to end, and the listener must go on to find meaning on his or her own.

TODAY CONSOLATION HAS LARGELY PASSED out of the modern vocabulary; music has other work to do beside consolation, and new vernaculars of understanding have taken the place of the religious. Loss and sorrow can now be understood as illnesses from which we can recover. This development, which began in Vienna in Mahler's time, has been called the triumph of the therapeutic.

When Mahler sought Freud's counsel in Leiden in August 1910, it was a meeting of two masters of the language of emotion. One had given form to the ascendant language of the talking cure, with its claims to science, its hostility to religious consolation, and its belief that grief, neurosis, anxiety, and sorrow could be cured by bringing emotion to utterance. The other was a master of the language inherited from Beethoven and Wagner, now in a desperate state of mind, tormented by his wife's infidelity, unable to finish his Tenth Symphony, driven to scrawling on his score, "My God why hast thou deserted me?" words of desolation as old as the Psalms.

They met for lunch and then walked up and down the canals for four hours: two Jews from Moravia, one in need of reassurance and comfort from the new science of the mind, the other seeking to capitalize on a celebrity encounter that he hoped would add to the prestige of a discipline still struggling at the edges of medical respectability.

It was a caricature of an analysis, of course, since Mahler did not spend any sessions on the couch. Perhaps he feared a cure would leach away the tensions that drove his art. In any event, there was no time: Mahler's heart condition had been diagnosed, and he believed he was a dying man. He was certainly a desperate one. Freud reassured him that Alma would not leave him, since her father fixation was the equal of his mother fixation. Mahler returned to work, comforted and reassured, and Freud came away impressed by Mahler's astonishingly quick grasp of the basic language of psychoanalysis and his acceptance of its insistence on returning to the primal scenes at Iglau.

Mahler reconciled himself to his wife's infidelities and plunged again into conducting, this time in New York, but he never completed the Tenth Symphony. His heart condition deteriorated, and in 1911 he returned to Vienna to die. He chose to be buried in the Grinzing cemetery, next to his daughter Marie. Days after his death, Freud presented the Mahler estate with a bill for his services. A callous or vulgar gesture, one might think, but it was Freud's way of insisting that the meeting at Leiden had been a medical consultation and should be acknowledged as such, through payment of a fee.

Freud admitted much later that he had not managed to dig more than a tunnel beneath the edifice of Mahler's neurosis. The edifice—made of sorrow and memory and hope—had been the place from which the music had come. Freud's tunnel never got close to the heart of it, nor to the sources of that immense consolation that Mahler's work has provided ever since to those who, in listening to him, suddenly think, here is someone who understands what I feel, someone who understands this loneliness, desperation, or sorrow, this exaltation that may soon turn to silence.

The new science of psychoanalysis promised to replace the false consolations of religion with self-knowledge achieved through therapy, yet even the inventor of the new faith had to confess its limitations. When Freud's own daughter died in the postwar influenza epidemic in 1920, he admitted sadly to a friend that her loss left him defenseless and alone. The language of psychoanalysis helped him to understand the blow but not to bear it:

> Since I am the deepest of unbelievers, I have no one to accuse and know that there is no place where one can lodge an accusation . . . [but] way deep down I sense the feeling of a deep narcissistic injury I shall not get over.

THE DEATHS THAT HAUNTED DOROTHEA von Ertmann, Friedrich Rückert, Gustav and Alma Mahler, and Sigmund Freud are now infrequent. Thirty years after Mahler's death, sulfa drugs and penicillin began to be used in hospitals, and the scarlet fevers that had carried off their children and blighted their lives became mere infections that prompt care could cure. Yet children still die, and their deaths can appear still more senseless and cruel when modern medicine proves to be of no avail. In the absence of consolation, only faith in medical miracles remains, and the search for them often ends in cruel disappointment.

As for Freud's talking cure, it once advanced with all the prestige of a science and the organizational energy of a cult. Now no longer the therapy of choice, it has been displaced by a host of competing therapeutic regimens that have come on the market to medicate misery.

If anything, music's importance as consolation has only grown in an age that medicates grief and treats sorrow as an illness. In moments of grief and despair, there is something unsayable about the experience that only music seems to express. Musicologists have spoken of the "floating intentionality" of music, this sense that music is about something but resists pinning down what precisely that something might be. Music calls on listeners to complete its implicit meaning, and when we do so, we have a feeling of understanding our own emotions that is central to the experience of consolation.

Music can have these tidal effects only when we are ready for them. In the first extremity of distress, we might not turn to music at all. A person in pain may have no time for beauty, for sound, for anything. The time when music can help might come years later, when you are sitting in a concert, listening to a musician play a passage, and you are swept away. Memories return, not now unbearable, but still so strong that you sit in the darkened hall, concealing tears from the people on either side, feeling gratitude that this music releases you so that the work of consolation can begin. This delayed effect, sometimes of years, of decades, teaches us that consolation may be the work of a lifetime.

IN THIS WORK, IN WHICH grief or regret slowly gives way to consolation, the dead play their part. They keep vigil by our sides. It is as if they would console us, if they only could.

A musician I know lost his own daughter in a single instant in a tragic accident many years ago. She was the eight-year-old he took to concerts, who sat with him and tapped her feet, her face rapt in attention. She was the one who seemed to have inherited whatever gift he had, and so they were especially close. When I asked him how he had dealt with her death, he said he kept working. There was nothing else to do. What did he think now, decades after her death? "I thought she had been spared suffering. Her life had been complete. It was full. She lived it. She was spared the rest."

Instead of lamenting a life cut short, he had learned, after many years, to think of his eight-year-old's time on earth as a life fully lived and moreover, one spared some of the griefs that he himself had suffered.

A working life in music had helped him to begin to live again. When I asked what music had consoled him, he found it hard to single out one piece because there were so many, but he settled on the final trio in Richard Strauss's *Der Rosenkavalier*, the soaring melancholy with which the Marschallin accepts her own aging, the death of love, and the triumph of her young rival. My musician friend did not mention the *Kindertotenlieder*. Perhaps it was too close for comfort. But then he added an afterthought. He had never forgotten his daughter, not for an instant, and he counted that as a victory. Every night, even now, he said, when he is about to perform, when he stands in the wings offstage, waiting to go on, she is there with him, a presence, a spirit, just there, visible to no one but him, a child watching silently as he moves forward onto the lighted stage.

Thirteen

The Calling

Max Weber and The Protestant Ethic

In June 1903, a thirty-nine-year-old German professor, traveling alone, stopped to visit the incomparable collection of Dutch art at the Mauritshuis in The Hague. He was recovering from a depressive illness that had forced him to give up work and abandon his professorship five years before. As he strolled through the collection, one painting, Rembrandt's *Saul and David*, completed sometime in the 1650s, caught his attention. The painting portrays the moment described in the first book of Samuel, chapter 19, verses 9–10:

> But an evil spirit from the Lord came on Saul as he was sitting in his house with his spear in his hand. While David was playing the lyre, Saul tried to pin him to the wall with his spear, but David eluded him as Saul drove the spear into the wall. That night David made good his escape.

In Rembrandt's vision of the scene, Saul's face is shown in profile, half-concealed by a thick curtain. Beyond the curtain is a region of blackness, which could serve as an emblem of his condition. He is wiping away his tears. David plays on, not looking at the king, his gaze concentrating on the strings of his lyre. The king looks away, haunted and desolate. He is tormented by jealousy of David, driven mad by the exploits of his protégé, who now plays at his command and seeks to calm his fury. The solace of music cannot reach him. Saul grips the spear. The lute is about to fall silent. We are a second away from an explosion. In an instant, the spear will slam into the wall.

Max Weber sent a postcard reproduction of the painting to Marianne, his wife, but he said that it did not do the painting justice:

> The one eye of the king which can be seen—he tearfully hides the rest of his face—tells us almost dreadfully how he had hoped the harp playing would make him forget that things were going downhill with him and how this hope had gone unfulfilled.

It was even more moving, he told Marianne, if you took into account Rembrandt's situation in the 1650s. After the death of his wife, Saskia, his property and pictures had been sold and he had gone into bankruptcy, living in solitude with his son and his faithful servant and lover Hendrickje, with old age approaching.

Marianne kept the postcard and was to mention it in the biography she wrote of her husband after his death. It seemed to cast a shaft of light into the darkness in his mind. The postcard told her he now had reactions, he was now engaged with the world, at least a little. He could identify with the courage of an artist still painting in the midst of aging, failure, and solitude. He could understand the agonized dividedness of the king, in tears at the soothing sound of the lyre yet unable to stop his hand from hurling the spear. Rembrandt, he was telling Marianne, had painted an unsparing portrait of what catastrophic depression was truly like: to yearn for comfort, yet to believe it was out of reach, to hear the music of the lyre yet feel oneself deaf to its beauty, to feel, at one and the same moment, tears of remorse and annihilating rage.

Neither Max nor Marianne mentioned another possible dimension to Weber's identification with the picture in the Mauritshuis. David was not Saul's son, of course—that was Jonathan, David's soul friend; but there must have been filial aspects in his close relationship to the king and his family; and those aspects, as they lurk behind Rembrandt's tense image, would have had painful resonances for a man recovering from a traumatic quarrel with his own father. In 1898, after years of conflict, Weber had forbidden his father to visit him in his home, so that his mother could come on her own and he could see her apart from his father. The father defied the ban, arrived, was duly banished by his son, and departed the house in a fury, only to die suddenly, alone, weeks later. Weber never forgave himself.

In Weber's postcard to Marianne, in the sympathy he displays toward Saul's anguish, we can see him, perhaps for the first time, becoming able to understand his own father's fury at being driven from his son's house. That is one possibility. Another is that Weber identifies with David. Hadn't Saul been driven to murderous rage by jealousy, by the taunting cries of the women in his court who sang that Saul had slain his thousands, but David his ten thousands? Hadn't Weber's father been jealous of the successful son, usurper of his place as his wife's favorite? Yet we know the son gained no victory in his battle with his father. Once the most brilliant young scholar of his generation, a prodigiously productive worker, on the ladder to a prestigious career in the most illustrious university system in the world, Weber suffered a total collapse after his father's death. For five years he was condemned to a life as a restless wanderer, living with an intolerable anguish. In the encounter with Rembrandt, in the postcard he sent to his wife, he had shared a glimpse into the roots of his condition, and this glimpse his wife took as an early sign of recovery.

One distinguishing symptom of Weber's illness was that he was unable to work. Any creative act like David's lute playing seemed cruelly beyond reach. He could not read, could not prepare lectures, and delivering them, he insisted to his mother, was impossible. She was baffled by his illness and believed he lacked the will or force of character to master his inner tempest. He struggled to explain himself to her:

> The inability to speak is purely physical, the nerves break down and when I look at my lecture notes I simply can't make sense of them.

He had been a formidable lecturer, with a dramatic delivery that led some listeners to predict he was destined for a political career. Now he was a shuffling invalid, unable to stand noise or company, chronically unable to sleep, and so weak, Marianne reported, that he couldn't even hang decorations on a Christmas tree. After several years in one sanatorium after another, the only way he could keep his devils at bay was through travel: to Italy, Spain, Portugal, and the Netherlands. His vagabond existence turned into an ironic reprise of his father's life. His father had been a self-indulgent dilettante—that at least had been how the son saw it, but now that the very springs of Weber's own work ethic had suddenly run dry, he felt himself to be a parody of the father he had both loved and despised.

After the trip to The Hague, Weber slowly began to recover. He found himself able to read and study again, and he began to focus his research on a transparently autobiographical theme: the roots of his own lost compulsion to work. Where, he wondered, had his own drive come from? Work had been his purpose in life as a young professor. Why was it now such torture?

Writing about these questions directly, in the form of autobiography or a "personal memoir," was out of the question. He was an embattled product of late Wilhelmine Germany's masculine codes, bound to dismiss the confessional or autobiographical mode as sophomoric or, worse, as feminine. One of his high-flying academic rivals, Werner Sombart, once asked Weber's advice about whether to write a directly autobiographical or "personal" book. Weber's reply is revealing:

> You want to write personal books. I am convinced that the distinctive personality . . . comes to expression invariably only when it is unintended, when it retreats behind the book and its objectivity, as all great masters have retreated behind their work. Where one wants to be personal . . . one almost always drifts into the path of the typical.

From 1903 to 1905, as his recovery gathered pace, Weber embarked on a course of reading that took him through Luther's German translation of the Bible, the writings of Benjamin Franklin, Richard Baxter, Jean Calvin, John Knox, the intellectual architects of the Protestant revolution. The mother he adored was of devout Protestant stock, and while he was not a believer himself, he knew how deeply its ethic had shaped him. This was where his own punishing asceticism had come from, and this was the spell that had to be broken. The scholarly essay that resulted ended seven years of silence, achieved a deeply cathartic examination of his own psyche, and turned out to be the most powerfully influential work he ever wrote.

The Protestant Ethic and the Spirit of Capitalism, published in

1905, launched a debate, which has gone on ever since, about the role of Protestantism in incubating the distinctive rationality and acquisitive energy that gave the capitalist West its long hegemony over the Rest. That debate, however important it was, was not the main point for Weber. His personal focus was upon the word *Beruf*, the word that Martin Luther, in his translation of Proverbs 22:29, had used to render the word for work or trade: "Do you see a man skilled in his calling? He can stand before Kings."

Instead of citing Genesis and the words that described labor as Adam's curse upon expulsion from the Garden, Luther had chosen to cite Proverbs, giving emphasis to its association of work with dignity and pride. In the word *Beruf* was the verb form *rufen*, meaning "to call." In using this word, he transformed the Protestant understanding of labor from a curse to a calling. In Luther's view, men were called by God to a vocation in which, through skill and effort, they proved themselves worthy of God's grace. This vision of work not only lifted Adam's curse, it also transformed the world itself from a place of exile into the realm in which man could build himself a home and earn salvation in the life hereafter. Weber summed up his understanding of the Protestant ethic this way:

> Only in the Protestant ethic of vocation does the world, despite all its creaturely imperfections, possess unique and religious significance as the object through which one fulfills his duties by rational behavior according to the will of an absolutely transcendental god.

For Weber, John Milton's concluding vision of Adam and Eve striding out of Paradise together, neither banished nor ashamed but taking possession of a whole new world, expressed the hope that was the core of the Protestant faith:

They, looking back, all th' Eastern side beheld
Of Paradise, so late their happy seat,
Waved over by that flaming brand; the gate
With dreadful faces thronged and fiery arms:
Some natural tears they dropped, but wiped them soon;
The world was all before them, where to choose
Their place of rest, and Providence their guide;
They, hand in hand, with wandering steps and slow,
Through Eden took their solitary way.

Milton's concluding lines express serene confidence that the human calling, our destiny on earth, is to transform the world and make it our home. For Weber, however, the Protestant idea of the calling was fraught with anxious ambiguity. How could a believer know for certain he had found a calling that was pleasing to the Lord?

It seems revealing of Weber's own state of mind that he was drawn not to Milton's hopeful answer, or to Luther's trusting faith, but to Jean Calvin, the author of the most uncompromising of all the possible Protestant answers to the question. For it was Calvin's doctrine of predestination that insisted that men would have to labor here below without any certainty that their vocation would prove worthy in God's sight. For a true Calvinist, no one could know for sure—not the preacher nor the community of believers in the church—for they too had no certainty of election, of God's salvation. What struck Weber to the heart was the "feeling of tremendous inner loneliness" of the Calvinist vision. It was a loneliness he recognized as his own.

He had always been drawn to the most austere and remote conceptions of God, like the one he found, for example, in the book of Job. It was in the "highest degree significant," he remarked, that when Job demanded that the voice out of the whirlwind justify himself, God at first didn't deem Job worthy of an answer.

If God was truly as Job had described him, then it was impossible to be certain that you had been called to your vocation. To live in truth, Weber came to believe, was to live without any consolation at all. This is what he meant when he spoke of the "disenchantment" of the world. To live in what he called the "capitalist cosmos" was to live without faith that your work in that cosmos was pleasing in God's eyes. Yet the idea that work could give meaning to a whole life continued to survive, in memory and culture, as a nostalgic residue of a vanishing faith. "The idea of vocation as duty," he wrote, "persists in our lives as a specter of former religious beliefs." If work was no longer sustained by faith, what remained was only remorseless duty without purpose.

In the lacerating final words of *The Protestant Ethic*, Weber quoted Nietzsche's phrases about modern man—"specialists without spirit, sensualists without heart: this nullity pretends to have reached a whole new level of humanity"—laying the whip of scorn across his own back.

But here was the paradox: in the process of painful self-discovery that led to the dark conclusion of *The Protestant Ethic*, Weber had rediscovered the satisfactions of scholarship, the delights of reading, the intoxication of feeling suddenly that he understood not only himself but also his times. In the lucidity that devoted study of the Protestant texts had given him, he began to break the hold of depression and find his way back to a precarious equilibrium.

He still could not return to a professorship—and did not do so for a further fifteen years—but polemical battles with other scholars proved to him that he was intellectually superior to his adversaries and destined to chart a scholarly course apart from the humdrum German academics of his time. Professors

were narrow specialists, while he was the mighty thinker ranging across disciplines—sociology, economics, and religion—
and daring to articulate, as no one had before, the disenchanted
spiritual emptiness of capitalist modernity.

His newfound confidence, which drew students from across
Germany to his lectures, was also underpinned by the masculine and nationalist culture of his time. His wife was a noted
feminist, but he never ventured out of the dark fortress of his
own masculinity. When World War I came, he was swept up in
the nationalist fervor of the hour, as Freud briefly was, believing
his country's cause was righteous and that the fatherland had
been forced into war. When later he saw Black and Asian troops,
subjects of the French and British Empires, fighting on the
western front, he was as chauvinist as any of his contemporaries,
writing with disgust that Germany was being attacked by lesser
races. For a white European man of his era, his self-confidence
depended on what looks in retrospect like a confection of racial
superiority, national chauvinism, and toxic masculinity.

In November 1918, however, this worldview collapsed with
the German defeat. The entire civilization that he had shared
with Mahler, Freud, and Nietzsche lay in ruins.

In Munich, where he lived, the Bavarian socialist republic had been proclaimed. The emperor had fled into exile. The
streets of the city were filled with demobilized soldiers, one
of them named Adolf Hitler. Rival political gangs on the left
and the right set up roadblocks and fought each other in the
streets. Money was worthless. The national government in
Berlin barely existed, and Germany was under occupation by
French, American, and British troops. Weber was now living
through the end of the world as he knew it, just what Boethius
and the Roman senatorial class had lived through with the end
of the Roman Empire.

Yet unlike them or most of his contemporaries who withdrew

into depression and inner exile, Weber felt that his moment
had come. The shattering of his world seemed to free him from
his inhibitions. His affair with Else von Richthofen, a longtime
friend of his wife, brought a long period of impotence to a close
and blossomed into a passionate relationship that Marianne
came to accept with resigned forbearance. Now in his fifties,
he threw himself into the melee of Weimar politics, fighting
for stronger powers for the president in the new Weimar constitution, advising the German delegation at the Versailles
conference, and, most of all, giving lectures to frightened and
disoriented students, who flocked to hear his advice on how to
orient themselves in a strange and frightening world. He was
no longer just a scholar. He had found his calling as a prophet
and a seer.

In November 1917, when Germany was still undefeated
but the Russian Revolutions of February and October were
already unleashing their furies, Weber was asked to lecture on
"spiritual and intellectual work as a calling" to a gathering of
left liberal students at the University of Munich. Any young
person setting out on a career, he told them, had to look reality in the face. Luck, chance, favoritism: all these, rather than
intellectual merit, determined success in an academic career.
Whenever he had issued such warnings in the past, he said,
"you always receive the same answer: of course, I live only for
my 'vocation.' " But a sense of calling rarely survived disillusion with the rank favoritism that prevailed in academic life.

An ambitious young scholar might yearn for a breakthrough
that would transform his understanding of the world, but the
very idea that science could uncover existential truth was itself
an illusion:

Apart from overgrown children who can still be found in the
natural sciences, who imagines nowadays that a knowledge

of astronomy or biology or physics or chemistry could teach
us anything about the meaning of the world?

When he was writing *The Protestant Ethic*, Weber had
mourned the ebbing away of religious consolation, but now he
was at war with the idea of consolation in any form, especially
the idea that modern science could provide men and women
with a purposive picture of the cosmos. He told the students
that he now agreed with Leo Tolstoy: "Life and death had lost
all meaning for a civilized person." While old peasants once
had died, without repining, content with their allotted span,
modern man was insatiable, lured onward by the fable of progress into believing that life was infinitely improvable. Modern men and women could never have "enough of life" in this
sense, could never rest content with what they had achieved.
As he warned students, they must forswear any hope that their
scientific conjectures would be confirmed. Final proofs might
be millennia away. Only someone with stoic acceptance of
this fact had a true vocation for science. Progress did occur in
knowledge, he told his students, but it had no power to console. Instead of despairing, he told them, they should under-
take scientific work with humility, accepting that even if their
work did achieve a permanent benefit, they were unlikely to
live to see it.

Weber seemed to exult in his own prophetic gloom, as acted
out on a platform before a frightened generation of German
youth trying to understand disaster and defeat. Once a recluse
in deep depression begging his mother to believe that lecturing
was torture, he was now packing halls with his speeches, counseling a minimalist lucidity that praised, above all things, what
he called *Sachlichkeit*—matter-of-fact realism and humility.

In dark times like these, Weber said, we were all like the
watchman in the book of Isaiah, chapter 21, helplessly witnessing

the fall of Babylon as all its gods and graven images shatter on the ground. But since we lived, he insisted, "in an age alien to God," we could not wait for God to save us. We had to wrestle with the "daemons" inside us and find a calling equal to the demands of the times.

This message, delivered in November 1917, had an even deeper resonance when on January 23, 1919, he addressed a huge crowd of left liberal students at the same university on "politics as a vocation."

On one side, he told the students, were the victorious leaders at Versailles, men like Clemenceau and Lloyd George, intoxicated with victory, animated by the implacable conviction that Germany must pay; on the other were conservative politicians in Germany, equally convinced that Germany had been stabbed in the back. In the streets of Munich and Berlin, Spartacists and Bolsheviks were promising a radiant tomorrow, if only the generals and the capitalist exploiters could be punished. As Weber was speaking, these political conflicts were hurtling toward a bloody denouement. In the days following his speech, paramilitary gangs of the Far Right would execute Karl Liebknecht and throw Rosa Luxemburg's body into a Berlin canal.

On all sides, Weber said, an ethics of conviction was running amok, a self-intoxication that was utterly heedless of consequences and indifferent to moral costs. Where, he asked, was an ethics of responsibility, a sober moderation, an ability to see the world as it actually was?

We must ask, he told the students, "what kind of a human being one must be to have the right to grasp the spokes of the wheel of history." Such a calling required a person with "passion, a sense of responsibility and a sense of proportion." Passion meant the opposite of "sterile excitement" or "the romanticism of the intellectually interesting." Such a person, he went on, must display "the ability to allow realities to impinge on you while maintaining an inner calm and composure." Weber was fascinated by charisma, but he despised charismatic rabble-rousers like Hitler, who were already learning their trade in the chaotic streets and beer halls of Munich. The charismatic politicians he admired—here he was fantasizing about himself—would balance a sense of reality with a dramatic sense of politics as theater and performance. This required a certain "distance," a refusal to be intoxicated by public acclaim. Politics was obsessively interesting to Weber precisely because it was beset by temptations he understood only too well: the lust for power, the vanity of demagoguery, and self-intoxication.

The calling of politics, in a collapsing world, was to assume responsibility to guide frightened men and women into the future. In this struggle for the future, he said, the Sermon on the Mount could no more serve as a guide than *The Communist Manifesto*. If Christian ethics alone were our guide, we might never have the courage to resist evil with force. If faith in a glorious communist future were our guide, he warned, ideology would trap us into colluding with evil.

Weber warned his young listeners that they must put aside any longing for salvation. There were no secure anchors in faith or ideology, only agonizing choices, beset by temptations of conviction, lust for power, and violent solutions. Reaching the peroration of his address, he reserved his highest praise for those who embraced politics with sober maturity and adamantine determination:

> I find it immeasurably moving when a mature human being—whether young or old in actual years is immaterial—who feels the responsibility he bears for the consequences of his own actions with his entire soul and who acts in harmony with an ethics of responsibility reaches the point where he says, "here I stand, I can do no other."

In citing the words attributed to Martin Luther at the Diet of Worms in 1521, in this, one of the final addresses of his life, Weber returned to the Protestant ideal of the calling. But it was a calling without any of the consolations of faith or the certainties of election.

As he ended his address, he said he hoped he would meet the students again in a decade's time, to see what they had made of their lives, but he feared that an "age of reaction" was dawning and "a polar night of icy darkness" was about to descend. These words, so often taken as a prophecy, did not actually represent his own despair. For he felt none at all—rather, he felt an elation at having found his calling at last as a prophet at the podium. It was this elation that enabled him to conclude by asking students to remember, "what is possible could never have been achieved unless people had tried again and again to achieve the impossible in this world." Here was the consolation of hope, which he offered to those young people, in dark times, provided they were prepared to shoulder the responsibilities of politics.

When he stepped off the stage, at the end of this prodigious evocation of polar night, he would have been euphoric. He joined his lover Else von Richthofen at a performance of *Tannhäuser*, and later they tasted the delights of love in a sleeping car on the way to Karslruhe. He became a professor again in Munich and pulled together his writings on the *Sociology of Religion* and his papers on *Economy and Society* that were to make his work an obligatory starting point for so much of twentieth-century social science. When he died at age fifty-six in the influenza pandemic in June 1920, both his wife, Marianne, and Else were at his side. No thinker of the twentieth century had been more inwardly troubled by the death of God, more bereft at the loss of the consolations of faith, and none had worked more strenuously to imagine a secularized version of the calling in which men and women would find meaning in their work without the certainty of God's grace. The burden he placed on himself, and on everyone who reads him, is first to grasp that each one of us must create for ourselves the purpose and hope to sustain us. This was how David Hume had found his vocation, but for Weber such internal, personal validation was never enough. More than any other thinker, it was Weber who made us ask: How could we be sure of our calling, if it turned out to be we—and we alone—who had called us to it? In 1919, at least, dark times themselves gave him the answer: the times themselves called him to inspire the next generation to embrace responsibility instead of taking flight in hatred or refuge in illusion.

Fourteen

The Consolations of Witness

Anna Akhmatova, Primo Levi, and Miklós Radnóti

It is Leningrad 1938. A long line of women, wrapped up against the cold, is queuing at the gates of Kresty prison, on the Arsenalnaya bank of the Neva River. The women wait every day and the gates often remain shut against them. Some have been coming to stand in the queue for as long as eighteen months. They do not even know if their men are still confined there or have simply disappeared. The line keeps growing. It is in the middle of the Yezhov terror: every night brings new arrests. Usually the women do not speak, knowing they cannot trust anyone. They just stand in a frozen torpor, waiting. But on this day, two women do exchange words. One whispers to the other— "Can you describe this?" The other whispers back, "I can." Then "something like a smile" crosses the first woman's face.

The woman who asked the question did not know the identity of the woman who answered, yet by pure chance she found the witness who would save the reality of that moment from oblivion. The poet Anna Akhmatova was in the queue at Kresty to see her son, Lev Gumilev, then under arrest. She was forty-nine years old, an impoverished widow, debarred from

publishing, living in one room in a communal flat carved out
of the decayed splendor of the Sheremetiev Palace.

Akhmatova placed her memory of the scene at the beginning of *Requiem*, the poetic cycle she wrote over the course
of twenty years to commemorate the victims—millions of
them—swept off the face of the earth or into the gulag by Stalin's regime:

> *I have woven you this wide shroud out of humble words*
> *I overheard you use. Everywhere, forever and always,*
> *I will never forget one single thing.*

Requiem was the monument she erected on behalf of every
woman who kept vigil outside the prison walls of Russia in the
1930s and on behalf of those confined inside, awaiting interrogation, torture, banishment, or a bullet in the back of the
head. She declared that if there ever was a monument raised in
her memory, it should be placed there, at the gates of Kresty
prison, where she had stood and waited with all the others.

We do not know whether the other woman in the queue
survived the siege of Leningrad or whether she ever saw the
man she was waiting to help. We know nothing of her fate,
only her smile, but thanks to the poem, circulated in manuscript since the 1940s and finally published in the 1960s, we
know that she hungered for her experience to be rescued from
forgetting. Thanks to her smile and to the genius of the woman
who saw it, a poem was written that puts everyone who reads it
under an obligation never to forget:

> *Now I will never manage to untangle*
> *Who is an animal and who a human being*
> *Nor how long I'll wait till the death sentence*
> *Is carried out.*

One of *Requiem*'s earliest readers in the West was Isaiah Berlin. He had read the work Akhmatova had written as a young woman in Tsarskoe Selo before and after the First World War, before she was banned. When he was in Leningrad in the autumn of 1945, on a visit as a British official, and discovered that she was still alive, he went to see her in the bare room in the Sheremetiev Palace. He was the first visitor from the West that she had seen in twenty years. She read to him in a matter-of-fact voice from a manuscript copy of *Requiem*:

> *The quiet Don is flowing quietly*
> *And the yellow moon enters my house.*
> *He enters wearing his hat askew and*
> *Meets a shadow, the yellow moon.*
> *This woman is not well,*
> *This woman is all alone.*
> *Husband in the grave, son jailed,*
> *Please offer a prayer for me.*

She read to Berlin, in the gathering darkness, breaking off at one point to exclaim quietly, "No, I cannot. It is no good, you come from a society of human beings, whereas here we are divided into human beings and . . ." She fell into a long silence. Later while they were sitting together, in near darkness, her son, Lev Gumilev, recently released from prison, came in and the three of them ate a dish of cold potatoes together. She spoke, Berlin later remembered, "without the slightest trace of self-pity, like a princess in exile, proud, unhappy, unapproachable in a calm, even voice, at times in words of moving eloquence." With war finally ended, with her son home and many of the poems in the *Requiem* cycle completed, she knew she had given voice to the torment of her people. It was a calling that she had not chosen, one that made her feel as desolate as the mad women of czarist times who had gathered below the Kremlin tower to wail in vain for their husbands' release. But it was a calling she was prepared to assume. As she said proudly, she had never chosen exile or escape, had never looked away from horror, and had fulfilled her duty as a witness.

AUSCHWITZ, SUMMER 1944. ON A hot Sunday afternoon, two young men in their twenties, one from northern Italy, the other from Strasbourg in Alsace, are walking through the camp to the kitchens to pick up a tureen of soup and carry it back to their barracks. They have both been in the camp for about six months and know its routines. They do not trust each other because you cannot trust anybody here, but Jean has picked Primo for the soup detail. It is the one moment they can stretch out, a brief hour of grace in an infernal routine of exhausting and degrading labor in a place where the smoke from the crematoria colors the sky.

The camp is a babble of languages, with Hungarian and Yiddish being the most prominent, but these two are conversing in French and German. When Jean, the Frenchman, says he would like to learn Italian, Primo, to his own surprise, begins reciting a few fragments from canto 26 of Dante's *Inferno* that he had memorized in high school. The canto tells the story of the Greek hero Ulysses who reaches the Gates of Hercules and exhorts his exhausted crew to go farther, to sail out beyond the gates into the wide-open sea. As the verses return to the Italian's memory, fragment by fragment, Jean becomes engaged in how to translate them best: *mare aperto*, should it be "open sea"? A *Blockführer* passes by on a bicycle. They freeze and remove their caps. Once he passes, they resume. When Ulysses "sets out" into the open sea, they argue about whether Dante's *misi mi* should be rendered as *je me mis* in French. Then, with a growing sense that they are sharing a text that contains a promise of freedom, Primo remembers the key lines—the exhortation delivered by Ulysses to convince his crew to set out beyond the Gates of Hercules, beyond the known world—

> *Consider well the seed that gave you birth*
> *You were not born to live your lives as brutes,*
> *But to be followers of virtue and knowledge.*

When these lines rise from the darkness of his memory, Primo feels as if he were hearing them for the first time, like the blast of a trumpet, like the voice of God. Jean begs him to repeat them and tell the rest, since they are approaching the kitchen. Primo struggles to remember the concluding lines. He closes his eyes, he bites his finger—it is no use. The cooks are shouting "soup and cabbage" in German and Hungarian, and behind them the men from the other barracks are clamoring to take their turn.

In Primo Levi's account of this scene, he does not tell us whether he managed to remember the ending. What matters is that the words reminded the two prisoners that they were not born to be brutes, and that there was another world, beyond the wire, where one day they might live as men.

This is undoubtedly why he felt such a surge of exaltation, but we also need to remember how Dante's tale actually ended. Ulysses and his crew did sail beyond the Gates of Hercules into the wide-open sea. Their mad journey continued into the darkness. They lost sight of the stars and the moon, then a storm struck and just as they saw an island looming up above them their ship foundered, turned over, and they all drowned. The last line of Dante's canto di Ulisse reads:

> *Until the sea again closed over us.*

———

HUNGARY, OCTOBER 1944. Farmworkers pause in their work in the fields to watch a column of men passing by on the road, a Hungarian labor service brigade, mostly composed of Jews, being marched back from a copper mine in Serbia across the Hungarian countryside. Their work uniforms are ragged; they are a brown and gray river of bodies, some stumbling and falling, others struggling to pick their fellows up and carry them along. Uniformed guards, mostly Hungarians, under the control of the German SS, patrol up and down, and the watching workers see men falling in the ditch, hear shots ring out, until the column disappears over the horizon.

As he stumbles along, one of the prisoners puts words together, assembles phrases, and commits them to memory. They have been on the march for days. In the distance, they can hear the thunder of the approaching Russian divisions. The war will surely be over soon, and they will make it home to their families. At night, lying on the bare ground of a brickyard, among the ragged sleeping men, he takes out a small notebook and writes down seven lines in a meticulously neat hand, conjuring into life the workers in the fields who had watched them pass. With laconic irony, he titles the poem "Picture Postcard":

> At *nine kilometers, the pall of burning*
> *Hayrick, homestead, farm.*
> *At the field's edge, the peasants, silent, smoking*
> *Pipes against the fear of harm.*
> *Here: a lake ruffled only by the step*
> *Of a tiny shepherdess is what the ruffled sheep*
> *Drink in their lowliness.*

He procured the notebook by bartering his last cigarettes with Serbian villagers who came to the wire of the Heidenau camp. On the march home, he keeps writing in the hope that he will see his wife, Fanni, again. Of her, he had written, "you whose calm is as the weight and sureness of a psalm." As he stumbles along, he dreams of her, of verandas, of plum jam, of the stillness of late summer in sun-dappled gardens.

He has survived months of hard labor in the copper mine, and when the guards started them on the march, he might have thought the journey would take him home, but as the days pass he begins to understand the truth. On the night of October 7–8, 1944, at a brickyard in Serbia, near the Hungarian border, the SS guards order the prisoners to lie down and empty their pockets of valuables. They machine-gun half their captives. A Budapest cabaret violinist topples to his knees and as the prisoner tries to help him the guards shoot the violinist in the neck. The prisoner falls beside him and lies still, not moving. He hears the guard speaking German just above his head. The SS and their Hungarian associates then force the survivors to their feet to resume the march. They are not going home, they now realize, but to labor camps in Germany. By October 24, they are halfway across Hungary, and he has time, at night, to write another "Picture Postcard":

> *The oxen drool saliva mixed with blood*
> *Each one of us is urinating blood.*
> *The squad stands about in knots, stinking, mad.*
> *Death, hideous, is blowing overhead.*

By now, they are marching northeast toward the border of the German Reich. The guards make them pitch camp on the tarmac of an abandoned airfield, and while the remnant of men lies sleeping, the prisoner takes a piece of cardboard he picked up on the road—on the back, an advertisement for cod-liver oil—and he writes another "Picture Postcard," this time describing his encounter with death days before:

> I fell beside him and his corpse turned over
> Tight already as a snapping string
> Shot in the neck. "And that's how you will end too."
> I whispered to myself, "Lie still, no moving.
> Now patience flowers in death." Then I could hear
> Der springt noch auf, *above, and very near.*
> Blood mixed with mud was drying on my ear.

He copies the seven lines into his notebook and dates it October 31, 1944. It is the last entry. One of the survivors of the column, who returned from Germany, later said that he last saw the prisoner, sitting alone on the tarmac of the airfield, staring down at his dilapidated boots.

On November 8, the Hungarian guards filled two carts full of prisoners no longer able to walk, among them the poet, and took them to local hospitals at a town near the German-Hungarian border. The hospitals turned the dying men away. Then the four Hungarian guards trundled the carts out to the woods outside of town, shot the prisoners in the backs of their heads, and tipped their bodies into a shallow grave.

In August 1946, the poet's wife, Fanni, was informed that bodies had been exhumed and some of her husband's personal effects had been found near the town where he had last been seen alive. These effects had been handed over to a local butcher, the leader of the town's Jewish community. When she went to the butcher shop, he gave her a brown paper parcel. When she unwrapped it, she found a wallet with his photograph and hers, his insurance card, a picture of his mother as a young woman, and the notebook. On the inside page was a message the poet had addressed in five languages—Hungarian, English, French, German, and Serbo-Croatian—informing anyone who found it that it contained the work of a Hungarian poet. When Fanni turned the pages, she found the "Postcards," written out in his steady, unvarying hand.

Fanni never recovered her husband's body or gave him a proper burial, but she did live long enough to see Miklós Radnóti recognized as one of the greatest poets of Hungary and Europe. There was indeed an answer to the last line of one of his poems: "But tell me, did the work survive?" His poetry is taught in Hungarian schools to this day. His act of witness also ensured that the suffering of his comrades in the labor service gang would not be forgotten. Like Akhmatova, like Levi, his act of witness was also a judgment that their countries still are reluctant to accept. Radnóti's work was incorporated into the national canon, but the uncomfortable fact remains that the guards who murdered him were Hungarian.

In the early 2000s, when Fanni was well into her eighties, her husband's biographer asked her whether the pain of losing him had diminished over time. She shook her head. Did she know, the biographer went on, the poem by Emily Dickinson?

> They say that "time assuages,"—
> Time never did assuage;
> An actual suffering strengthens,
> As sinews do, with age.
> Time is a test of trouble,
> But not a remedy.
> If such it prove, it prove too
> There was no malady.

Fanni nodded again. Yes, she did know the poem.

———

FOR ANYONE BORN IN THE decade after the war's end, as I was, these figures—and other witnesses of the two twentieth-century tyrannies—became touchstones of moral judgment. We turned to them to understand the history from which our parents came and from which our own world emerged. It was a past that put paid to any possibility, at least for me, that I could ever be consoled by Condorcet's faith in progress or Marx's faith in revolution.

What these survivors had endured gave them the authority once accorded to saints. Except, of course, that they didn't want to be thought of as saints. Still, I could not help but think of them in this way, for they exercised the moral authority of saints. Like them, they had suffered for a faith, not a belief in paradise or salvation, but instead a resolute conviction that hell existed and that they had an obligation to chronicle it.

Their act of witness was not just a vindication of art but also an affirmation of allegiance to a tradition, stretching back in time, for example, to Dante, whose courage in exile six hundred years before had been an inspiration to both Akhmatova and Levi. To write poetry was to assert their belonging to a fellowship of witness, across the centuries, that made sense of the human project as a whole, and if it did this, it was a fellowship they hoped would extend into the future.

Consolation, as I am using it here, was for them a form of political hope. They wanted to win the vital political battle of the future, over what meaning their nations and peoples would give to the horror they had endured. They wanted victims to be remembered and to ensure that their once all-powerful tormentors would be consigned to infamy.

Their passionate belief that history would not forget the suffering they had chronicled was a consoling thought, and not just for them. We, their readers, also hope that history is given meaning by virtue of their exemplary courage. They had wrung poetry from extremity; they had preserved the memory of the persecuted; they had kept faith with writing, with lucidity, in the midst of terror.

Their greatness of spirit, their determination to remember, consoled us for being members of a human family that had done this to them. We allowed ourselves to believe that their acts of witness could weigh in the balance against the horror they described, as if the heroic memory of one woman outside the prison could make up for what happened inside its gates and for the archipelago of oppression of which it was a part. In my generation's way of thinking, or at least in mine, there was a hidden desire for absolution. In paying tribute to their greatness of spirit, we appropriated their greatness as if it were our own.

They were saints, too, because they had faith in us, the generations who would come after them. They would have given in, surely, had they not held on to the conviction that their writings would survive and find readers who would take their truths to heart. They even hoped, as saints do, that our faith would move mountains, that once we had taken their truth to heart, such torments would never happen again.

We were their consolation. When they composed verses on death marches, when they remembered poetry in the camps, when they memorialized all those who had kept vigil in the cold, they were sustained by the hope that we—the succeeding generations—would ensure that they had not spoken truth in vain. They were consoled by the thought that we would remember them.

But have we?

The last survivors of the Holocaust and Stalin's terror are dying, and what they endured is passing from memory into the contested domain of history, and from there, into the still more uncertain terrain of opinion. More and more people actually think they have a choice about whether to believe these things happened. The ruler of contemporary Russia, whose father worked for Stalin's killers, has made nostalgia for Stalin the official ideology of his regime. He has said the destruction of the Soviet empire was the greatest catastrophe of the twentieth century. Poor Akhmatova—one can only be glad that she died not knowing how faithless her heirs would be.

Such faithless heirs—and they also include Holocaust deniers and anti-Semites, racists and hate-mongers—force us to ask whether the faith of these saints has been misplaced. Those of my own generation, who came to adulthood schooled in their unsparing testimony, may now feel something akin to shame. We have become unwilling witnesses to the creation of a new alternative reality in which what they witnessed and suffered is disbelieved.

If the meaning they stood for had won the battle, the once popular slogan—Never Again—would not now ring so hollow. New genocides would not have returned. This crime, it turned out, was not some elemental rupture with history, but the reenactment of a persistent historical temptation to create by force a world without enemies. Stalin and Hitler understood the appeal of this utopia, and it captivated millions of believers in the twentieth century. The same demonic utopia is bound to remain a permanent temptation in politics in the twenty-first and beyond.

It is just as well, really, that none of these saints lived to see who their heirs might be and that none of us will live to see how the story of our own times turns out. History has no consolations to offer because it never ends and its meaning is never settled, not even by witnesses as heroic and courageous as these. History may have no consolation to offer, but it does leave us with duties. Since they had faith in us, we should keep faith with them and defend the truths they bequeathed to us.

At the end of his life, Primo Levi wrote an incomparable memoir, *The Drowned and the Saved*, about being a witness. It begins with an epigraph from Coleridge:

> *Since then, at an uncertain hour,*
> *That agony returns:*
> *And till my ghastly tale is told,*
> *This heart within me burns.*

Levi lived long enough to see many of his fellow survivors die and for the Holocaust to slowly transform from a lived memory to a historical fact, and then, more disturbingly, into a myth. He did not spare himself in the struggle against this tide of amnesia and willful distortion. He answered the letters from Germans who wrote him ignorant or self-deceiving responses to his books. He showed up at schools and learned to listen patiently to children asking him, in small voices, why he hadn't been able to escape. One little boy could not believe that escape was impossible. So Levi drew him a map of the camp, with the barbed wire and the guard posts marked in. The little boy was still not convinced. "This is how you should do it," he said, and with a few energetic arrows and lines, the little boy tried to show Levi how. In this and so many other encounters, Levi as witness had to struggle with the disbelief in evil that is the chief illusion of happy lives.

He despised the moral kitsch that turned all Holocaust survivors into heroes. He knew otherwise. He chronicled the "grey zone," the ambiguous world of compromise he inhabited as a scientist spared from the crematorium by virtue of his technical skills. He even admitted that his year in Auschwitz was when he felt most fiercely alive. He viewed his own survival as a privilege for which he felt ashamed. He became convinced that the best had drowned, while the worst had been saved. He struggled with shame from the first moment of his release on that January day in 1945, when Russian soldiers on horseback crossed the wire into the camp and came upon wretched men in ragged striped uniforms dying in the dirty snow. Levi saw in his rescuers' eyes a deep embarrassment, as if they didn't want to acknowledge that these prisoners too were men.

He never stopped thinking through the responsibilities he had as a witness, never ceased to interrogate the role he had unwillingly embraced. When a fellow prisoner whom he met told him that Providence had saved him in order to be such a witness, Levi recalled bitterly, "Such an opinion seemed monstrous to me. It pained me as when one touches an exposed nerve and kindled the doubt I spoke of before: I might be alive in the place of another, at the expense of another."

In 1988, exhausted and depressed by age, a recent prostate operation, and the unremitting burden of caring for both his aged mother and his mother-in-law, Levi took his own life, hurling himself down the stairwell of the apartment in Turin where he had lived most of his life. Many of his readers allowed themselves to be disappointed that he had given up, that his role as a witness no longer gave him a reason to go on. One such reader wrote at the time:

> No one wants to believe it [that he committed suicide], not just for his sake, but for our own. It was as though Primo Levi held up a light for us—almost the only human being who did, in that worst place and time. It is as though . . . he helped us to regain our self-esteem. And if he laid down that light himself, was he not saying that he no longer believed in it—that he no longer believed in us?

He had carried so many burdens. He should not have been asked to carry that one as well.

Fifteen

To Live Outside Grace

Albert Camus's The Plague

In January 1942, in the North African city of Oran, a twenty-eight-year-old journalist and writer, who had been battling tuberculosis since adolescence, began spitting up blood. His wife, Francine, rushed him to a physician. Dr. Cohen used a needle to inject nitrogen into his chest cavity to collapse the lung, a treatment that was thought at the time to give the diseased organ a chance to recover. When he got home, the writer whispered, "I thought I was done for that time." Dr. Cohen told him his best hope of a cure was to escape the damp climate of Oran and rest and recover in the mountain air. Francine's relatives recommended a remote village in central France. It took them eight months to get there, but by August they had installed themselves in Le Panelier, a hamlet high in the Vivarais range, with a fringe of pines on the ridges all around and a kindly woman who gave them room and board.

By October he was feeling better, and Francine returned to her teaching job in Oran, while he completed his rest cure. Then on November 7, British and American forces landed in North Africa, and four days later the Germans occupied the whole of

France. He had booked his passage home, but returning now was out of the question. The writer was trapped in a remote hamlet, in an alien landscape, far from his family and the sun, water, and light of the Mediterranean, under German occupation.

It was here, alone with his illness, that Albert Camus began writing *The Plague*. He had already published *The Stranger* and *The Myth of Sisyphus*, but the themes of these two early books— exile in one's own life, the gulf between a man's need to understand "and the unreasonable silence of the world"—were no longer literary abstractions. They had become his reality. In his notebooks, he struggled, as he put it, to maintain "the unity of his personality." For the first time, he was living as a real exile, not a metaphorical one, severed from the two connections that had made sense of his life—his mother and his wife. Every time he coughed and tasted blood in his mouth, he felt his life ebbing away. In his notebook, he sought to find words for his desolation:

> What lights up the world and makes it bearable is the feeling which we usually have of our links with it—and more particularly what joins us to other people. . . . But on the days when . . . we realize that most of them have their backs to us . . . when we thus imagine how contingent and accidental everything in what we call a love or a friendship is, then the world goes back to darkness and we to that great cold from which human tenderness had for a moment rescued us.

Between November 1942 and September 1943, when he left for Paris to take a job offered by Gaston Gallimard, his publisher, the young writer sought the only consolation available to him: to give meaning to experiences that otherwise would have overwhelmed him.

If the process of how a writer consoles himself by putting words on a page is mysterious, even more so is the process by which he finds the metaphors that allow him to represent his own anguish. It is difficult to uncover how the idea of the plague came to preoccupy Camus's thoughts. He had made note of a typhus epidemic in Algeria in 1941, and he had jotted down in his notebook an odd phrase, *la peste libératrice*, a reference to an essay Antonin Artaud had written about the theater in the 1930s. How could a plague be liberating? Perhaps because the struggle against it could give purpose to disordered lives.

Camus began to see the German occupation as a plague, a moral infestation that cast everyone into a state of isolation and mutual suspicion. As he recorded in his notebook,

> Imagine an outbreak of typhus or of plague, things like that happen, they've happened before. In a way it's plausible. Well then, everything's changed, it's the desert that comes to you.

He began reading works from the desert, the Old Testament prophets who had called down the plague as God's punishment for human disobedience. He copied out Leviticus 26:25: "And I will bring a sword against you to execute the vengeance of the covenant. Though you withdraw into your cities, I will send a pestilence among you, and you will be delivered into the hand of the enemy."

As he read the Old Testament prophets who, like him, had wondered how pestilence could belong in a world ordered by a just God, he thought he understood their dire theodicies. "Man has had the power to become God's equal," he wrote, "and God has feared him and kept him in subjection." But if plagues had long been understood as punishments for human hubris, what about the plagues of today? How could one understand the catastrophe of occupation and defeat? How could Europe have plunged itself into such cruelty and violence? All around him, in the collaborationist and even the resistance press, despondent Frenchmen were coming to the conclusion that they had deserved their defeat in 1940. The Hebrew prophet's question— how to give meaning to the implacable wrath, if not of God, then of history—now pressed in upon everyone.

Camus read with an increasing sense of direction, following leads in footnotes, remembering texts from his days at the lycée and then university in Algiers: accounts of the Marseille plague of 1720, the plague in Florence that provided the setting for Boccaccio's *Decameron*, the plagues in Spain that led to the persecutions of the Jews, and recent journalistic accounts of plagues in China only twenty years earlier. In Daniel Defoe's *A Journal of the Plague Year*, published in 1722, he found a sentence that he used as an epigraph for *The Plague*:

> it is as reasonable to represent one kind of imprisonment
> by another, as it is to represent anything that really exists
> by that which exists not.

He was in a double imprisonment—illness and occupation— and the only remedy was to write himself out of it, "to represent one kind of imprisonment by another." He turned for inspiration to Melville's *Moby-Dick* and found there an example of how to organize an entire fiction around a single metaphor. His reading was voracious, and then when he could read no more, he wandered the hilly paths around Le Panelier, watching the leaves blow across the steep upland pastures. He came home and in the dark rooms of the farmhouse where he lodged, he wrote, "This strange wind that always runs along the edge of woods. Man's curious ideal: in the very bosom of nature, to make a dwelling for himself." At home in North Africa, swimming

in the sea had given him perfect oneness with nature. Now
he was walking alone in rainy fields a thousand miles from
home.

In order to make fiction come to life, he put his memories
of Oran to use: the smell of the narrow streets, the sun on shut-
ters, the chatter from cafés, sunbathing naked in the dunes,
drinking lemonade and feeling the sting of carbonated bub-
bles in his throat. He had to keep from being dragged down
into hopeless nostalgia, to keep at bay family memories—the
oversized raincoats his fierce grandmother bought him, his
seamstress aunt counting out buttons on the table, the bleak
poverty of his mother's room in Algiers. He managed to work
this very struggle with memory into the book that was slowly
taking shape:

> It was undoubtedly the feeling of exile—that sensation of
> a void which never left us, that irrational longing to hark
> back to the past or else to speed up the march of time, and
> those keen shafts of memory that stung like fire.

In creating the early scenes of the novel, when the plague
descends upon Oran, Camus used his own tormented awakening to the illusions about continuity and stability that had
been stripped away when his wife departed and the German
occupation began:

> Mothers and children, lovers, husbands and wives, who had
> a few days previously taken it for granted that their parting
> would be a short one, who had kissed each other goodbye
> on the platform and exchanged a few trivial remarks, sure
> as they were of seeing each other again after a few days,
> or at most, a few weeks, duped by our blind human faith
> in the near future and little if at all diverted from their

normal interests by this leave-taking—all these people found themselves, without the least warning, hopelessly cut off, prevented from seeing each other again, or even communicating with each other.

Instead of remaining trapped in the idea that his own condition was particular to himself, he began to understand that he shared his fate with others. When he went by train to the grim industrial town of Saint-Étienne for his pneumothorax injections, he studied his fellow passengers with a new curiosity, watching in particular an old peasant couple, "her face as wrinkled as parchment, his smooth face lit up by two clear eyes and a white moustache," clad in shiny and mended clothes, clutching worn-out suitcases. He began to move beyond solitary self-absorption into a fleeting compassion, an early glimmering of solidarity with strangers.

In North Africa, as a prodigiously gifted young man on the sidelines, he had written about the absurd; now he was living it. He knew he had to find a way to capture what it felt like to live in a time without hope, without narrative, without prospects of escape. He slowly discarded the noncombatant's disengagement that had been possible in Oran. Remaining a bystander had become untenable.

He wanted to make a claim, no longer about himself, but about the human situation: how you built shelter and home and cultivated relations of friendship and love, and how suddenly, without warning, these could be ripped apart. As he confided to his notebook in November 1942:

At the heart of an incomprehensible world, they had patiently built up a private, fully human universe in which their days were shared out between tenderness and habit. And now it was doubtless not enough to be separated from the world itself; the plague also had to separate them from their modest daily creations. After having blinded their minds, it tore out their hearts.

He would write fictional dialogue and then step back and address himself as if to clarify the ideas his art was struggling to make real:

> I want to express by means of the plague the suffocation from which we all suffered and the atmosphere of threat and exile in which we lived. At the same time, I want to extend this interpretation to the notion of existence in general.

All around him, resistance to the suffocating weight of occupation began to rise to the surface. In the winter and spring of 1943, he ventured out by train from his mountain retreat to Lyon. Through leads provided by Gaston Gallimard, his publisher in Paris, he made his first contacts with Pascal Pia, Francis Ponge, René Leynaud, and Louis Aragon. They were beginning to express their revolt through writing, in clandestine journals like *Confluences* or *Les Cahiers du Sud*. Camus did not always realize that these people were also organizing sabotage missions, blowing up railway lines, and making night pickups of matériel dropped from British planes. Around this time, he also befriended Raymond-Léopold Bruckberger, a jovial Dominican friar who was already an active resistant, and he wrote his first piece of writing for the resistance cause, his *Letters to a German Friend*.

It was based on a story Camus may have heard from Bruckberger, in which a German prison chaplain is accompanying a dozen French prisoners, including a teenage boy, in the truck taking them to their execution. The priest sits with the prisoners at the back of the truck and befriends the boy, offering him what comfort he can. Camus imagined their dialogue:

> "I didn't do anything," says the boy. Yes, says the priest, but that's not the question. "You've got to get ready to die." "Why doesn't anyone understand?" the boy says. "I'm your friend, and maybe I do understand. But it's late. I will be with you and so will God too. You'll see. It'll be easy."

Then, when the priest's back is momentarily turned, and the soldiers driving the truck are occupied in keeping to the road, the boy wiggles through a gap between the canvas and the truck and jumps, struggling to his feet and making off into the fields. Only the priest sees him, but he immediately taps on the truck cabin and orders the drivers to stop. The soldiers drag the boy back. The journey resumes. The priest officiates at the boy's last rites. The execution takes place.

No French priest, Camus wrote, would have done such a thing: consoling a frightened boy and then delivering him up to certain death. That, he exclaimed to the imagined German friend of these letters, was the coldness of heart that made them enemies.

This fury at false consolation was not a new note. It had already featured in his writing. In *The Stranger*, as Meursault awaits his death, he is visited by a priest who seeks to console him, only to be met with a cry of rage. What was new in *Letters to a German Friend* was that this rage was now accompanied by a deep commitment, for the first time, to actively join the resistance to the occupation.

While Camus was still at Le Panelier, the book he began as an attempt to capture the silent oppression of occupation now

became a book about resistance in the face of evil. One character, Bernard Rieux, the plague doctor, whose name Camus
borrowed from that of a doctor in a local town, gradually took
center stage as protagonist and narrator of the story.

As *The Plague* became the story of Rieux's resistance and
Camus's too, the writer's understanding of resistance was
framed by the desperate realities of 1942 and 1943. D-Day was
still a year away. Those who joined the resistance in this period
did so more in desperation than in hope. This inspired but also
fascinated Camus. He himself was struggling against an illness that did not then have a cure. How was it that men could
resist even when they knew victory was impossible? Explor-
ing this issue became central to his depiction of Rieux's battle
against the plague. In the novel, Rieux cannot cure anyone of
the plague; all he can do is comfort the dying. A growing sense
of futility crushes him, and in a dialogue with his friend Tarrou, Rieux begins to question a God who creates an illness that
defeats all efforts to cure it:

> "After all," the doctor repeated, then hesitated again, fix-
> ing his eyes on Tarrou, "it's something that a man of your
> sort can understand most likely, but, since the order of the
> world is shaped by death, mightn't it be better for God
> if we refuse to believe in Him, and struggle with all our
> might against death, without raising our eyes towards the
> heaven where He sits in silence?"
>
> Tarrou nodded.
>
> "Yes, but your victories will never be lasting; that's
> all."
>
> Rieux's face darkened.
>
> "Yes, I know that. But that's no reason for giving up
> the struggle."

"No reason, I agree. . . . Only, I now can picture what this plague must mean for you."

"Yes. A never-ending defeat."

This theme of resistance as an absurd encounter with "never-ending defeat" had been present in his *Myth of Sisyphus*, but Camus's handling of the theme in his earlier works had been a young man's five-finger exercises with grave and serious ideas. Now in Le Panelier in the spring of 1943, the question of why one should resist fate, even if the outcome might be hopeless, became a matter of life and death.

As Camus well knew, most of his contemporaries went along with the tide. In his trips to Lyon or Saint-Étienne, or when reading the newspapers from Paris, he could see how many of his contemporaries had accepted occupation and adjusted themselves to its realities. Even he had done so, to a small but significant degree, allowing Gallimard to publish *The Myth of Sisyphus* in 1943 without the chapter on Kafka, because German censors objected to any writing that touched on the thoughts of a Jew. Camus later published the entire book in an underground edition, with the Kafka chapter included, but in 1943 allowing it to appear mutilated by German censors took Camus into what Primo Levi was to call the "grey zone."

The central moral question all around him was why some people chose to aid, abet, or apologize for the occupation, while others rose in resistance. As the novel took shape, as the characters created themselves, Camus made a significant choice: he refused to judge or condemn his characters' choices, allowing them to express all the moral ambiguities he could see around him. A character called Rambert, for example, captures the part of Camus himself, whose first instinct had been to flee home to Algeria. When escape becomes impossible, however, Rambert decides to remain and joins the "sanitary brigades" fighting the plague. Other characters remain bystanders, while still others capitalize on the situation—the character Cottard slips into the black market to make a penny out of others' misery. The writer's detachment toward these choices did not come easily, but what rescued the book from becoming a tract for the times, a piece of resistance literature trapped in its own period, was precisely the way in which Camus's narrator refused judgment and condemnation.

There was one attitude toward the plague, however, that the writer did not allow to pass without judgment. The consolation offered by the German priest in *Letters to a German Friend* had revolted him, and now in the novel, the priest Paneloux begins to take shape as Dr. Rieux's chief antagonist. It is Paneloux to whom Camus gives a sermon calling on the dying city to seek consolation through repentance:

> A small still flame, in the dark core of human suffering . . . illuminates the shadowed paths that lead towards deliverance. It reveals the will of God in action, unfailingly transforming the dark valley of fears and groans towards the holy silence, the well-spring of all life. This, my friends, is the vast consolation I would hold out to you, so that when you leave this House of God you will carry away with you not only words of wrath, but a message, too, of comfort for your hearts.

Camus's narrator reports Paneloux's sermon with dry restraint, but Camus's own feelings about religious consolation surface in a subsequent scene, in which Paneloux and Rieux watch together through the night by the bed of a child screaming, writhing, and dying in agony. When the child's suffering is finally over, Rieux can stand no more, and as he angrily strides out of the hospital, he exclaims to Paneloux:

"Ah! That child anyhow was innocent—and you know it as well as I do."

Paneloux replies, clearly shaken:

"Perhaps we should love what we cannot understand."

To which Rieux responds,

"No father, I have a very different idea of love. And until my dying day I shall refuse to love a scheme of things in which children are put to torture."

Later in the novel, Paneloux gives a second sermon, in which he admits that the child's death has backed him up against a wall, forcing him either to accept Christ's promise of redemption or to reject it utterly. Paneloux makes his choice—he remains with faith, but it is a faith now chastened by suffering:

"My brothers, a time of testing has come for us all. We must believe everything or deny everything."

After the child's death, Paneloux says, and Rieux does not dissent, "We're working side by side for something that unites us—beyond blasphemy and beyond prayers." In this scene of two exhausted men harrowed by the death of a child, Camus seems to be saying, to himself as much as to his contemporaries, that in the face of evil and suffering, the old quarrel between the party of faith and the party of progress and science, between those who offer consolation and those who revolt against it, is irrelevant. Both beliefs are abstractions, and both can only fall silent when life turns merciless and unjust. In the face of death and evil, what came to matter most for Camus was not who was right, but who comforted the suffering.

One of the most moving characters in the book is the one who speaks least. Dr. Rieux's aging mother sits quietly, hour by hour, keeping watch over the slow, agonizing death of Rieux's friend Tarrou,

> her hands folded on her lap; in the dim light of the room she seemed no more than a darker patch of shadow. . . . Bending above the bed, she smoothed out the counterpane and as she straightened up, laid her hand for a moment on his moist tangled hair.

From his own mother, back in Algiers—a poor widow, an illiterate woman born half deaf who made her living as a seamstress and cleaner—Camus had learned that the most enduring comfort could be wordless. Indeed, there were moments when words were too much. You just had to sit there by the bed and hold someone's hand, give them water, change their clothes, remove their wastes, help to reduce their suffering. This was the only comfort that mattered.

When he left Le Panelier for good in September 1943 and went to Paris to take up an office with his publisher Gallimard and work on the clandestine newspaper *Combat*, Camus took the half-finished manuscript with him. It became harder and harder to complete it as, once again, history took over: D-Day, then the joyful, terrifying liberation of Paris. In August 1944, he assumed editorial direction of *Combat*. He was now thirty years old, meeting Sartre and de Beauvoir for the first time, falling in love with the actress Maria Casarès. He was the handsome outsider whom everybody in Paris wanted to meet, and yet always, thanks to his writing, thanks to his Algerian origins, he remained apart, even as he entered the most turbulent period of political engagement of his entire life. The manuscript, which he had begun in poverty, illness, and isolation in 1942, now had to be completed as he became a celebrity whose editorials in *Combat* became a touchstone for the Parisian intellectual elite.

Here the manuscript came to his rescue, for in completing it he could withdraw from the growing clamor around him and use it to define his own distance from the fashionable intellectuals of his time. In Dr. Rieux, he found a character who could express his own disenchantment with the bad faith that accompanied the lust for vengeance against wartime collaborators. Like Max Weber before him, Camus came to despise the self-righteous ethics of conviction that sprang so easily from the lips of his intellectual friends after the liberation. Where was the sober ethics of responsibility that the times actually needed? As he drew *The Plague* to a close, Camus had Rieux say, as he walks among the crowds of people in the city, "he had a feeling no peace was possible to him henceforth, any more than there can be an armistice for a mother bereaved of her son or for a man who buries his friend." As Rieux watches the crowds celebrating the infection's mysterious retreat, he delivers a warning, not just for his times, but for our own:

> He knew what those jubilant crowds did not know but could have learned from books: that the plague bacillus never dies or disappears for good; that it can lie dormant for years and years in furniture and linen-chests; that it bides its time in bedrooms, cellars, trunks and bookshelves; and that perhaps the day would come when, for the bane and the enlightenment of men, it roused up its rats again and sent them forth to die in a happy city.

The Plague finally was published in 1947. The French intellectuals who welcomed Camus into the world of Saint-Germain-
des-Prés in 1944 and 1945—Simone de Beauvoir, Jean-Paul
Sartre, and Roland Barthes—were condescending about the
young Algerian's book when it appeared, believing that Camus
had been mistaken to identify the plague as a "natural virus"
and instead should have "situated" it in its historical moment
and turned it into an accusation against the corrupt classes and
parties who had made the French collapse possible. Camus
refused this path, believing that his message was not linked to
any particular time.

The Plague's publication led, a decade later, to the Nobel
Prize, an honor he came to feel was a disaster for himself and
for his writing. It was an irony of which he was keenly aware
that the most productive, imaginative, and resourceful period
he had ever known as an artist had been in that winter of
1942–43, when he had been penniless, alone, and exiled, and
in the deepest sense had needed the writing that became *The
Plague*. At the end of his life, he was struggling to return to
the sources of his creativity—that bare-bones yet inextinguish-
ably happy childhood with his silent mother in a small flat
in working-class Algiers—and he was carrying with him the
first 160 pages of a manuscript called *The First Man*, which he
hoped would silence the critics who said he was a burnt-out
case, when on January 4, 1960, he died instantly in a car accident near Sens, on the outskirts of Paris.

IN 2020, WHEN OUR OWN time came, we read or reread *The
Plague,* clearing it off shelves everywhere, this time with a
shock of recognition that a piece of fiction could have so clearly
foreseen our situation and the refuge we took in illusion—the
deceptions of our leaders, the inequalities of fate and fortune

that prosperity enabled us to ignore, the lip service paid to the idea that "we were all in this together," the far less noble reality. The pandemic brought home our equal vulnerability, but in Camus's words, "nobody wanted that kind of equality."

Reading Camus again helped us to open our hearts to those like Rieux who were fighting, at the cost of their lives, to keep us safe. Camus would not have been surprised to see the windows of apartments in New York, Milan, Paris, London, and Barcelona opening at an appointed hour for complete strangers to applaud other strangers, suited up in personal protection equipment, who were, at that moment, struggling to save mothers, fathers, sons, and daughters, in hospitals across town.

Camus's insistence on the plague's absurdity, its meaninglessness, was perhaps the harder of his messages to accept. It challenged the consolation we had derived, even without realizing it, from illusions we may have had about the onward and upward path of progress. Here was a virus that seemed to plunge us back in time to 1918–20, to 1720 in Marseilles, or 1665 in London. Instead of running forward, time seemed to be running backward to a past we thought was irrevocably behind us. The awakening did not stop there. The death toll laid bare the illusion that we had sufficient hospitals, beds, ventilators to deal with any public health risk. It exposed the shocking fragility of our systems of social care for the aged and the indigent, just as Camus had told us it would.

So suddenly, by force of loss and misfortune, in the winter, spring, summer, and autumn of 2020, as our world seemed to plummet into darkness and silence, we read Camus again with unwelcome recognition. We had so much less control of history than we supposed, so much less control of illness than we imagined. The speed with which our society was brought to a standstill acted to humble us all and put into question every secular faith.

What we discovered—and Camus also told us this would happen—was our reliance upon and our need for each other. There was no consolation other than that, no faith other than the conviction, reinforced by our observance of the devotion of care workers and doctors and volunteers everywhere, that we would not let each other die if we could possibly help it.

At the end of Camus's novel, Rieux reflects on what he had learned from his time in hell:

> The evil that is in the world always comes out of ignorance, and good intentions may do as much harm as malevolence, if they lack understanding. On the whole, men are more good than bad.

How can a pandemic possibly tell us that? Yet Camus insisted upon it, because such a faith, however unverifiable, is basic to any idea of hope. It is a passage that recalls the question raised by Primo Levi's life: whether the virtue of the few men like him consoles us for the cruelty and cowardice of the many. Dr. Rieux hopes so, and Camus did too, but that is all the consolation he would allow us.

In 1945, as the war ended, Camus wrote a passage in his notebooks that he entitled "Meaning of My Work":

> So many men lack grace. How can one live without grace? We must really get down to it and do what Christianity has never done: concern ourselves with the damned.

In one of his last interviews, in 1959, an embattled Camus exclaimed, in answer to a journalist's hostile question:

> I don't see why I should apologize for being interested in those who live outside Grace. It is high time we began

concerning ourselves with them, since they are the most numerous.

We are not angels, we are not blessed, Camus is saying. There is nothing to prevent the plague from erupting and scything through our certainties. This, he wanted us to understand, is what it means to "live outside Grace." It means living beyond an ultimate certainty or final consolation, beyond any belief that history has any meaning that a human being can understand. But he did not leave it there. To live outside Grace is not to live without hope or examples of how one should live. There are always good examples, and the ones he wanted us to see were very real and very specific: an old woman silently watching by the bedside of a stranger, keeping him company in the night, so he would not die alone.

Sixteen

Living in Truth

Václav Havel's Letters to Olga

He has been dead now for some time, and his life—as a playwright, essayist, dissident, political prisoner, and finally president of his country—has receded from many memories. He belongs to a past that cannot be recovered now, the heroic moment of transition—when the Berlin Wall came down, when Nelson Mandela walked free, when we dared to think history would turn out differently than it has. Václav Havel is most often remembered today for one remark, his answer to a journalist who interviewed him about the wellsprings of his life in 1986, three years before he led his country into freedom:

> Hope is definitely not the same thing as optimism. It is not the conviction that something will turn out well, but the certainty that something makes sense, regardless of how it turns out.

This remark has taken on a life of its own and figures to this day in speeches by people who quote it because it inspires them to stick with apparently hopeless causes. It is a remark with the authority of a whole life behind it. Through three decades, through failure, imprisonment, and self-doubt, he had stuck with a cause that, to his own astonishment, was to lead him to the presidency.

In the warm glow of retrospect, it's easy to assume that figures like Mandela and Havel always believed victory would be theirs one day, but there were times, both for Mandela and for Havel, when hope seemed truly gone. Their steadfastness is better understood as a very human victory over despair.

In Havel's case, those sentences about hope were meant, at least in 1986, as another salvo in a bitter argument with the great Czech writer Milan Kundera about whether change was possible in Communist Czechoslovakia. Kundera's novel *The Unbearable Lightness of Being* had immortalized the moral atmosphere in Prague after 1968, when Havel, then in his thirties, was circulating petitions for the release of political prisoners who had been arrested after Soviet tanks occupied his country. Kundera has one of the characters in his novel say that it was futile to sign such petitions. They would not secure anyone's release. Nearly twenty years later, Kundera's position, or at least the position of his character, still rankled. Petitions made a difference, Havel insisted, especially if you were in prison. Knowing that someone was trying, however hopelessly, to get you released helped you survive. How could Kundera have known that? Since 1975, he had been safely in Paris, while Havel had stayed in Prague and done prison time for defying the regime as the leading spokesman for the entire dissident movement. Worse, in abandoning faith in such gestures, Kundera had succumbed to a fatalism that made any politics seem like a waste of time. As an intellectual Marxist who had once believed he had his hands on the steering wheel of history, Kundera was now purveying a world-weary resignation in his fiction, writing that history was "a clever divinity that could only destroy us, cheat us, misuse, or at best play jokes on us."

Havel had no time for Kundera's detachment. History, he told his interviewer, "is not something that takes place elsewhere: it takes place here. We all contribute to making it"— Kundera with his novels, the journalist with his interviews, the dissidents with their petitions. If we all make history, we can also inflect its path, each in our own small way. This had been Havel's path: dogged refusal to bow to the regime and years in prison. Three years after that interview—when Havel stood on the balcony in Wenceslas Square in front of 250,000 people and the Communist regime slunk away in defeat, he might well have felt that history had ended up on his side. Yet he was too chastened by his experience to allow himself much euphoria. In a life of dissident commitment, he had learned that human beings do make their history, but not as they intend, nor even as they hope.

If that is what he came to believe, how then did he keep hope alive?

Havel himself asked this question, over and over, but never more so than in the summer of 1982, when he was in Bory prison, in the third year of his sentence for defying the Communist regime. He never liked to talk about his time in prison, but for a forty-year-old middle-class intellectual with soft hands, it was a rude awakening. He had been detained before, in 1977, but this was his first experience of prison labor. At Heřmanice prison, he had to struggle to make his quota in the scrap iron yard, learning how to use an acetylene torch. At other times, his job was to dismantle electrical cables in the greasy filth and cold of an unheated machine shed. The prison warden singled out his most famous prisoner for special abuse and sent him to "the hole" for trying to talk a fellow prisoner

out of suicide. When he was transferred to Bory prison, he
worked in the prison laundry, stuffing semen-stained sheets
into the washing machines.

The other prisoners—mostly petty criminals—generally
left him alone, but life with them was suffocatingly close and
ultimately exhausting. In order to survive, he remained silent,
wary, locked inside his own head, the only place where he could
be free. He dreamed of life outside, haunted by odors from his
childhood—the way his dog smelled when he came out of a
muddy river swim and shook himself; the dry smell of theater
costumes on the racks of the Theatre on the Balustrade where
he had worked in his twenties; the smell of hay in the Czech
countryside beyond the prison walls. He lived for Saturday
night, when he could find a quiet moment on his bunk and
write a four-page letter to his wife, Olga.

One night in May 1982, along with the other prisoners, he
was watching the nightly weather report on television, delivered by a woman from the state meteorological service. In the
middle of her report, suddenly the sound cut out and the woman
stood there, aware that something was wrong but unable to do
anything about it. As Havel reported in a letter to Olga,

> the mantle of routine fell away and before us there sud-
> denly stood a confused, unhappy and terribly embarrassed
> woman: she stopped talking, looked in desperation at us,
> then somewhere off to the side, but there was no help
> from that direction. She could scarcely hold back her tears.
> Exposed to the view of millions, yet desperately alone,
> thrown into an unfamiliar, unexpected and unresolvable
> situation, incapable of conveying through mime that she
> was above it all (by shrugging her shoulders and smiling,
> for instance) drowning in embarrassment, she stood there
> in all the primordial nakedness of human helplessness.

Here was a moment he could identify with, the terrifying moment when you "dry," when you forget your lines and stand naked in front of an audience, your persona dropping away, revealing the quaking human being beneath. The other prisoners may well have been whistling or hooting in malicious glee to see the humbling of a loyal servant of the regime—lip service to the party line was obligatory even in the Czech meteorological service—but Havel was so filled with compassion that he wanted, absurdly, to reach out and stroke her hair.

The scene, he told Olga, touched the core of his being. He wrote Olga that he felt responsible "for everything"—crazy as it might seem—including the silent suffering of this stranger. Why did he feel responsible for her? Because in her naked embarrassment, he saw himself. "Responsibility," he realized once again, had to be the anchor of his life.

At the time, Havel had been reading an essay his brother Ivan had sent him, called "No Identity," by the French philosopher Emmanuel Levinas. Levinas too had been in prison. A soldier in the French army, he was captured in 1940 and sent to a prisoner of war camp in Germany, where he labored in a forestry brigade for five years. A Lithuanian Jew, he escaped the death camps only because the Germans had to acknowledge that he was a prisoner of war, protected by the Geneva Conventions. Levinas came to understand his imprisonment as a servitude in the ancient meaning of the Hebrew Bible. He cited Psalm 119: "I am a stranger on the earth, do not hide from me your commandments." In the essay, he wrote, "the condition of being strangers and slaves in the land of Egypt brings man closer to his neighbor. In their condition of being strangers, men seek one another. No one is at home. The memory of this servitude creates humanity." Havel read these words with a shock of recognition. He also noted Levinas's remark:

Responsibility does establish identity, but we are not responsible because of our identity; instead we have an identity
because we are responsible.

This remark of Levinas helped Havel understand his upsurge
of compassion for the television meteorologist: they were kin,
and he had a responsibility to her, native to his very being.
In the same way, he now realized, when he used to get on a
streetcar in Prague late at night, he always put a coin in the
slot, even if the conductor wasn't looking, even if there were
no passengers looking on either. He did so because he felt an
invigilating eye that was not his own but an absolute standard
of conduct to which he felt accountable.

No, he told Olga, in one of the many letters he devoted
to thinking through the impact of Levinas's essay, it was not
God who was watching, but "this intimate-universal partner
of mine—who is sometimes my conscience, sometimes my
hope, sometimes my freedom and sometimes the mystery of
the world." Whatever it was, it was too intimate to worship,
and besides, Havel was not a practicing Christian. Neverthe-
less, religious categories were the ones he used when thinking
through his deepest longings. He felt he was "continuously,
always" facing judgment. "Nothing that has happened can ever
un-happen, everything remains . . . and I too remain there—
condemned to be with myself till the end of time, just as I am."

For a man struggling with anguish at the thought that all
his sacrifices as a dissident had been in vain, a man suddenly
moved to tears by a stranger's plight and feeling responsible for
her and for others, all this came as a liberating gust of purpose.
With purpose came hope and a feeling of personal redemption.

Once this breakthrough occurred, other more intimate
emotions rose to the surface. He had to face the fact that he was

utterly dependent on Olga. She—and his brother Ivan—were his only contacts with the outside world. She was the one who visited every quarter, who delivered the parcel with Earl Grey tea and cigarettes and shaving lotion, along with news and gossip from his circle of dissidents and theater people.

She was his first love, a working-class woman—"as straight as a ruler." He met her in Prague in the late 1950s when she was a theater usher three years his senior and he an adolescent apprentice stagehand. Her adamantine character proved irresistible to the brilliant, voluble, uncertain, middle-class young man. Besides, his mother feared and disliked her, which sealed a pact of rebellion between the two young lovers. By the time of his imprisonment, they had been together for more than twenty years and her blunt and cutting assessments of people came to be his touchstone. She was his first reader, his fiercest critic, his muse, but by the time he went to prison, years of his infidelities had left their marriage in tatters.

When the police came to arrest him, he was not at home with Olga, but with Anna Kohoutová, the ex-wife of a dissident friend. When he entered prison, Olga's forbearance, even though he always confessed his infidelities, was exhausted. Her letters to him were infrequent, and no wonder. He filled the letters with demands—this toothpaste, not that, this type of tea, not that—and in one even asked Olga to pass a friendly message to Anna. Their early meetings were tense with emotions neither felt like sharing, still less with the watching guards. She punished him in the only way she could: with imperious silence, leaving him to beg her for replies. Prison taught him how vulnerable he was, how much he needed her. He took to saying that she had become his rock, his one certainty. She never deserted him, but she would not have been above manipulating his guilt. Squirm he did, but any man who took strength from adherence to moral principles had no choice but to stay with a woman who reminded him, lest he forget, what kind of man he ought to be.

Moral authority is one thing; love and desire another. The letters are cold documents, records of an indissoluble bond, but one based on an unsparing reckoning with each other. When his friends asked him why the *Letters to Olga* were so impersonal, so rarely offering her words of comfort, reassurance, and, yes, love, he replied that people had to remember the letters had to pass the prison censor. Besides, he added, he and Olga had "never made a habit of professing our feelings for each other. We're both reticent, though this reticence has a different source in each of us: pride in her case, shame in mine."

He sought her forgiveness, but he also sought to forgive himself. He was haunted by an episode that went back to his first detention in Ruzyně prison, January–May 1977, awaiting trial for his role as a dissident spokesman. He was questioned by a clever interrogator who, in Havel's rueful words, exploited his every weakness: his middle-class eagerness to please, his cleverness, and his sense of intellectual superiority. He played on these to extract from Havel an agreement to step aside as spokesman for the dissident movement in return for early release. Havel could excuse himself for being frightened and disoriented; what he couldn't forgive was that he had thought he had outwitted his interrogator. He realized, too late, that he had disgraced himself in the eyes of the dissident circles in Prague. When he was released, his friends were understanding, but he went through the darkest period of his life: "weeks, months, years in fact of silent desperation, self-castigation, shame, inner humiliation, reproach and uncomprehending questioning." In perhaps the closest moment in their entire exchange, he confessed that only Olga had any inkling of how desperate he had been.

This all-too-human lapse, unlike his infidelities, compromised the core of his moral authority as the spokesman of a movement that, after all, had precious little other than moral authority to give it weight. As he neared the end of his sentence, he knew that he would be incapable of resuming leadership outside if he failed to stanch the shame that seeped from this unhealed wound. With the help of Levinas and the catharsis of compassion for the weatherwoman, he had rediscovered the roots of his commitment to others. Now he had to forgive himself for a critical failure to live by what he believed.

"Living in truth" left him no margin for false consolation. To forgive himself, he had to take responsibility, all the way down to the depths of his being, for his weakness and failure in the interrogation rooms of Ruzyně prison. In the climactic passage of *Letters to Olga*, he wrote:

> It is not hard to stand behind one's successes. But to accept responsibility for one's failures, to accept them unreservedly as failures that are truly one's own, that cannot be shifted somewhere else or onto something else, and actively to accept—without regard for any worldly interests, no matter how well disguised, or for well-meant advice—the price that has to be paid for it: that is devilishly hard! But only thence does the road lead—as my experience, I hope, has persuaded me—to the renewal of sovereignty over my own affairs, to a radically new insight into the mysterious gravity of my existence as an uncertain enterprise, and to its transcendental meaning.

To own failure was to stop pretending that the person responsible was a discarded self and to accept that this person was always and eternally you. To accept this failed self was to stop pushing your shame away. This was what it truly took to "live in truth."

It was also to understand, going forward, that he could never take his own virtue for granted, that he must be aware how vulnerable he was. All it had taken in that interrogation room at Ruzyně, he said, was a "moment of inattention," of "careless trust that one is what one is." He would never trust what he was again. His life no longer made sense to him as a destiny but rather as a maze of perilous choices stretching out into the future, in which every misstep or wrong turn carried the risk of ultimate betrayal.

By the summer of 1982, his letters were being passed around the Havels' circle in Prague, and it was his idea that some of them should be published in a samizdat edition. Calling them *Letters to Olga* acknowledged her role as his confessor. A philosopher friend wrote an introduction, which made the connection with Boethius. The letters were thus introduced as a contemporary *Consolation of Philosophy*. The similarities and differences between the two texts are worth noting. In both a man seeks consolation from a woman—in Boethius's case from Philosophia, in Havel's from a real human being, but one he had betrayed. In Boethius, the consolation he seeks is to be at peace with his fate. In Havel, the consolation he craves is forgiveness.

Havel's remark about hope and his injunction "to live in truth" deserve their authority because he paid for them through a laborious reckoning with himself. Having accepted that there were no excuses, none, that would justify his moment of weakness before the interrogator, he came to the end of imprisonment believing he had earned the right to return to freedom because he had forgiven himself.

After he was released from prison in early 1983, "living in truth" didn't become any easier. Some incorrigible elements of his character did not change. He resumed his affair with Anna, and then with another woman, and Olga took up with another man. Yet he never left Olga. She remained, to the end, his rock, his confidante, and his judge.

Within seven years of leaving jail, he was president of his country. At first, he was euphoric at the chance to shape history and flattered by the attention that his extraordinary life attracted in the capitals of the world. In Washington and London, Paris and Berlin, he was showered with prizes and doctorates, but there was always a detached part of himself that looked on like a spectator. He parodied his own life cheerfully: "little Honza—although everyone tells him it's hopeless—beats his head against the wall for so long that the wall eventually collapses and he becomes king and rules and rules and rules for thirteen long years."

His life story became a cliché that gave hope to others, and that may have been his justification for staying in the presidency so long, but even his closest friends wondered why he stuck it out. So much of his time in office was a via dolorosa, but he trudged uphill all the way. The country split in two during his presidency; he was routinely outfoxed by Prime Minister Václav Klaus; he warned his people, in eloquent speeches, to beware of the corruption, selfishness, and spiritual emptiness, but the people didn't listen. In 1996, Olga died of cancer. He remarried soon after, and his choice, a much younger actress, attracted derision. He was adamant: her love and her determination to get him medical attention during one frightening episode had saved his life, and wasn't he entitled to a little happiness?

Criticisms of him mounted, yet he did not leave Prague Castle. All day long, the exercise of power confirmed, he said, "that you really exist, that you have your own undeniable identity, that with every word and deed you are leaving a highly visible mark on the world." At the same time, power robbed him of his self: his speeches became defensive and formulaic;

his associates stopped telling him the truth; he no longer had any time to be himself or even be with himself. If he had made "living in truth" the test of an authentic life, now in the twilight of his years in power, often chronically depressed, he must have wondered, more and more often, whether he was living a lie.

After he finally stepped down in 2003, he did enjoy a victory lap in Washington. The Americans gave him an office at the Library of Congress and a house in Georgetown. The great and the good came to Madeleine Albright's house to meet him, and he discoursed, in his inimitable English, on the state of world affairs. The American president received him at the White House, and he enjoyed it all, even those wry moments in the afterlife of a famous person when a complete stranger mistakes you for someone else. In an elevator in the US Capitol, a young man told him that he had always been his idol; after Havel thanked him, the young man asked him whether he had really written *The Unbearable Lightness of Being*. To be mistaken for one of your main antagonists was, Havel thought, "a truly Kunderian situation."

His humor and self-deprecation carried him through the later years, but at the end, he was more and more often alone, in the country house at Hrádeček that he had shared with Olga, musing to himself that he was running away from the public, from politics, from people, perhaps even from his new wife, and perhaps even from himself.

He wondered why he kept puttering about the house, keeping it tidy, why "everything had to be aligned with everything, nothing can be left hanging over the edge of a table or be crooked." Why did he keep the refrigerator filled when he could eat scarcely any of the food? It was as if he were constantly expecting someone to visit. But who? A beautiful woman? A savior? Old friends? In fact, he didn't really want to see anyone anymore.

He thought he knew why. "I am constantly preparing for the last judgment, for the highest court from which nothing can be hidden, which appreciates everything that should be appreciated, and which will, of course, notice anything that is not in its place."

The last judge would notice little things like that, he thought, because he would be a stickler like him. But then why should he care? Because, he said, "my existence ruffled the surface of Being" and the little ripple he had left—as dissident, prisoner, and president—had changed the world. So his life must be judged, evaluated, weighed in the balance. He would stay here alone, "just a bundle of nerves" waiting for the reckoning. When it came, six years later, he was in his country house, with only a nursing sister to watch him breathe his last. For all his faults, few men who made history were more unrelenting in their self-examination. An extrovert who had learned introspection in prison, he found a way to live in truth, as best he could, and to inspire others to do the same. At the end, he would have waited for the judge's sentence, knowing there was nothing he could be judged for that he had not, long since, judged himself for. In that knowledge, there might have been some consolation.

Seventeen

The Good Death

Cicely Saunders and the Hospice

Of my mother's last hours, nearly thirty years ago, I remember mostly the sounds: the squeak of shoes on the linoleum in the hospital corridor outside her room, the monitors and machines pinging and clicking, a radio somewhere in the distance, and the hoarse rasping of her breathing as she blindly tossed and turned. My brother stood at the head of her bed and tried to massage her shoulders, and I sat by her trying to keep hold of her hand. She couldn't have known we were there. After some time, I can't remember how long, a young Asian doctor in green scrubs came in, flipped open the chart at the foot of her bed, surveyed the scene, and asked if she needed another injection. Her breathing had just ceased; she was lying inert on her side. She no longer needed anything at all. The doctor gave us a bemused shake of his head, the nurses ushered us out, and I never saw my mother again.

When my father suffered a sudden heart attack during a visit to the little town in Quebec where his Russian mother and father had lived the last years of their lives, he was taken by ambulance to the intensive care ward of a hospital forty minutes away. My brother, then living in Toronto, managed to reach the hospital and visit him, but when visiting hours were over, he had to leave him alone, hooked up to drips and monitors, looking bereft and frightened. He died that night. I was on the other side of the Atlantic and couldn't get there in time.

These hospital deaths left me with an enduring sorrow. I wish my parents could have had a good death, where we could have been together and talked, one last time. But there was no time, and there was also no place. That hospital ward, that intensive care unit, was no place for consolation. In the absence of such a place, death leaves deep scars on the living.

IN THE MID-TWENTIETH CENTURY, PHYSICIANS, nurses, and patients on both sides of the Atlantic sought to change how we die. They had to change how medicine understood the physician's role, and how we all understand what awaits us at the end of life. For many doctors, perhaps including the ones who treated my parents, death was failure. If a patient was dying, if no further treatment was possible, then hope was gone, and a doctor should leave the rest to nurses. What a new generation of physicians and nurses began to understand was that even when no further treatment was possible, hope still remained—if not for a cure then for making peace with life, for reconciliation with estranged children, for healing old psychic wounds, for putting affairs in order and leaving existence with a sense that everything had been taken care of. Dying was not the end of hope: even in the shadow of death there was yet more to accomplish and to resolve. In this insight lay the possibility of consolation and potential for an institution where it could take place.

Many people contributed to this change, but no one made a more significant contribution than an English doctor named

Cicely Saunders. She reinvented an old institution, the hospice, which dated back to the Middle Ages, and created a twentieth-century version in which advances in the medical treatment of terminal pain and the compassionate nursing of dying patients were combined in a new institutional setting that allowed the dying the time to be reconciled with death and to meet it with as much serenity as possible. In this way, she helped create a new secular practice of consolation, crafted from nursing, psychology, pain management, and therapy. Like Elisabeth Kübler-Ross in the United States, Saunders believed that most of us, faced with the prospect of death, begin with resistance and denial, but nearly all of us reach a stage of reconciliation with our fate. In this, Kübler-Ross and Saunders believed, there was hope for escaping the fear of death itself. Each drew upon the traditions described in this book—for Saunders it was Job, the Psalms, and Camus; for Kübler-Ross, Freud, Jung, and their disciples—but each turned also to a source most of their male physician colleagues had ignored: the words of their dying patients. They discovered that the anguish of dying was not just about the pain and the fear. It was also the feeling, sometimes desperate, sometimes enraged, that they were not being listened to and were even being denied the truth. What the dying needed was to talk about their lives, to make sense of them, to forgive themselves and others, to reconcile themselves to the ending of it all. Forcing these issues into the center of medical practice required Saunders to confront the entrenched gender-based division of labor in the hospital medicine of the 1960s. In the hospitals of that era, therapy and treatment remained the domain of mostly male doctors, pain medication was the job of mostly female nurses, and consolation was left to the chaplains. Saunders collapsed these roles and helped create a new practice of palliative care in which these roles were combined, and consolation became as important to medical practice as good nursing and pain medication. Thanks to the palliative care movement that she helped to create, there are now hospices in most countries in the world and palliative care in most hospitals.

CICELY SAUNDERS BEGAN HER LIFE in medicine in wartime London, training as a nurse, but it was after the war that she began to understand that her life's work was in caring for the dying. It began by accident. One morning in January 1948, when she was working as a medical social worker at St Thomas' hospital in London, Saunders received a call from a landlady in Soho telling her that one of her recently discharged patients had collapsed. When she got to his lodgings, the patient, David Tasma, was being loaded into an ambulance. He asked her if he was dying. No one else had told him the truth. She told him that yes, his bowel cancer was terminal. He asked whether she would visit him. "What else could I do?" she remembered thinking.

She visited him nearly every evening for the next two months in a crowded general ward of a London hospital, listening to his whispered words amid the noise of dishes and trolleys and footfalls and groans on either side of them. He was a Polish Jew, only forty years old, who had arrived in London before the war and worked as a waiter at Biedak's kosher restaurant in Denmark Street. He had lost all of his family during the war and now faced death alone except for this tall, upper-middle-class thirty-year-old spinster at his bedside. He confessed that he felt he was dying without having lived, without, as she later said, "leaving even a ripple on the pool." Her visits were the only proof that he mattered to anybody.

In the noisy ward, separated from the other patients only by curtains, she began talking about how there must be a better place than this for dying patients. She shared some early thoughts about a place where patients would have better pain medication, more privacy, family visits, and help with sorting out their affairs. Brightening, he told her he had a life insurance policy and would make her a beneficiary so she could create such a place. She tried to dissuade him, but he persisted. He was the grandson of rabbis, he told her, but the faith of his forefathers had left no anchor he could hold on to. She was a fervent evangelical Christian and hoped she could convert him, but he said he liked her too much to "believe just because I like you."

As he weakened, he asked her to "say something to comfort me" and she began reciting "the Lord is my shepherd" from the twenty-third Psalm. When he asked her to go on, she recited the words from Psalm 95, "Oh come let us sing unto the Lord," and then from Psalm 121, "I will lift up mine eyes to the hills." He asked for more, but when she reached into her bag and pulled out the Bible to read to him, he shook his head and said, "I only want what is in your mind and in your heart." On February 25, she visited him as he drifted into unconsciousness. She said goodbye and took the bus home, learning when she called the hospital the next day that he had died an hour after she left; she had been the last person he had seen.

Saunders dated the beginning of her life's work to those weeks in David Tasma's company. After he died, she wanted to leave social work to go into nursing, but a doctor told her to become a physician since, as he put it, "most doctors desert their dying patients," and she would be one who wouldn't. Besides, he said, there was so much to learn about pain control. She went back to school and, after qualifying, began working as a physician at a Catholic hospice in London. It embodied the compassionate practices of a nursing tradition that dated back to medieval times, but was almost, as she put it, "entirely innocent" of modern advances in pain control. She made pain management her specialty. At that time, patients could secure pain relief only if they were actually suffering; it was as if they had to "earn" their medications. She substituted a regimen of regular but light doses of medication that sought to anticipate pain and remove it, if possible, altogether. She demonstrated that this approach would not create drug dependency. More importantly, if patients could be helped to remain conscious and pain free, they would have the time to come to terms with their deaths. She understood that for cancer patients, pain control was the essential precondition for any process of reckoning with the end of a life.

In the summer of 1960, she had her second life-changing encounter, with another Polish patient named Antoni Michniewicz, an aristocratic and highly educated engineer dying of bone cancer. He was fifty-eight, fifteen years her senior. Over a period of six months, their relationship grew ever more confessional. It was she who told him his illness was terminal. Instead of turning away or reacting with despair, he looked at her tenderly and asked whether it had been difficult for her to tell him. She said it had been very difficult.

When he told her that he had fallen in love with her, she later recalled, "my world was suddenly unmade without warning." It was a relationship between physician and patient that violated every professional norm, but the Catholic nurses protected her and allowed the relationship to develop. She visited him every evening, and they sat in a six-person bay, with only curtains separating them from other patients, and talked with the quiet intensity that final moments make possible. He kissed her hand, and she held it to his face. He admired her watch. It was the one left to her by David Tasma. "I can give you nothing," he told her, "nothing but sorrow." She whispered, "There has not been anyone like you."

He was a devout Catholic, she an evangelical Protestant,

and their religious faith sustained them both in his final weeks as he rapidly lost weight and began to slip into longer periods of unconsciousness. He died one evening in August when she had just gone out to look in on another patient. The next day, when she came in for her hospital rounds, his bed was empty and she stood in the doorway, unable to move.

She had accompanied a man to the edge of death and had fallen deeply and lastingly in love. Their weeks together, she later said, were her *Liebestod*. Their time together transformed her sense of what was possible when time was running out. "Time isn't a matter of length," she told an interviewer years later. "It's a matter of depth." When dying patients told her they had run out of time, she replied that there was always enough time, if you could be with someone to share it.

After Antoni's death, she was tormented by dreams of him and wrote agonizing descriptions of imagined encounters with him in the afterlife. At the same time, she entered the most intellectually productive period of her life, when she put up the scaffolding of ideas and practices on which her later work was to be built. She read voraciously: the Jewish philosopher Martin Buber, Viktor Frankl's Holocaust memoir, *Man's Search for Meaning*, Søren Kierkegaard's *The Gospel of Sufferings*, together with the work of American physicians from the 1930s whose studies of the dying had been ignored. For spiritual comfort, she turned to the French religious mystic Teilhard de Chardin; for psychological insights, she read Nietzsche, that connoisseur of spiritual and mental anguish, and Camus's *The Plague*, paying particular attention to the scene in which the Jesuit and the doctor, after trying in vain to save a dying child, confess that despite their different faiths they are enlisted in the same battle to save the living. For her, the scene was only too real. Once, on a nursing ward in wartime London, she had spent a long night listening to the wails of a child dying of spinal meningitis. Fifty years later, she recalled, she could still hear the sound.

She was the rare doctor who had also been a nurse, someone who knew about the indignities of untended pain and the loneliness of final illness, but who also knew how much difference a quiet routine, a hot water bottle, a tuck-in at night could make to a dying person:

> Dying patients usually like to be propped up a little or to be on their sides. They only remain flat on their backs because they cannot move or ask. They need pillows so arranged that their heads do not fall forwards. They are often frightened of the dark and long for light and fresh air. They get little comfort from oxygen and hate a mask. Their tossings are often attempts to throw off the bed-clothes which must be light.

This matter-of-fact attention to detail was the form that compassion took with her, the same humble attention to detail that Tolstoy achieved in his unforgettable story *The Death of Ivan Ilyich*, in which the one person who actually comforts the dying state counselor in his lonely hours of agony is the old servant who sits with him night after night, massaging his feet. Saunders knew how to massage feet, treat bedsores, turn patients over, prevent the humiliating irritations and infections from catheters. She had a warm sense of humor about her patients: the old men who would beg her not to wash them all over, since, as they whispered, "they washed me too much" in some other hospital, or the old alcoholics dying of cancer on the hospice wards who would sneak out to drink in the pub, only to sneak back into bed at night, thinking she hadn't noticed. As she watched them die, she learned not to fear it for herself. She also learned to tell the relatives at the bedside never to talk as if the patient wasn't there, since though they might be unconscious they could still hear.

She became pragmatic about the vexed relation between consolation and truth. She had told both David and Antoni the truth, but in other cases, she was in favor of gentle prevarication. Every patient was different. Everyone had a different tolerance for reality. "The door of hope must be shut slowly and gently," she wrote, since false hope was no consolation at all. Thanks to *The Plague*, thanks to hours spent at the bedsides of atheist or agnostic patients, she came to accept that she had no business preaching religious hope to the dying when medical hope was gone. The hospice she established was a community, she said, but "of the unlike," united not by shared belief but by shared respect for the dying and their individual needs.

She also knew enough about doctors and about her own fears to understand that many of them couldn't tell patients the truth because they couldn't tell themselves the truth. As she sardonically remarked:

Man's powers of self-deception are almost unbelievable. A doctor can fail to recognize symptoms in himself which would be quite diagnostic to him in anyone else and may remain in complete ignorance of his impending death.

In the mid-1960s, in a grief-stricken period of her own life—after the deaths of her father and Antoni—she published her first account of what came to be her central insight about the dying. Their pain, she said, was not just physical. It was also social, psychological, and metaphysical. Patients in their last days worried about their children, their financial affairs; they cast anguished looks back at their lives and wondered whether they had lived at all; they were consumed by regret and guilt for acts and omissions sometimes deep in the past. Their pain was "total": an overwhelming combination of afflictions of body and soul. As always, she gave credit for this insight to one of her patients, a working-class woman named Mrs. Hinson, who, when asked where it hurt, had told her, "Well doctor, the pain began in my back, but now it seems that all of me is wrong."

If "all of me is wrong," palliative care had to embrace counseling, therapy, financial advice, interventions with the family, as well as pain medication and compassionate nursing. Consolation was all these things, but it was mostly about listening. "Watch with me," Christ told his disciples while he prayed in the garden of Gethsemane. Instead of watching, they fell asleep, and he was left alone to face the truth that God commanded him to suffer and die. "Watch with me" became the phrase Saunders used to express what consolation meant. It meant being there, watching through the night, so that you would hear the dying speak. What they wanted, as one dying man told her, was "for someone to look as if she is trying to understand me." She was a compassionate listener but also an unsentimental one. "We can never really understand another person any more than we can alter the hard thing that is happening"—but at least she could keep watch.

In 1967, with the confidence of someone who knew exactly what she wanted, Cicely Saunders succeeded in financing and opening St Christopher's Hospice, a sixty-bed facility in south London. Over the next forty years, it pioneered the scientific evaluation of advanced pain remedies, trained thousands of physicians and nurses in palliative care, and provided end-of-life care for patients and their families in the working-class neighborhoods around it. A stained-glass window was installed to commemorate David Tasma's founding gift. Doctors came from around the world, and one of them, Balfour Mount from

Montreal, coined the term "palliative care" to describe the new medical specialty that Saunders and her team were shaping in their daily practice on the wards.

Instead of believing, as we often do, that dying is the loneliest moment of our lives, Saunders understood that it was among the most public and social moments of our existence, and that it demanded an institutional setting that would respect its social, familial, and public character. She understood not only that the dying needed a place where consolation would become possible, but that the dying wanted to use their final days to console others and that the giving of consolation was essential to the receiving of it.

I MET HER ONLY ONCE, at St Christopher's Hospice one afternoon in 1996. She was a tall, wide-shouldered woman in her late sixties, with well-permed white hair, wearing robust tweeds and a ruffled blouse with a brooch. She spoke with the precise, cut-glass enunciation of the English upper-middle classes of an earlier age and looked like a recognizable English type: a justice of the peace, a fixture at county fetes and church auxiliary meetings. She offered me a whiskey and poured a large one herself. She was a fiercely intelligent woman, with an intellectual curiosity and range of learning at odds with the image she created of a down-to-earth English countrywoman. She was also an unreconstructed romantic, whose ready laughter and girlish delight echoed in the hallways as she escorted me through the corridors of St Christopher's, pointing with pride and love to the many oil paintings on the walls that, she explained, had been the work of her Polish husband ("my third Pole") who had died a year before, after fifteen years of marriage.

What made her remarkable was her capacity to bring together a practice of palliative care—in the hospice setting, in hospitals, and in the home—that by then she knew, with justifiable pride, had made the ending of life bearable for millions of people around the world.

She was also formidable in argument, especially on the subject of euthanasia. Everything she had devoted her life to building was threatened by the growing belief that "dying with dignity" should mean choosing to end your life when life no longer seemed bearable. It was wrong, she said, to call this death with dignity. The doctor who delivered a lethal injection was betraying his Hippocratic oath, and patients who accepted it were succumbing to an illusion that they would soon sink into degrading dependency. The nurse in her rebelled at this. Even for patients struck down by motor neuron disease, it was possible to preserve their dignity and agency to the very last. She stuck to these beliefs all her life. More than forty years before, she had written, "we cannot claim to dispose directly of life. It is not for us to say that the suffering is fruitless nor that there is nothing more for the patient to do or learn in this life. Man is not the master and possessor of his body and his existence." Her ideas about consolation depended on this belief: that we are not masters of our bodies, and that the task facing us is to make peace with the large portion of our life that is not in our power.

Whether in fact we all can reach a stage of acceptance of our own deaths, whether we can attain that moment of peace and reconciliation that she thought was the natural progression, are questions each of us will answer only when the time comes. But Cicely Saunders did understand that being consoled in our final hours is possible only if we never give up hope of giving our death meaning to those we love. We can die for them, she thought, and we can do that, she understood, only if we are left in peace to do so, in a place that respects the importance of those last hours together.

In her final years, she developed a cancer, which slowly spread and which she bore with fortitude and wry humor. It was difficult to keep the truth from her. She wanted to see the X-rays, and she lived the last year of her life hoping, as she admitted, "that the cancer is going to turn up somewhere else," since it would be "tiresome," she thought, to keep hanging on. In her last months, she returned to St Christopher's, this time as a patient, and died there, receiving all the palliative care she had perfected in her practice for others, on July 14, 2005, at the age of eighty-seven. She had devoted fifty years of her life to identifying every necessary component of a good death: relief from pain, a quiet contemplative setting, the presence of loved ones, time to reflect on the shape of a life and the prospect of an end to suffering; I hope that she, who did so much to secure this for others, was able to achieve it, in the end, for herself.

Epilogue

When my parents died within three years of each other, thirty years ago, I spent a long time in a state of desolation. They had been the audience before whom I played out my life, and with those two seats in the theater suddenly empty, the play itself seemed to have little point. I grieved for them, but in some disabling way, I was inconsolable.

Even now, I cannot reconstruct exactly how I recovered my bearings. I did fall in love again and found someone who understood and forgives, who loves with her whole heart. Being with my two children, watching them grow up, seeing in their faces the traces of my mother and father, helped to restore hope that they lived on in them. I began dreaming about my parents again. I saw my father walking by the seashore in the waves, bending down from time to time to pick up a shell. I saw my mother smoothing a new red dress at her knee and asking me how she looked. I began talking about them with my brother, discovering how differently he remembered everything, and through that process began to fix down, as one places a photo in an album, the indelible memories that were mine. Now, thirty years later, time has done its work. Nothing hurts the way it once did, and I now feel that they will always remain a benevolent presence in my life. On the windowsill of my room, catching the light as I write, is a figure of a dancing horse—at least that's what it looks like to me—carved from a gnarled root of Canadian spruce by my father on a summer's day at the cottage in Georgian Bay more than sixty years ago. I look at it and think, at last free of the sadness and anger that sometimes came between us, how grateful I am that he was my father and that I am his son. Just as I am haunted no longer by the memory of my mother at the end of her life—lost to us, unable to speak, unable to remember our names—and recall instead that laughing woman so full of life and hope who sang Judy Garland songs while she cooked us dinner when we got home from school, the artist who painted the portrait of me, age eight, which hangs on the wall over my wife's desk now and seems a true likeness of the person I have been all my life.

In this reckoning with their deaths, I learned that consolation is both a conscious process by which we seek meaning for our losses and at the same time a deeply unconscious undertaking, in the recesses of our souls, in which we recover hope. It is the most arduous but also the most rewarding work we do, and we cannot escape it. We cannot live in hope without reckoning with death, or with loss and failure.

Some of my failures have been private, others very public. In the stages of recovery that follow, you begin with self-pity, until it dawns on you that there are many worse things in life. In the next stage, you tell yourself that you gave it your best, though it remains painful to admit that your best wasn't nearly good enough. Then you try to let it all go, only to discover that there isn't a day when you don't wish you had been less naive and self-deceiving. But at the end of this journey, you finally understand, as Havel did, that you have to take ownership of the entire person you once were, take some pride in what you tried to do, and take responsibility only for those portions of your failure that were yours alone. In this slow, circuitous, barely conscious way, you come to be consoled. You can even learn to be grateful for what failure has taught you about yourself.

Failure is a great teacher, and so too is aging. As I have grown older, at least one false consolation has dropped away. Of all the advantages that loving parents, class, race, education, and citizenship conferred on me, the most incorrigible entitlement was existential: that I was somehow special. I had been given an all-access pass that gave me free passage through life. This was absurd, of course, but it was an illusion that sustained a great deal of what I tried to do. Failure and age gradually teach most of us otherwise. You shed any illusion of a special status that confers immunity from folly and misfortune and come to accept, willingly or otherwise, that you are like everyone else, prey to delusion, self-deception, and all the ills that flesh is heir to. You realize that the all-access pass will have to be handed in, and that in any case there is a door ahead that it will not open. It takes some time to accept the emergent sense of solidarity with the rest of humankind that begins to dawn when you do hand in that pass, when you realize that your previous liberal protestations of abstract solidarity had been so false, when it finally hits you that you are yoked together with all others in a common fate. But these realizations are an unavoidable part of getting older, and they become a kind of consolation. You may not be special, but you do belong. This is not so bleak or so difficult to accept. It might even make you a little more attentive to the misfortunes and calamities of others and more alive to the ancient wisdom that has always been there to warn us not to be so vain and foolish.

Doubtless, these are some of the experiences that led to the making of this book. Writing it was a reckoning with my losses, in the company of these living presences who, in their writing, shared with me the hours of trial in which they tried to find a pathway to hope. The consolation they offer, it seems to me, lies in their example, in their courage and lucidity, and in their determination to leave something behind that might console us. "Did the work survive?" the poet asked in 1944, as history closed in upon him. Yes it did, and we are the better for it. Their company restored to me a sense of the unbroken continuity, and the occasional grandeur, of the human experience. Thanks to their example, I learned we are never alone when we face pain and loss. There is always someone who has been there before, who can share the experience. That, I hope, will be as consoling to you as it has been to me.

Though I have described three ancient doctrines of consolation—the Hebrew, the Christian, the Stoic—together with a fourth modern one, the idea of progress that led Marx to put his faith in revolution, this has been a book about people. It is not doctrines that console us in the end, but people: their example, their singularity, their courage and steadfastness, their being with us when we need them most. In dark times, nothing so abstract as faith in History, Progress, Salvation, or Revolution will do us much good. These are doctrines. It is people we need, people whose examples show us what it means to go on, to keep going, despite everything.

I will end with one such person, a luminous example, the poet Czesław Miłosz, whom my wife and I met at his house in Berkeley, California, on a bright January day in 1998. Shared pleasure in his poetry was one of the links that had bound us together as a new couple. His poem "After Paradise" would be the one that I would recite to Zsuzsanna at our wedding ceremony in 1999, my voice catching on the last line, "which this love of yours suddenly transformed," since it expressed perfectly what she has meant to me.

The poet was eighty-seven when we met him, a small man
with unforgettable deep-set blue eyes beneath bushy eyebrows.
He had an agility of body and an irresistible charm that belied
his age. He was alone in the house on Grizzly Peak Boulevard
in which he had lived, as a professor at Berkeley, for nearly forty
years, and it felt empty since he was leaving soon and moving
back to Kraków in his native Poland. We went down the stairs
into a large, bare sitting room, and Zsuzsanna asked him if
he would read to us. He read in a formal way, bent over the
book we gave him to use, in a low, husky, but precise voice, in
English, taking obvious pleasure in reading his own words, his
eyes flashing delight when Zsuzsanna asked him to read some
more. As his voice filled the room, every word had the authority of a life's experience. This was the poet whose "Campo dei
Fiori" and "A Poor Christian Looks at the Ghetto" had found
words for watching, unscathed but helpless, as Polish Jews
were slaughtered in Warsaw in 1943; a man who chose exile,
first in France, then in America, because he could not live in
truth in the Communist Poland of the 1950s; an author whose
The Captive Mind had been among the first to analyze the spiritual abjection of the Communist system; a teacher who had
mastered a new language in exile and had taught Slavic literature and Polish poetry since the 1960s, sometimes despairing
that he would ever see a free Poland again; a husband who had
nursed his invalid wife only to watch helplessly as she wasted
away and died; a father who endured being threatened at gun-
point by his psychotic son; an artist who had been awarded
the Nobel Prize in 1980 but had confessed to a friend that
he would have exchanged it for a healthy wife and a healthy
son; a man who had found love again, in his eighties, and who
had held on to hope through every trial thanks to his unshak-
able connection to the flowing spring of his native tongue. He
was now returning home at last. He read us one poem that

Zsuzsanna and I knew by heart. It had been composed in this very house, with a view of the San Francisco Bay from the garden. For both of us, it is the enduring description of what it is to feel consoled, to be reconciled to one's losses, to have come to terms with one's shame and regrets, and to feel, despite everything, alive to the beauty of life. He wrote it in 1970, before some of the losses that were yet to befall him, and this only made plain how much consolation remains the work of a lifetime, constantly recommenced, though it can be savored in a single moment. The poem that captures this moment is called "Gift." Consolation is always a gift, a form of grace we do not always deserve, but which, when we receive it, even for a fleeting instant, makes our lives worth living:

> A *day so happy.*
> *Fog lifted early, I worked in the garden.*
> *Hummingbirds were stopping over honeysuckle flowers.*
> *There was no thing on earth I wanted to possess.*
> *I knew no one worth my envying him.*
> *Whatever evil I had suffered, I forgot.*
> *To think that once I was the same man did not embarrass me.*
> *In my body I felt no pain.*
> *When straightening up, I saw the blue sea and sails.*

NOTES AND FURTHER READING

Introduction: After Paradise

On the general theme of consolation, I should begin with Alain de Botton's use of Boethius and his attempt to restore popular philosophy to its role in providing consolation in his *The Consolations of Philosophy* (London: Penguin, 2000). I learned a great deal from Rivkah Zim's study of consolation as a literary form in *The Consolations of Writing: Literary Strategies of Resistance from Boethius to Primo Levi* (Princeton, NJ: Princeton University Press, 2014). There are many books about how to console yourself in the face of your own mortality: for example, Andrew Stark's *The Consolations of Mortality: Making Sense of Death* (New Haven, CT: Yale University Press, 2016); the excellent compilation edited by Kevin Young, *The Art of Losing: Poems of Grief and Healing* (New York: Bloomsbury, 2010); and another fine collection of consoling poetry and prose in P. J. Kavanagh, ed., *A Book of Consolations* (London: Harper Collins, 1992). For a profound meditation upon mortality by an observant and compassionate doctor, see Atul Gawande, *Being Mortal: Medicine and What Matters in the End* (New York: Metropolitan, 2014). I also learned an immense amount about the history of death and dying, and its attendant rituals of consolation, from Thomas Laqueur's *The Work of the*

Dead: A Cultural History of Mortal Remains (Princeton, NJ: Princeton University Press, 2015).

Chapter One:
The Voice in the Whirlwind: The Book of Job and the Book of Psalms

Though the quotations from the book of Job are taken exclusively from the King James Version of the Bible, I am deeply indebted, in both this chapter and the next, to the work of Robert Alter, as a translator, literary critic, and textual analyst. I made particular use of his introduction to his translation of the book of Job. See Robert Alter, ed., *The Hebrew Bible*, vol. 3 (New York: Norton, 2019), 457–65. A demanding study of the book of Job is Paul Ricoeur's "On Consolation," in *The Religious Significance of Atheism*, by Alasdair MacIntyre and Paul Ricoeur (New York: Columbia University Press, 1968). I also learned greatly from Moshe Halbertal's essay, "Job, the Mourner," in *The Book of Job: Aesthetics, Ethics, Hermeneutics*, ed. Leora Batnitzky and Ilana Pardes (Amsterdam: De Gruyter, 2014).

My reading of the Psalms is indebted to Robert Alter's introduction and translation of the Psalms in *The Hebrew Bible,* vol. 3 (New York: Norton, 2019), 3–27. I also consulted Walter Brueggemann and William H. Bellinger Jr., *Psalms (New Cambridge Bible Commentary)* (New York: Cambridge University Press, 2014). I learned from the following great readings of the Psalms: Dietrich Bonhoeffer, *Psalms: The Prayer Book of the Bible* (Minneapolis: Augsburg Fortress Publishers, 1970); and Thomas Merton, *Praying the Psalms* (St. Cloud, MN: The Order of St. Benedict, 1955).

Chapter Two:
Waiting for the Messiah: Paul's Epistles

The basic sources for Paul's life and teaching, of course, are his Epistles and the Acts of the Apostles. All quotations are taken from these sources in the New International Version. In addition, I benefited greatly from modern Pauline scholarship, especially N. T. Wright, *Paul: A Biography* (London: Harper One, 2018). I also consulted

E. P. Sanders, *Paul: A Very Short Introduction* (New York: Oxford University Press, 1991); and James D. G. Dunn, ed., *The Cambridge Companion to St Paul* (New York: Cambridge University Press, 2011). On the formation of the Bible and its history, I commend John Barton, *A History of the Bible: The Book and Its Faiths* (London: Allen Lane, 2019); and Paula Fredriksen, *Paul: The Pagans' Apostle* (New Haven, CT: Yale University Press, 2017).

Chapter Three:
Cicero's Tears: Letters on the Death of His Daughter

Susan Treggiari's *Terentia, Tullia and Publilia: The Women of Cicero's Family* (New York: Routledge, 2007) pulls together what we know about the women in Cicero's family. The quotations from Cicero are from his letters to his friend Atticus. See Marcus Tullius Cicero, *Letters to Atticus (Complete)*, trans. E. O. Winstedt, 3 vols. (repr., Washington, DC: Library of Alexandria, n.d.). I also used Cicero, *Tusculan Disputations: Treatises on the Nature of the Gods and on the Commonwealth* (Berlin: Tredition Classics, 2006); and Cicero, *On Duties,* ed. M. T. Griffin and E. M. Atkins (New York: Cambridge University Press, 1991). For Cicero's biography, I used Anthony Everitt, *Cicero: The Life and Times of Rome's Greatest Politician* (London: Random House, 2003); and Kathryn Tempest, *Cicero: Politics and Persuasion in Ancient Rome* (London: Bloomsbury, 2013).

For further examples of *Consolatio* as a genre, see Plutarch, *In Consolation to His Wife,* trans. Robin Waterfield (London: Penguin Great Ideas, 1992); and Lucius Annaeus Seneca, "Of Consolation to Helvia" and "Of Consolation to Polybius," in *Consolations from a Stoic*, trans. Aubrey Stewart (London: Enhanced Media, 2017).

Chapter Four:
Facing the Barbarians: Marcus Aurelius's *Meditations*

All quotations from the *Meditations* are taken from Marcus Aurelius, *Meditations, with Selected Correspondence*, trans. Robin Hard (New York: Oxford World Classics, 2011). On his life, see Frank McLynn, *Marcus Aurelius: A Life* (New York: Perseus, 2010); Marcel van Ackeren, ed.,

A Companion to Marcus Aurelius (London: Wiley Blackwell, 2012); and Pierre Hadot, *The Inner Citadel: The Meditations of Marcus Aurelius*, trans. Michael Chase (Cambridge, MA: Harvard University Press, 2001). I particularly commend R. B. Rutherford, *The Meditations of Marcus Aurelius: A Study* (New York: Oxford University Press, 1989).

For the young Marcus Aurelius, I turned to the correspondence with Marcus Cornelius Fronto, *Correspondence*, ed. and trans. C. R. Haines, 2 vols. (London: William Heinemann, 1919). On the posthumous judgment of Marcus Aurelius, see C. Suetonius Tranquillus, *The Lives of the Twelve Caesars*, trans. Alexander Thomson, rev. T. Forrester (London: George Bell and Son, 1909); and Tacitus, *The Annals of Imperial Rome*, trans. Michael Grant (London: Penguin, 1956; repr. 1996). On the barbarians, I consulted Peter Heather, *Empires and Barbarians: The Fall of Rome and the Birth of Europe* (New York: Oxford University Press, 2009).

Chapter Five:
The Consolations of Philosophy: Boethius and Dante

The quotations from the *Consolation* are taken from Boethius, *The Consolation of Philosophy*, trans. Victor Watts (London: Penguin, 1969, 1999). The quotations from Boethius's *Theological Tractates* are from Boethius, *The Theological Tractates*, trans. H. F. Stewart and E. K. Rand (London: William Heinemann, 1918), https://www.ccel.org/ccel/boethius/tracts.pdf.

For Theoderic's reign and the twilight of the Roman Empire, I consulted Jonathan J. Arnold, *Theoderic and the Roman Imperial Restoration* (New York: Cambridge University Press, 2014); Peter Heather, *Empires and Barbarians: The Fall of Rome and the Birth of Europe* (New York: Oxford University Press, 2010); and James J. O'Donnell, *The Ruins of the Roman Empire: A New History* (New York: Harper Collins, 2008). I greatly enjoyed Judith Herrin's *Ravenna: Capital of Empire, Crucible of Europe* (Princeton, NJ: Princeton University Press, 2020) for its re-creation of the religious and political atmosphere of Theoderic's reign.

See also James J. O'Donnell, *Cassiodorus* (Berkeley: University of California Press, 1979); Thomas Hodgkin, *The Letters of Cassiodorus*

(London: Henry Frowde, 1886); and Procopius, *History of the Wars*, trans. H. B. Dewing, vol. 3 of 7 (London: Heinemann, 1919), https://www.gutenberg.org/files/20298/20298-h/20298-h.htm.

On the milieu of Theoderic's court see the anonymous collection of documents and reports known as *Anonymus Valesianus*: Bill Thayer, "The History of King Theodoric," Anonymus Valesianus, http://penelope.uchicago.edu/Thayer/E/Roman/Texts/Excerpta_Valesiana /2*.html.

For studies of Boethius's intellectual preoccupations and philosophy, see Henry Chadwick, *Boethius: The Consolations of Music, Logic, Theology, and Philosophy* (New York: Oxford University Press, 1981); Margaret Gibson, ed., *Boethius: His Life, Thought and Influence* (New York: Oxford University Press, 1981); John Magee, "Boethius," in *The Cambridge History of Philosophy in Late Antiquity*, ed. Lloyd P. Gerson (New York: Cambridge University Press, 2010), chap. 43; Kevin Uhalde, "Justice and Equality," in *The Oxford Handbook of Late Antiquity*, ed. Scott Fitzgerald Johnson (New York: Oxford University Press, 2012); and John Moorhead, *Theoderic in Italy* (Oxford, UK: Clarendon Press, 1992).

On Edward Gibbon's comments on Boethius, see his *History of the Decline and Fall of the Roman Empire*, vol. 2, chap. 39 (London: Strahan & Cadell, 1781).

On Dante's relation to Boethius, see Angelo Gualtieri, "Lady Philosophy in Boethius and Dante," *Comparative Literature* 23, no. 2 (Spring 1971): 141–50; Dante's verses on Boethius are from *The Divine Comedy*, trans. Steve Ellis (London: Vintage, 2019), *Paradiso*, canto 10, lines 127–29. See also Barbara Reynolds, *Dante: The Poet, the Thinker, the Man* (London: Bloomsbury Academic, 2006); Zygmunt G. Barański and Simon Gilson, eds., *The Cambridge Companion to Dante's 'Commedia'* (New York: Cambridge University Press, 2019); Winthrop Wetherbee, "The *Consolation* and Medieval Literature," in *The Cambridge Companion to Boethius*, ed. John Marenbon (New York: Cambridge University Press, 2009), 279–302. I also found an unpublished doctoral thesis by Victoria Goddard, "Poetry and Philosophy in Boethius and Dante" (PhD diss., University of Toronto, 2011), particularly helpful.

Chapter Six:
The Painting of Time: El Greco's *The Burial of the Count of Orgaz*

The painting and the church of Santo Tomé can be viewed at the website of the church of Santo Tomé, www.santotome.org/el-greco.

I made use of Fernando Marias, *El Greco: Life and Work—A New History* (London: Thames and Hudson, 2013); Rebecca Long, ed., *El Greco: Ambition and Defiance* (New Haven, CT: Yale University Press, 2020); and David Davies, ed., *El Greco* (London: National Gallery Company, 2003), published in conjunction with an exhibition of the same title, organized jointly by the Metropolitan Museum of Art, New York, and the National Gallery, London, and presented in New York in 2003 and in London in 2004. On the Spanish imperial context, the classic study is J. H. Elliott, *Imperial Spain, 1469–1716* (London: Penguin, 2002).

The two detailed studies of the painting that I consulted were Sarah Schroth, "Burial of the Count of Orgaz," in *Studies in the History of Art*, vol. 11, ed. Jonathan Brown, *Figures of Thought: El Greco as Interpreter of History, Tradition, and Ideas* (Washington, DC: National Gallery of Art, 1982), 1–17, II, VI; and Franz Philipp, "El Greco's Entombment of the Count of Orgaz and Spanish Medieval Tomb Art," *Journal of the Warburg and Courtauld Institutes* 44 (1981): 76–89.

Chapter Seven:
The Body's Wisdom: Michel de Montaigne's Last Essays

All quotations from Montaigne are taken from three essays in Book III written between 1586 and 1588, "Of Diversion," "Of Physiognomy," and "Of Experience," in Michel de Montaigne, *The Complete Works*, trans. Donald Frame (New York: Everyman's Library, Alfred A. Knopf, 2003). On Montaigne's life, see Philippe Desan, *Montaigne: A Life*, trans. Steven Rendall and Lisa Neal (Princeton, NJ: Princeton University Press, 2017); Donald Frame, *Montaigne: A Biography* (New York: Harcourt Brace, 1965); and Sarah Bakewell, *How to Live, or, A Life of Montaigne in One Question and Twenty Attempts at an Answer* (New York: Other Press, 2011). On Montaigne's study decorations, see George Hoffmann, "Montaigne's Nudes: The Lost

Tower Paintings Rediscovered," *Yale French Studies* 110 (2006): 122–33. Finally, on his relationship with Marie de Gournay, see Maryanne Cline Horowitz, "Marie de Gournay, Editor of the *Essais* of Michel de Montaigne: A Case-Study in Mentor-Protégée Friendship," *Sixteenth Century Journal* 17, no. 3 (Fall 1986): 271–84.

Chapter Eight:
The Unsent Letter: David Hume's *My Own Life*

This chapter builds on a previous essay of mine: "Metaphysics and the Market: Hume and Boswell," in *The Needs of Strangers* (London: Chatto and Windus, 1984). The details of Hume's early life are to be found in E. C. Mossner, *The Life of David Hume* (Oxford, UK: Oxford University Press, 1954, 1980). Hume's unsent letter is in *The Letters of David Hume*, vol. 1, ed. J. Y. T. Greig (Oxford, UK: Oxford University Press, 2011). All quotations from Hume's *My Own Life* are taken from the facsimile edition, edited by Iain Gordon Brown (Edinburgh: Royal Society of Edinburgh, 2014).

All quotations from Hume's *Enquiries*, *Treatise*, *Natural History*, and *Political Writings* are taken from the following editions: David Hume, *Enquiries Concerning Human Understanding and Concerning the Principles of Morals*, 3rd ed., ed. L. A. Selby-Bigge and P. H. Nidditch (Oxford: Clarendon Press, 1975); David Hume, *A Treatise of Human Nature*, 2nd ed., ed. L. A. Selby-Bigge and P. H. Nidditch (Oxford: Clarendon Press, 1978); David Hume, *The Natural History of Religion*, ed. A. Wayne Colver, and *Dialogues Concerning Natural Religion*, ed. John Vladimir Price (in one volume, Oxford: Clarendon Press, 1976); David Hume, *Political Writings*, ed. Stuart Warner and D. W. Livingston (Indianapolis: Hackett, 1994). For his references to Lucian, see Lucian, "Dialogues of the Dead," in *Lucian*, vol. 7, trans. M. D. Macleod (Cambridge, MA: Loeb Classical Library, Harvard University Press, 1961). Adam Smith's letter on Hume's death is to be found at "Letter from Adam Smith to William Strahan," November 9, 1776, in Dennis C. Rasmussen, ed., *Adam Smith and the Death of David Hume: The Letter to Strahan and Related Texts* (New York: Rowman and Littlefield, 2018). See also James A. Harris, *Hume: An Intellectual Biography* (New York: Cambridge University Press, 2015);

and Dennis C. Rasmussen, *The Infidel and the Professor: David Hume, Adam Smith, and the Friendship That Shaped Modern Thought* (Princeton, NJ: Princeton University Press, 2017).

Chapter Nine:
The Consolations of History: Condorcet's *A Sketch for a Historical Picture of the Progress of the Human Mind*

All quotations from Condorcet's *Sketch* are taken from *Condorcet: Political Writings*, ed. Steven Lukes and Nadia Urbinati (New York: Cambridge University Press, 2012). I learned from Elisabeth Badinter and Robert Badinter, *Condorcet: Un intellectuel en politique* (Paris: Fayard, 1988). Key documents relating to his confinement and flight in 1794, including the letter from his landlady, are to be found in Jean François Eugène Robinet, *Condorcet: Sa Vie, Son Œuvre, 1743–1794* (1893, repr., Geneva: Slatkine Reprints, 1968). Keith Michael Baker has made the study of Condorcet his life. See his *Condorcet: From Natural Philosophy to Social Mathematics* (Chicago: University of Chicago Press, 1982); see also his "On Condorcet's 'Sketch,' " *Daedalus* 133, no. 3 (Summer 2004): 56–64. On Condorcet's relation to the Scottish Enlightenment and his political and economic thinking, see Emma Rothschild, *Economic Sentiments: Adam Smith, Condorcet, and the Enlightenment* (Cambridge, MA: Harvard University Press, 2001); for Rothschild's effort to rescue Condorcet from his caricatures as a relentless rationalist ideologue, see her "Condorcet and the Conflict of Values," *The Historical Journal* 39, no. 3 (September 1996): 677–701. Jacques-Louis David's portrait of the Abbé Sieyès is in the Harvard Art Galleries: Jacques-Louis David, *Emmanuel Joseph Sieyès (1748–1836)*, 1817, oil on canvas, 97.8 × 74 cm, Harvard Art Museums/Fogg Museum, bequest of Grenville L. Winthrop, https://hvrd.art/o/299809.

Chapter Ten:
The Heart of a Heartless World: Karl Marx and *The Communist Manifesto*

All quotations from Marx are taken from *Karl Marx: Early Writings*, trans. Rodney Livingstone and Gregor Benton, intro. Lucio Colletti

(London: Penguin, 1975). For Marx's biography, I returned to Isaiah Berlin's *Karl Marx: His Life and Environment*, 4th ed., intro. Alan Ryan (New York: Oxford University Press, 1978); my largest debt, however, is to Gareth Stedman Jones for his *Karl Marx: Greatness and Illusion* (London: Harvard University Press, 2016); I also benefited from Shlomo Avineri's *Karl Marx: Philosophy and Revolution* (New Haven, CT: Yale University Press, 2019). On Marx and religion, see Alasdair MacIntyre, *Marxism and Christianity* (London: Duckworth, 1968); and David McLellan, *Marxism and Religion* (New York: Harper and Row, 1987). On Marx and Lincoln, see Robin Blackburn, *An Unfinished Revolution: Karl Marx and Abraham Lincoln* (London: Verso, 2011).

Chapter Eleven:
War and Consolation: Abraham Lincoln's Second Inaugural Address

All quotations from Abraham Lincoln are taken from *Abraham Lincoln: Speeches and Writings*, vol. 2, *1859–1865*, ed. Don E. Fehrenbacher (New York: Library of America, 1989). See also Ronald C. White, *Lincoln's Greatest Speech: The Second Inaugural* (New York: Simon and Schuster, 2002). I learned from the following works as well: Adam Gopnik, *Angels and Ages: A Short Book about Darwin, Lincoln, and Modern Life* (New York: Knopf, 2009); William Lee Miller, *Lincoln's Virtues: An Ethical Biography* (New York: Knopf, 2002); Jay Winik, *April 1865: The Month That Saved America* (New York: Harper Collins, 2001); Doris Kearns Goodwin, *Team of Rivals: The Political Genius of Abraham Lincoln* (New York: Simon and Schuster, 2005); Drew Gilpin Faust, *This Republic of Suffering: Death and the American Civil War* (New York: Knopf, 2008); Eric Foner, *The Fiery Trial: Abraham Lincoln and American Slavery* (New York: Norton, 2010); and Ronald C. White Jr., *A. Lincoln: A Biography* (New York: Random House, 2009).

Chapter Twelve:
Songs on the Death of Children: Gustav Mahler's *Kindertotenlieder*

The story of Dorothea von Ertmann is told in Maynard Solomon, "The Healing Power of Music," in *Late Beethoven: Music, Thought,*

Imagination (Berkeley: University of California Press, 2003). On Mahler's life, I used the standard biography by Henry-Louis de La Grange, *Gustav Mahler*, especially vol. 2, *Vienna: The Years of Challenge (1897–1904)* (New York: Oxford University Press, 1995). On the death of Alma and Gustav's daughter, I used *Gustav Mahler: Letters to His Wife*, ed. Henry-Louis de La Grange and Günther Weiss, in collaboration with Knud Martner, rev. and trans. Antony Beaumont (London: Faber, 2004). I also used Natalie Bauer-Lechner, *Recollections of Gustav Mahler*, trans. Dika Newlin, ed. Peter Franklin (London: Faber, 2013).

On Mahler's Vienna milieu, I depended upon Leon Botstein, "Whose Gustav Mahler? Reception, Interpretation, and History," in *Mahler and His World*, ed. Karen Painter (Princeton, NJ: Princeton University Press, 2002), 1–54. On the *Kindertotenlieder*, I have relied upon Donald Mitchell, *Gustav Mahler: Songs and Symphonies of Life and Death* (London: Boydell Press, 1985); Donald Mitchell and Andrew Nicholson, eds., *The Mahler Companion* (New York: Oxford University Press, 1999); and Theodor W. Adorno, *Mahler: A Musical Physiognomy* (Chicago: University of Chicago Press, 1992). For a study of the *Kindertotenlieder*, see Randal Rushing, "Gustav Mahler's *Kindertotenlieder*: Subject and Textual Choices and Alterations of the Friedrich Rückert Poems, A Lecture Recital, Together with Three Recitals of Selected Works of F. Schubert, J. Offenbach, G. Finzi, and F. Mendelssohn" (PhD diss., University of North Texas, 2002). On Freud's encounter with Mahler in Leiden, I have used the account in Ernest Jones, *The Life and Work of Sigmund Freud*, ed. Lionel Trilling and Steven Marcus (New York: Basic Books, 1961). Freud's own attitude toward consolation, religious or otherwise, emerges in his "The Future of an Illusion," in *Sigmund Freud*, vol. 12, *Civilization, Society and Religion*, Pelican Freud Library (London: Penguin, 1975), 179–242. On the psychology and philosophy of music, I have learned from Elizabeth Helmuth Margulis, *The Psychology of Music: A Very Short Introduction* (New York: Oxford University Press, 2019); and especially from Martha C. Nussbaum, "Music and Emotion," chap. 5 in *Upheavals of Thought: The Intelligence of Emotions* (New York: Cambridge University Press, 2001). I am indebted, most of all, to the following recordings: Dame Janet Baker, mezzo-soprano, and Sir John Barbirolli, conductor, *Janet Baker Sings Mahler: Kindertotenlieder, 5 Rücketlieder, Lieder eines fahrenden Gesellen*, Great Recordings of the Century, EMI Classics, 1999; and Bruno Walter, conductor, and Kathleen Ferrier, contralto, Vienna Philharmonic Orchestra, *Das Lied von der Erde*, Vienna, 1952.

Chapter Thirteen:
The Calling: Max Weber and *The Protestant Ethic*

Rembrandt's painting *Saul and David* can be viewed at the Mauritshuis in The Hague: Rembrandt van Rijn, *Saul and David*, c. 1651–54 and c. 1655–58, oil on canvas, 130 × 164.5 cm, Mauritshuis, The Hague, https://www.mauritshuis.nl/en/explore/the-collection/artworks/saul-and-david-621/. On Weber's life, I have depended on Joachim Radkau, *Max Weber: A Biography*, trans. Patrick Camiller (Cambridge, UK: Polity Press, 2009), chap. 18; and especially upon the biography by his wife: Marianne Weber, *Max Weber: A Biography*, intro. Guenther Roth, trans. and ed. Harry Zohn (London: Transaction Publishers, 1988), chaps. 19–20. On Munich 1919, I learned from the work of Thomas Weber, especially *Hitler's First War: Adolf Hitler, the Men of the List Regiment, and the First World War* (New York: Oxford University Press, 2010). On the shape of his thought, see Fritz Ringer, *Max Weber: An Intellectual Biography* (Chicago: University of Chicago Press, 2004); Arthur Mitzman, *The Iron Cage: An Historical Interpretation of Max Weber*, with a new introduction (London: Routledge, 1985, 2017); and Terry Maley, *Democracy and the Political in Max Weber's Thought* (Toronto: University of Toronto, 2011). All quotations from Weber are taken from the following editions of his works: Max Weber, *The Protestant Ethic and the "Spirit" of Capitalism and Other Writings*, ed. Peter Baehr and Gordon C. Wells (London: Penguin, 2002); Max Weber, *The Sociology of Religion*, trans. Ephraim Fischoff, intro. Talcott Parsons (1922; Boston: Beacon Press, 1964); Max Weber, *The Vocation Lectures: "Science as a Vocation"; "Politics as a Vocation,"* ed. David Owen and Tracy B. Strong, trans. Rodney Livingstone (Indianapolis: Hackett, 2004); and Max Weber, *Political*

Writings, ed. Peter Lassman and Ronald Speirs, Cambridge Texts in the History of Political Thought (New York: Cambridge University Press, 1994).

Chapter Fourteen:
The Consolations of Witness: Anna Akhmatova, Primo Levi, and Miklós Radnóti

For Akhmatova, I relied on *The Complete Poems of Anna Akhmatova*, trans. Judith Hemschemeyer, ed. Roberta Reeder (Somerville, MA: Zephyr Press, 1992); Lydia Chukovskaya, *The Akhmatova Journals*, vol. 1, *1938–1941*, trans. Milena Michalski and Sylva Rubashova (London: Harvill, 1994); Nadezhda Mandelstam, *Hope Against Hope*, trans. Max Hayward (London: Penguin, 1971); Isaiah Berlin, *Personal Impressions: Twentieth-Century Portraits*, 3rd ed., ed. Henry Hardy (London: Pimlico, 2018); and my own description of Berlin's meeting with Akhmatova in my *Isaiah Berlin: A Life* (London: Chatto and Windus, 1998).

For Miklós Radnóti, see Miklós Radnóti, *The Complete Poetry in Hungarian and English*, trans. Gabor Barabas, foreword by Győző Ferencz (Jefferson, NC: McFarland, 2014); see also Zsuzsanna Ozsváth, *In the Footsteps of Orpheus: The Life and Times of Miklós Radnóti* (Bloomington: Indiana University Press, 2000). For the "postcards" quoted in the text, I used the translations in Miklós Radnóti, *Foamy Sky: The Major Poems of Miklós Radnóti, a Bilingual Edition*, trans. Zsuzsanna Ozsváth and Frederick Turner (Budapest: Corvina, 2014).

For Primo Levi, I depended on Primo Levi, *The Complete Works*, 3 vols., ed. Ann Goldstein (New York: Liveright, Norton, 2015), and in particular vol. 1, *If This Is a Man*, trans. Stuart Woolf (originally published 1947), in which "The Canto of Ulysses" story appears, and vol. 3, *The Drowned and the Saved*, trans. Michael F. Moore (originally published 1986). An essential critical counterpoint to Levi's reckoning with Auschwitz is Jean Améry, *At the Mind's Limits: Contemplations by a Survivor on Auschwitz and Its Realities*, trans. Sidney Rosenfeld and Stella P. Rosenfeld (Bloomington: Indiana University Press, 1980). For Levi's life, I used the following biographies: Myriam Anissimov, *Primo Levi: Tragedy of an Optimist*, trans. Steve Cox (Woodstock, NY:

Overlook Press, 2000); and Carole Angier, *The Double Bond: Primo Levi: A Biography* (London: Viking Penguin, 2002).

Chapter Fifteen:
To Live Outside Grace: Albert Camus's *The Plague*

On Camus's life, see Herbert Lottman, *Albert Camus: A Biography* (New York: Doubleday, 1979); and Olivier Todd, *Albert Camus: A Life* (New York: Carroll and Graf, 2000). See also Edward J. Hughes, ed., *The Cambridge Companion to Camus* (New York: Cambridge University Press, 2007). I especially valued the essay on Camus in Tony Judt, *The Burden of Responsibility: Blum, Camus, Aron, and the French Twentieth Century* (Chicago: University of Chicago Press, 1998). On the genesis of *The Plague*, the key source is Albert Camus, *Carnets, 1942–51*, trans. Philip Thody (London: Hamish Hamilton, 1966). I also used Albert Camus, *Lettres à un ami allemand* (Paris: Gallimard, 1948, 1972); Albert Camus, *Camus à Combat: Éditoriaux et articles d'Albert Camus, 1944–1947*, ed. Jacqueline Lévi-Valensi (Paris: Gallimard, 2002); and Albert Camus, *Carnets, III, Mars 1951–Décembre 1959* (Paris: Gallimard, 1989).

Chapter Sixteen:
Living in Truth: Václav Havel's *Letters to Olga*

All quotations from Havel in prison are from Václav Havel, *Letters to Olga*, trans. Paul Wilson (London: Faber and Faber, 1988). I also used the following collections of interviews and essays by Havel: Václav Havel, *Disturbing the Peace: A Conversation with Karel Hvížďala*, trans. Paul Wilson (London: Faber and Faber, 1990); Václav Havel, *Summer Meditations on Politics, Morality and Civility in a Time of Transition*, trans. Paul Wilson (London: Faber and Faber, 1992); and Václav Havel, *Václav Havel, or, Living in Truth*, ed. Jan Vladislav (London: Faber and Faber, 1987). The essay by Emmanuel Levinas that Havel read in prison is "No Identity," in *Collected Philosophical Papers*, trans. Alphonso Lingis (Pittsburgh: Duquesne University Press, 1998). See also Benjamin Ivry, "A Loving Levinas on War," *Forward*, February 10, 2010, https://forward.com/culture/125385/a-loving-levinas-on

-war/. I am especially indebted to the biography by Michael Žantovský, *Havel: A Life* (London: Atlantic Books, 2014).

Chapter Seventeen:
The Good Death: Cicely Saunders and the Hospice

David Clark's *Cicely Saunders: A Life and Legacy* (New York: Oxford University Press, 2018), together with his edited edition, *Cicely Saunders: Selected Writing, 1958–2004* (New York: Oxford University Press, 2006), were essential reading. I also commend a 1983 interview with Cicely Saunders: Dame Cicely Saunders, interview by Judith Chalmers, aired May 16, 1983, on Thames Television, YouTube video, 21:53, https://www.youtube.com/watch?v=KA3Uc3hBFoY.

Epilogue

All quotations of Czesław Miłosz are taken from Czesław Miłosz, *New and Collected Poems, 1931–2000* (New York: Harper Collins, 2001). For his life, see Andrzej Franaszek, *Miłosz: A Biography*, ed. and trans. Aleksandra Parker and Michael Parker (Cambridge, MA: Harvard University Press, 2019).

INDEX